No More Lies

NO MORE LIES

The Myth and the
Reality of American History

BY RICHARD CLAXTON GREGORY

Edited by James R. McGraw

PERENNIAL LIBRARY
Harper & Row, Publishers
New York, Evanston, San Francisco, London

Grateful acknowledgment is made for permission to use the following:

Excerpts reprinted by permission of the Macmillan Company from *The Negro Revolution*, by Robert Goldston. Copyright © 1968 by Robert Goldston.

Excerpt from *The Right of Revolution*, by Truman Nelson. Copyright © 1968 by Truman Nelson. Reprinted by permission of Beacon Press.

Excerpt from *The Rich and the Super-Rich*, by Ferdinand Lundberg, published by Lyle Stuart.

Excerpts reprinted by permission of G. P. Putnam's Sons from *The Historians' History of the United States*, by Andrews Berky and James P. Shenton. Copyright © 1966 by Andrews Berky and James P. Shenton.

Excerpts from *The Peculiar Institution*, by Kenneth M. Stampp. Copyright © 1956 by Kenneth M. Stampp. Reprinted by permission of Alfred A. Knopf, Inc.

Excerpt from *Before the Mayflower: The History of Black America*, by Lerone Bennett, Jr. Copyright © 1962, 1968 by Johnson Publishing Company. Reprinted by permission of Johnson Publishing Company.

"Pretty Colored Snake" (p. 119) and excerpts from *The New Indians*, by Stan Steiner. Copyright © 1968 by Stan Steiner. Reprinted by permission of Harper & Row, Publishers, Inc.

Excerpt from an interview with Arnold Toynbee in *Look*, May 18, 1969. Copyright © 1969 by Cowles Communications, Inc.

Excerpts from *To Be a Slave*, by Julius Lester. Copyright © 1968 by Julius Lester. Reprinted by permission of Dial Press.

Excerpts from *Look Out, Whitey! Black Power's Gon' Get Your Mama*. Copyright © 1968 by Julius Lester. Reprinted by permission of Dial Press.

First PERENNIAL LIBRARY edition published 1972.

STANDARD BOOK NUMBER: 06–080236–7

This book is dedicated to Women's Liberation, the movement of the 1970's which will make all Americans proud to call the Statue of Liberty their momma. The book is further dedicated to the Indian Americans who once owned the harbor in which Miss Liberty stands and all of the land her children now occupy.

CONTENTS

ACKNOWLEDGMENTS

First of all a word of appreciation to Jeannette Hopkins of Harper & Row for her patience, understanding, and accommodation with regard to my hectic and unpredictable schedule. A further special word of thanks to Leedie Miller, her able assistant.

Thanks also to Judy Messel, Susan Stallings, Francis Johnson, A. Donald Bourgeois, James Baker, Brahim Ben Benu, Theadrick Lumpkin, Jean Williams, Leon Watts, Bob Johnson, editor of *JET* magazine, and Harry Moses whose research efforts made the preparation of this manuscript possible.

And as always James Sanders and James R. McGraw were on hand to help in so many ways.

Finally, my love and appreciation to my wife Lillian and the kids—Michelle, Lynne, Pamela, Paula, Stephanie, Gregory, Miss, and Christian (who was born during the latter stages of the writing of this book)— for their tolerance of an absentee father retired to his room to read, talk, tape, and type.

DICK GREGORY

No More Lies

> "God forbid we should ever be twenty years without . . . a rebellion."
>
> THOMAS JEFFERSON, 1787

> "This country, with its institutions, belongs to the people who inhabit it. Whenever they shall grow weary of the existing government, they can exercise their constitutional right of amending it, or their revolutionary right to dismember or overthrow it."
>
> ABRAHAM LINCOLN, 1861

Introduction

FOR WHITE ONLY

I became interested in American history quite by accident. I remember I was back in grade school, happy being a good "nigger," singing the blues and not causing any trouble. The principal came into class one day and announced, "The Board of Education says you can't graduate unless you read and memorize the Declaration of Independence."

I was a typical rebellious youngster, so I looked up and said, "The Decla . . . who? Man, us black folks don't want to read any of that old white stuff." The principal answered, "Well, you won't graduate." Naturally I replied, "Then lay it on me right now."

So I started reading, "We hold these Truths to be self-evident, that all Men are created equal." You can imagine how those words sounded to my young, black, ghetto ears. But wanting to graduate, I kept right on reading until I got to the section which said:

—That whenever any Form of Government becomes destructive of these ends, it is the Right of the People to alter or to abolish it when a long train of abuses and usurpations, pursuing invariably the same Object, evinces a design to reduce them under absolute Despotism, it is their right, it is their *duty*, to throw off such Government, and to provide new Guards for their future security.

I dropped my book, ran to the principal's office, broke breathlessly through the door, and gasped, "Have you got any more of this stuff layin' around?" Reading that Declaration of Independence made me want to take a look at the United States Constitution to see what else I might have missed!

But later I discovered that the founding fathers obviously made a mistake in writing their Declaration of Independence. Thomas Jefferson neglected to label it "For White Only." Without that label the Declaration of Independence becomes a dangerous document—in the black ghettos of America, on the Indian reservations, in the grape fields of California where Mexican-American workers are struggling for human dignity, in the Puerto Rican slums and ghettos; in short, wherever America's long train of abuses is most painfully felt and the system's usurpations of human rights have become most despotic. It is dangerous for white America to insist that basic American documents be read by the black, poor, and oppressed, because such people are just naive enough to go out and do what the founding fathers said oppressed people should do.

Evidently white America does not realize the danger, because it makes the same mistake today—forgetting to carefully label *how, where,* and *by whom* certain American teaching should be applied. For example, can white America really be insane enough to believe that black soldiers can be drafted into military service, sent to basic training and taught to be guerrillas, shipped ten thousand miles to Vietnam with orders to kill foreigners to liberate other foreigners, without realizing that those same black soldiers will return home to apply their instruction to liberate their own parents? If so, it is a dangerous mistake. America must realize she is not dealing with World War II black folks anymore—soldiers who can be turned on and off at random.

White America has developed a peculiar population blindness in recalling and reciting American history. Traditional American history is a myth and can only be accepted when read with blinders that block out the facts. The strange recitation begins with Columbus "discovering" America. Not only is that bold lie taught in ghetto schools in America, but little Indian children in reservation schools are given the same lesson.

Even George Washington, the "father of our country," is not revered in this nation's memory because he spent considerable time in prayer or sang "We shall Overcome" to the British soldiers. George Washington is a national hero because he fought against oppression, drove out the British, and killed every one of them he could get his hands on. Yet white America, seeing history through those peculiar blinders, would rather talk about little nonviolent George who had guilt feelings about molesting a cherry tree.

The continuing myth of American history dignifies the illicit acts of some and condemns the same acts when others do them. Many Americans have a hard time understanding the actions of the poor, the oppressed, and the young, because they really do not know, or admit, their own history. In the past Americans condemned Indian massacres. Today they bemoan the black crime rate and place the statements of militant black leaders and radical young whites in the category of treason. Yet white folks are stirred by similar words memorized by every school child. "Give me liberty or give me death." Who said that? Rap Brown? Eldridge Cleaver? Jerry Rubin? "Don't shoot until you see the whites [of their eyes]." Who said that? Stokely Carmichael? Huey P. Newton? Abbie Hoffman?

America continues to condemn radical black and white youth for not respecting the police. American history books proudly recite the exploits of a white man named Paul Revere who, during the days when the British were the police, rode through the white community and said, "Get a gun, white folks, the police are coming." Most Americans can understand those original White Panthers. But the Black Panthers make them forget about their own history.

Rioting and looting in the black ghettos of America are held up as horrible examples of lawlessness on the rampage. Yet the history books enthusiastically tell of a group of patriotic white folks in Boston who dressed themselves up as *Indians* no less, boarded that foreign ship, and dumped all the tea in the water. How can anyone who proudly remembers that moment in history have nerve enough to call black folks hoodlums? The lawlessness in the Boston harbor, for which white folks wanted Indians to take the rap, is honored in our national memory as the Boston Tea Party. If that terminology is legitimate, every time black folks steal a television set during a ghetto rebellion, it should be called a Saturday Night Fish Fry. Why do you suppose white America is so upset about black looting? Because black folks have enough sense to take the loot home with them?

Many white folks seem to feel that being born black means inheriting criminal tendencies. They will say black folks are 11 per cent of the population but represent 90 per cent of certain crimes. If that statistic really meant anything, no white man could sit down in night club, restaurant, or theater without being mugged. Incidentally, I've always contested America's arithmetic. Who counts us black folks? The census takers, and most of them are white, so they are not too eager to go into the black community to count noses. I think they count all the white folks and then say black folks are 11 per cent of them. Check the crime myth for yourself. Names such as Jesse James, Al Capone, John Dillinger, "Baby Face" Nelson, Ma Barker, and Bonnie and Clyde come to mind. You will not find a black face among them. And isn't it odd that J. Edgar Hoover, the FBI, and local police are able to arrest members of the Black Panther party all over the country but can't seem to get their hands very often on the Mafia or the Minutemen?

The inequity of population distribution has a significance for the crime rate, too. Black folks are crowded and compressed into tiny islands of land, called ghettos, in urban areas all over America. White folks, by and large, are scattered throughout the remaining suburban and rural areas. It is only natural that black folks end up snatching more pocketbooks per acre.

Think, for example, what would happen if there were only 200 automobiles in the world. Ten automobiles would be placed in Harlem, and the remaining 190 would be scattered throughout the rest of the world, one to a country. Quite naturally there would be more automobile accidents in Harlem for the simple reason there would be more cars to hit. Yet white American mythology would end up explaining, "Black folks are accident-prone. They're reckless." Of course, white folks have always said black folks are shiftless, which in itself could cause a lot of accidents in the absence of an automatic transmission.

Crowding of the black population into urban ghettos has created dilapidated housing, dirty streets, a polluted human environment. Because of this, white America calls the compressed ghetto dwellers "niggers." If white America ever penetrates that particular mythology, a shocking discovery will be made. I personally will accept white America's terminology and statistics. If dirtying up an overcrowded black ghetto neighborhood makes black folks "niggers," white Americans who, though enjoying a more scattered population distribution, have ended up polluting the water, the lakes, streams and rivers, the air we all breathe, and recently even the moon, must be "superniggers."

Many white Americans sincerely believe that black Americans have a natural odor. I would not categorically assert that black folks don't stink. I would merely suggest that you do your own research. Check and see how many billions of dollars white Americans spend each year for deodorants. Then turn on the television set, wait for a deodorant commercial, and see if you can find a black armpit. If black folks are doing all the stinking, and white folks are buying all the deodorants, who really stinks in my country?

White America has curiously become the victim of the very myths it has created. It is one thing to tell a lie and quite another thing to believe it. Since the days of slavery, white mythology has insisted that black people were of inferior stock. But a quick glance at social reality in America will show that white folks do not believe the inferior stock myth.

If I marry a woman of any ethnic background—Italian, Chinese, Puerto Rican, Irish, or whatever—a child produced through that union will be considered black in the eyes of white America. The child will be said to have "Negro blood," will be considered "a Negro" and frequently called "a nigger." The same pattern holds true for any black woman who marries a man of any other ethnic background. Black genes are considered so socially (if not biologically) dominant that a child is designated black regardless of the mixture. Does that sound like inferior stock to you?

Because of the inferior stock myth, nothing upsets average American white folks more than to see a black man with a white woman. The blond, blue-eyed white lady has been projected on every level of the mass media. She has become the sexual symbol for America, and black folks are Americans, too.

Every time I see an advertisement for a new automobile, and black folks do like to drive new cars, there is a white lady dangling the keys enticingly by the open door. Such an advertisement leads me to believe I should take the white lady along with the car to make sure my gears shift right. When I see a white lady holding a bottle of Pepsi Cola urging me to "come alive, and have a Pepsi, honey," it's only natural to assume I will want the Pepsi and the lady, too.

I go into my black apartment, sit down in my black living room, in front of my black television set, with my black wife and my black kids, and all of a sudden here comes a white lady dancing across the screen, half naked, saying, "Buy a Playtex living bra." Can white America actually believe that sex objects used in advertising will tempt only the white segment of the intended market?

American mythology begins to program young black minds at a very early age. When I was a little kid growing up in the ghetto of St. Louis, I used to go to the movie theater every night. The theater was warmer in the winter than it was at home, and cooler in the summer. Children under the age of twelve, accompanied by their parents, were admitted free. So I would just move up next to an adult standing in line and become their instant child. I had a young, fresh mind, ready to be programmed. Black folks were not allowed to attend the movie in the white neighborhood, but white America brought the white lady to the black neighborhood. The first people I can remember seeing make love on the movie screen were Ava Gardner and Humphrey Bogart in *The Barefoot Contessa*. I was too young to know what they were doing, but I had enough sense to know I was going to grow up and do it one day. I remember nudging my little friend during a love scene and saying, "I'm sure going to get me one of those when I grow up." My friend said, "Which one—him or her?" I said, "I don't know. I may try them both."

I'm grown up now, and the mythology is still in operation. White America is still upset at seeing a black man with a white lady. I hope white America gets more and more upset, so more and more *black* ladies will appear in the movies and more and more *black* ladies will advertise products. If that happens, white America will soon realize that black men were not born desiring white women. Such a phenomenon has taken careful and systematic programming.

White America also got upset when black folks raised the clenched fist salute and the cry "Black Power!" White folks would not have been upset if black folks had started shouting "Brown Strength!" White folks would have been greeting us on the street every day saying, "Hey, my brother, Brown Strength!" But the two words together—"black" and "power"—really upset white folks. Why? Because white America has corrupted those two words. Any honest evaluation of government and big business will show how "power" has been corrupted in this country. And the word "black" has been defined by white America as dirty, evil, and mean. A tiny lie is called "a little white lie." A hit record a decade or so ago was entitled "Those Little White Lies." But a big lie is called a "dirty, black lie." Angel food cake is white. Devil's food cake is black. There is nothing blacker than a tornado, until it gets ready to whirl through the white lady's kitchen on the Ajax television commercial; then it becomes a "white tornado," and cleans everything in sight. America's rhetoric perpetrates the myth every day that white is clean and pure, and black is dirty and evil.

Most white folks don't realize they gave black folks the idea for the clenched fist salute. Did you ever buy a box of baking soda? On the box you will see a big white arm raised clenching a hammer in the fist. All black folks did was take the hammer out, change the color of the arm and tone the muscle down a little bit.

White America's favorite myth is the myth of non-violence, which really means that oppressed people should not use violence against the oppressor. Think of the only country in the history of the world that dropped atomic bombs on other human beings now coming to black folks, poor folks, and young folks telling them to be nonviolent! Truman Nelson in *The Right of Revolution* describes that hypocrisy in all of its true horror:

They [black people] remember the bomb one of our liberal Presidents dropped on Hiroshima on August 6, 1945, from a bright blue sky at 8:15 in the morning. There was a blinding flash; the fireball dropped to the ground. A wind blew furiously through the streets of the city. It was a wind that could be seen, a wind of solid flame, dense enough to liquefy the stones of its channel. Everyone it touched died instantly, but people a mile away felt their skins peel off and hang down like strips of cloth. This happened in utter darkness. Thirty minutes later it got light again, and there was a heavy rainfall of black water which was deadly poison. There were other phases of torture. A whirlwind came up at one o'clock, separating what was left of the half-liquefied buildings and hurling the fragments around like projectiles.

Some 200,000 people were killed in a matter of minutes, and the President was sent an enthusiastic cable saying, "Operated on this morning, stop, diagnosis not yet complete but results exceed expectations, stop . . . interest extends great distance." Three days later, on August 9, 1945, the President of the United States ordered another bomb dropped, this time on Nagasaki.

It exploded just above Uragami Cathedral. The results did not "exceed" but were, perhaps, equal to the "expectations." There was now a predictable pattern; first, tremendous heat, about 50,000,000 degrees centigrade. Then this cooled slightly, and the blast came which blew the people who had not been burned into extinction and which was mingled with the destruction of all the buildings at the hypercenter of the explosion. About 100,000 people were killed at once, but another 200,000 of Hiroshima and Nagasaki people have been dying slowly and painfully for the last twenty-two years.

Here then are two primitive bombs which killed 300,000 people rather quickly and kept another 200,000 in a lifelong concentration camp in which the daily tortures of pain and nausea are inflicted upon them without the necessity of guards, dogs, torture chambers, planned starvation, or uncounted miles of rusting barbed wire.

The myth of nonviolence touches me very closely personally. I am totally committed to the concept of nonviolence. To me "Thou Shalt Not Kill" includes anything with life in it, so consequently I have become a vegetarian. But even so I feel that white America should never be allowed to utter the word "nonviolence" as long as the Indian is trapped up on the reservation. No group of people has been more nonviolent than the Indians over the past few decades. The sad reality in

America is that Indians would have to go on the warpath for America to listen truly to their demands. America really respects violence, and she only pays attention when someone is staring at her down the muzzle of a gun. Black folks know that America does not believe in nonviolence. We have watched a succession of Presidents send guns and bombs to Vietnam to free a foreigner; we know what white folks would do to free their own families.

I speak on more than three hundred college and university campuses each year, and I am constantly reminded that America has presented young people with so many problems to solve that youth had nothing to do with creating. We older folks spend twenty-four hours a day lying to young people. Then when the youth catch us in the lie, we say it is a generation gap. It is not a generation gap; it is a moral gap. The ecology fad represents older America's latest trick. We say, "The number one problem facing America today is the problem of air and water pollution." The number one problem facing America today is *moral* pollution. The same moral pollution which keeps the smoke up in the air also keeps the Indian on the reservation.

So youth in America today are saying to their elders, "No more lies!" The gradual process of social evolution in America has produced a new "black" mood with regard to social problems and racial relationships which is hard for the white mythology to understand. Perhaps a simple illustration will help. Think of the process of social evolution in America as a giant pendulum swinging back and forth. For more than three hundred years the American white man has been riding on that pendulum.

Up until the present moment in American history, the black man has been chasing the swinging pendulum trying to hitch a ride also. During the years of slavery and after the Emancipation Proclamation the black man chased the pendulum by trying to mimic the white man, trying to be as much like him as possible. But over the years the black man used up so much energy chasing the pendulum that he never had quite enough strength to jump on. Just when the pendulum seemed to be clearly within his grasp, the black man jumped and missed and the pendulum began to swing back the other way. And the black man started chasing once again.

The white man ridiculed the black man's nappy hair, so the black man developed his own social "process" and straightened out the hair hangup. Then the white man ridiculed the black man's thick lips, so the black man grew a moustache to cover that problem. The black man did everything he could to develop white attitudes, to try to think white—think white, be white—and the black man thought surely he would be able to catch the pendulum when he became "white" enough.

But the "whitening process" did not work. The pendulum slipped out of the black man's grasp and began to swing back the other way. So the black man began to develop a new strategy. He pleaded with the white man, appealing to his conscience. The civil rights movement was a plea for integration, for a fair and equal share of the American Dream. It was a plea for inclusion, a moral claim socially and politically supported by the rhetoric of the Declaration of Independence and the United States Constitution.

During the chase the black man saw certain signs that perhaps the white man was listening—the Civil Rights Act, the Housing Act, the Voting Rights Act, and the Supreme Court decision on school desegregation. The black man saw that the rights acts looked good on paper but were nullified by lack of implementation. He saw that the white man was more concerned about the "inciting to riot" section of the 1968 act than he was with fair housing.

To add insult to injury, the black man saw another thing happening. Each time the pendulum completed its swing, the white man picked up another rider—the Irishman, the Italian, the Jew, and so on. Still the black man could not climb on board.

So the black man began to analyze the arc. He noticed that even though the pendulum swung away, it always swung back. The black man suddenly realized that he was dissipating all of his energy and strength *chasing* the pendulum. So the black man decided to stop chasing and wait.

During his period of waiting the black man has decided to address himself to his *own* problems. He has begun looking to his own history, his own culture, and his own neighborhood. The black man is developing authentic black attitudes. He has pride and sees beauty in his blackness. Rather than pleading for inclusion into the white man's neighborhood, the black man is tackling the problems of his *own* neighborhood and demanding the right to solve those problems. He is demanding that the black community control its schools and its health, police and fire services, as well as the planning, strategy, and construction decisions that vitally affect life in the black community.

As the black man waits, he begins to see the tricks the white man used to keep him involved in the chase. The white man ridiculed the black man for the way he talked. And the black man used to be embarrassed when he would count "one, two, three, *fo'*." The white man would say, "You colored folks sure do talk funny." Then the black man went to England and heard the English language as it should be spoken. And he came home realizing that white folks can't speak the English language properly either.

The black man knows that the process of social evolution dictates that the pendulum will swing back to him one day. When it does, he will be ready to encounter that white rider. But the black man sees that he will not be alone when he meets him. He looks at the 1968 Democratic Convention in Chicago and notices that the sons and daughters of the white man are jumping off the pendulum already. A new phase of social evolution has developed where white folks are battling in the streets over black folks—what was supposed to have happened during the Civil War.

There are those who say that the American pendulum has swung about as far right as it can get. If so, it will soon start swinging back. And when it does, black folks, and their young white, Puerto Rican, Chicano (Mexican-American), Indian, and Oriental allies will be ready.

Blackness is no longer a color, you see; it is an attitude.

> ". . . where blood is once begun to be shed,
> it is seldom staunched of a long time after."
>
> JOHN ROBINSON, 1623

1

THE MYTH OF THE PURITAN PILGRIM

or "Sit Down You're Rockin' the Rock"

"So they committed themselves to the will of God & resolved to proseede," explains William Bradford, second Governor of the Plymouth Plantation (yes, folks, that's what he called it!) and one of the leaders of the *Mayflower* group of "church resisters." His words stand as the classic articulation of the myth of the Puritan Pilgrim as it survives today.

Though the settlers who arrived in Plymouth were not the first American colonists from England, or even the most important and influential in New England, Plymouth Rock and the *Mayflower* are the symbols of the Pilgrim myth. And that myth goes something like this.

THE MYTH

The Puritans were a party in the Church of England who wanted to go all the way in carrying out the Protestant Reformation. They wanted to establish both a religion and a way of life based upon a strict interpretation of the Bible; that is, living and worshiping as the Bible would suggest—without all the frills the Church had added. The Church of England, a high-church and formal structure just a shade left of the Vatican, did not make it with the Puritans. However, King James I and his law-and-order men did not take well to an "underground church," just as Department of Justice staffers are not likely to go to Fathers Dan and Phil Berrigan, George Clements, James Groppi, or the Reverend James Bevel for confession today. So after repeated busts and harassments the God-seeking Puritans split to Holland, where freedom of worship was respected, and formed the English Congregational Church in Leyden. But all the while they longed for an unmolested home under the English flag. They felt like "pilgrims and strangers" in a foreign land, and they were worried that their kids were losing contact with English culture. William Bradford felt the Dutch language was "uncouth."

America seemed to be the answer. The Puritans got permission from the Virginia Company's London branch, found some financial backing from a group of English merchants known as the "Adventurers," and set sail in the *Mayflower*. Even the voyage across seemed to prove that God was on the side of the Puritan Pilgrims. They had originally planned to make the voyage to American in two ships. But the second ship, the *Speedwell,* didn't live up to its name, proving to be neither "well" nor "speedy" as it kept springing leaks, so the entire Pilgrim group had to crowd on the *May-*

flower, which wasn't in any too good a shape itself. That the leaky ship made it from England to America with a 180-ton burden proved divine sympathy was with the undertaking.

After a long, hard sixty-five-day journey, the Puritan Pilgrims finally landed on the New England shores, considerably north of Virginia, and decided to settle along what is now Plymouth harbor. Thus it turned out to be a real "mass" movement. They arrived en masse, in Mass, running away from Mass.

Only courage and devotion kept the little band of Pilgrims alive. Though ill-equipped to make it on their own in an unfamiliar land, lacking both talent and resources, they somehow survived. Pilgrim rhetoric says God provided the survival kit. Governor Bradford said, "They knew they were pilgrims, and looked not much on those things, but lift up their eyes to the heavens, their dearest country." And William Brewster boasted, "It is not with us as with other men, who small things can discourage, or small discontentments cause to wish themselves at home again."

Surviving the first winter in the settlement of New Plymouth stands as one of the first "profiles in American courage." Think of the odds, the myth perpetrators tell us. Mishaps and delays caused the Puritan Pilgrims to land in the midst of one of those terrible New England winters. Not only did nature prove to be hostile, but all the time, as one historian put it, there were "dusky savages skulking among the trees." More than half of the band of settlers died that first winter, and "at one time the living were scarcely able to bury the dead." (Of course, if the Puritans *really* took the Bible seriously, that shouldn't have caused any concern. After all, Jesus said, "Let the dead bury the dead."

No ship arrived with additional supplies for a whole

year. Yet when the good ship *Fortune* did arrive, with thirty-five new mouths to feed, not one of the original survivors wanted to make the trip back to England when the *Fortune* set sail again. Such is the stuff the Pilgrim fathers were made of.

And, the myth continues, the Pilgrims were also the fathers of the democratic form of government America holds so dear. Upon arriving in the New World, the Pilgrims drew up the Mayflower Compact, which stated that they would be ruled by the will of the majority until England made permanent provision for the new colony.

Pulitzer-prize winning historians Henry Steele Commager and Samuel Eliot Morrison sum it up this way in *The Growth of the American Republic*:

But they [the Puritan Pilgrims] never lost heart or considered giving up and going home. These simple folks were exalted to the stature of statesmen and prophets in their narrow sphere, because they ardently believed, and so greatly dared, and firmly endured. They set forth in acts as in words the stout-hearted idealism in action that Americans admire; that is why Plymouth Rock has become a symbol.

And Governor Bradford concluded in his annals:

Thus out of small beginnings greater things have been produced by his hand that made all things of nothing, and gives being to all things that are; and as one small candle may light a thousand; so the light here kindled hath shone unto many, yea, in some sort, to our whole nation.

So the Puritan Pilgrims, though later to be replaced by the founding fathers of the American Revolution, still remain most dear to American mythology. America the God-fearing and God-loving nation was founded by those who shared that fear and love. America is specially blessed because of her religious origins. "Land where our fathers died; land of the pilgrims' pride; from every mountainside; let freedom ring."

And every Thanksgiving little kids in public school assemblies re-enact that first New England feast, complete with funny hats and costumes, and always, of course, carrying muskets.

THE ROCK IS ROCKY

Of course there were too many slaves in the English colonies for the Plymouth Rock myth to sit well in the black community. To black folks the myth says, "Here was a man searching for religious freedom and the right to worship as he pleased, and on his way over to find God, he stole *us*." It is a strange man who wants to establish a way of life as the Bible suggests and begins that new way of life by keeping some slaves.

But even white folks should realize the shaky foundation upon which Plymouth Rock rests. The Puritan Pilgrims arrived in Plymouth quite by accident. Call it divine intervention if you want to, but God had to pull some pretty shady deals with the Indians to make it happen.

When the Puritan Pilgrims were looking to the New World for a place to settle, their first choice was Guiana, which Sir Walter Raleigh had described so alluringly. But they soon decided that a tropical climate would not be the best for industrious Puritans. Besides, the new colony would be dangerously exposed to the Spaniards, who had proved themselves not very friendly to another group of God-seekers, the Huguenots, whom they had wiped out in Florida.

Second choice was Virginia, but the Puritans soon remembered that Episcopal (Church of England) ideas had already taken root there. New England was considered too cold, but the land around the Delaware River seemed ideal. Through the help of Sir Edwin Sandys, who was sympathetic to the Puritans, negotiations were completed with the London Company for a grant of land in the Delaware River area.

Quite the opposite from nature being hostile, if it hadn't been for certain acts of nature, Plymouth Rock would never have happened. Storms and foul weather so confused accurate measurings of latitude and longitude that the Puritans ended up in Cape Cod. Since they were not in an area under the jurisdiction of the London Company, they tried to head south but were again turned back by natural hazards. So Plymouth became the best possible site for settling considering the circumstances. Even though their land grant was no good, the Puritans thought they could easily obtain a new grant from the Plymouth Company.

Nature's unforeseen change of the Puritans' travel plans probably saved their lives. It so happens that some three years before the Puritan Pilgrims landed, a terrible pestilence had swept over the New England area and killed, according to some estimates, half of the Indian population between the Penobscot river and Narragansett bay. Many of the Wampanoag Indians in the area attributed this calamity to their having killed two or three white fishermen the year before. So when the Pilgrims landed, the Indians were reluctant to deal with the invaders, thinking that all white folks might have the power of the plague at their disposal. Those "dusky savages skulking among the trees" were merely looking out for the plague demon. Just keeping an eye on white folks.

When the Pilgrims landed, the Indians held a powwow and went through elaborate rituals, conjuring up every kind of curse imaginable, but they were superstitious enough not to resort to physical methods of attack. Thus began a phenomenon which was later to become a byword in America—religiously inspired strategic nonviolence. So the Indians left the Puritan Pilgrims alone that crucial first winter.

But that was all the time the white folks needed. At the first sight of Indians scurrying in the bushes, a platform was built on the nearest hill and a few cannon were placed there to cover the neighboring valleys and plains. By the end of summer the platform had become a fort, overlooking and protecting the harbor and the rapidly growing village.

Imagine what would have happened to the Plymouth Rock myth if nature had not intervened. The Puritan Pilgrims would have landed on course in the lands between the Hudson and the Delaware. They probably would have had problems with the Dutch. If not, they would have found themselves in the territory of the Susquehannock Indians, at the time one of the most powerful tribes on the continent. And the Susquehannocks did not have hangups about the plague demon.

PURIFYING THE PURE

What kind of stock were these Pilgrim ancestors white folks have been trying to trace their ancestry back to for over three hunded years? First of all, there is some argument among historians that the Plymouth Rock folks were Puritans at all. Some say they were Separatists, not Puritans, the latter group being the settlers of the Massachusetts Bay Colony. Those Massachusetts folks proclaimed a more "pure" rhetoric, seeing themselves and their colonial enterprise as a "beacon of light for all mankind." I suppose that really means making the Indian's territory "safe for democracy."

But it is clear that the *Mayflower* group had no other motives for settling down in the New World than looking out for number one. They didn't see themselves on a missionary crusade to convert the Indians as other pilgrims did. They just wanted a bit of land in which they could do their own thing. What that thing was to be we shall soon see. But whether or not Puritans or Separatists is the proper designation for the Plymouth Rock group matters little, because fewer than half of the *Mayflower* arrivals were pilgrims anyway. Captain Miles Standish was a non-Pilgrim hired to serve as military adviser, along with two hired seamen and fourteen indentured servants and hired artisans, thus forming the first military-industrial complex.

Brother Standish was responsible for originating an American problem which many people feel is still paramount today—the use of outside agitators who encourage looting and stealing. When the *Mayflower* first docked in Provincetown, Standish led a few expeditions inland to explore. When Standish and his men came across some corn buried by the Indians in underground barns, they couldn't resist the urge to "cop" their new find, thus giving a very early answer to the Indian's question of whether or not he could trust the white man. Governor Bradford later said that planting the stolen kernels of corn the following spring is what saved the Pilgrim fathers from starvation. Of course, a few bushels of corn were minor compared to what the white man would later steal from the Indian.

But at least Brother Standish didn't steal Indians themselves, as an earlier white invader in the same area, George Weymouth, had done. Weymouth and his traveling buddy, James Rosier, worked for English promoters who were trying to drum up enthusiasm for settling in the New World. Colonization was seen as good business primarily, and religious considerations only came in second. To the English capitalists, if religion could get folks over there, fine. The main thing was to get white folks settled over in the land of the Indians with a tie to England, so that money-making goods would flow into the mother country.

Weymouth and Rosier did some trading with the Indians to get them used to the idea. Or, as Weymouth said, the English "wished to bring [the Indians] to an understanding of exchange" so that "they might conceive the intent of our comming to them to be for no other end." Since the English planned eventually to get as much of the Indians' land as possible, they wanted to make that later job easier—or again, as Weymouth said, to treat the Indians "with as great kindness as we could devise" without regard to profit.

But one day Weymouth and Rosier got the feeling that the Indians were setting them up for an ambush. Probably because of their own guilt, their [white folks'] fears came out in them, and on the suspicion of ambush alone they decided that the natives belonged "in the ranke of other Salvages, who have beene by travellers in most discoveries found very treacherous." So the two Englishmen cut out, kidnaping a few Indians to take with them, and headed back for home shores.

Back in England, Ferdinando Georges, head man in Plymouth, was very pleased with the Indian catch. He saw them as very good for promotion. The Indians were taught the English language and then were used to make speeches about the riches of the New World and the good life to be found there. Such Madison Avenue hustling paid off. The New World was described as a veritable paradise; rivers filled with fish, jumping out in Charlie Tuna fashion just begging to be caught; turkeys falling out of the trees before you could shoot them; animals eager to give up their furs; and all manner of utopian delights.

People remembered Thomas More's description of a utopia located somewhere in the New World, and America seemed to be it. All kinds of folks were attracted to going there, not just the God-seekers. Convicts from the jails of Middlesex and other counties in England for example. As early as 1617 convicted criminals were saved from the gallows in England to "yeilde a profitable service to the Commonwealth in parts abroad." By 1670 the good folks in Virginia were quite upset at the great number of "fellons and other desperate villianes sent hither from the prisons of England." They petitioned their council for law and order to prevent the "barbarous designs and felonious practices of these wicked men," and to see to it that English promoters stopped sending "jailbirds" into the New World.

America also proved to be a convenient "fresh air fund" for England—get the kids off the streets and into the colonies. Poor folks in general and kids in particular, with whom England was "pestered," were sent to the colonies. King James himself sent off a group of "Duty boys" on the ship *Duty*: "divers young people" of whom the king wrote to Sir Thomas Smith, a leading English promoter, January 13, 1619, "who wanting imployment doe live idle and followe the Court." Some towns saw America as a convenient answer to the poverty problem, recognizing that a one-way ticket was a cheap form of relief and a good way of getting rid of indigents.

Thus in the colonization of America the English government and the capitalists worked hand in hand. Colonization was good for business and a way of getting rid of undesirables. King James was glad to get rid of the Pilgrim fathers because he had vowed either to whip them into line or to run them out of the country. After all, they were dissenters, opponents of the Church establishment. Anything the promoters could do to make the trip enticing had governmental approval.

It is like the "Join the Army—See the World" slogan syndrome today. Hearing that propaganda, one would think army life is just one big vacation. The army promoters do not tell you about the war. When the real word of war filters back, young folks are not so easily enticed. It was the same with the criminals and children in England when the word came back about the sufferings and hardships in the New World. The vital statistics of colonization, those who died either in or on the way to the New World, were so appalling that "some of the children designed by the City [of London]" refused to make the trip. To die from epidemics and getting acclimated to life in America was not a happy prospect even to vagrants and criminals; and to many such folks the thought of the trip over was no better than life in prison or death on the gallows.

Even today, the army is used as a way out for youthful offenders. Teen-age gang leaders are told, "The best place for you is in the army." Soldiers go into the service for various reasons—to avoid being drafted, to get army pay because they can't get a job at home, and so on—not just for the pure patriotic reasons of duty to or love of one's country. Just as colonists came to America for various reasons other than the search for religious freedom that the myth of American history extols.

Of course the English promoters had an advantage over the army promoters today. The English didn't have to buck television. Had there been a news team with cameras in the colonies and on the ships going over, most people would have given up on the colonizing idea when they saw the first TV special. Army promoters have faced the problem of Huntley and Brinkley, or Walter Cronkite, bringing the Vietnam war into every American living room each night. Young folks see the killing at first hand. And they are not about to fall for the "Join the Army—See the World" line.

People underestimate the power and influence of television. Many folks are upset about crime in the streets and rioters looting television sets. They ought to see it as retribution, since television is largely responsible for such acts in the first place. I don't know what kind of a hoodlum I might have been if we had had television when I was a kid. I went to bed hungry every night, unless I was lucky enough to grab a biscuit my brothers didn't see me take. But if I had gone to bed and turned on the *Tonight* show, where one commercial showed me more food than our family saw in a month, who knows how much stealing I might have done the next day. And in a country, the richest country in the world, where more than a quarter of the population goes to bed each night underfed aand hungry, crime in the streets could be seen as reparations. Nobody in America should be allowed to walk the streets safe until the problem of hunger is solved.

Think of the insult to poor folks in America when the government pays Senator Eastland of Mississippi $10,-000 a month not to plant food crops and pays a poor black baby in Mississippi $8 a month to survive. As long as that continues, crime in the streets of Washington, D.C., will never begin to equal the crime on Capitol Hill.

The way Americans seem to think today, about the only way to end hunger in America would be for Secretary of Defense Melvin Laird to go on national television and say we are falling behind the Russians in feeding folks. Just let a team of Russian sociologists go into hunger-ridden areas of America and say the same things publicly that certain United States senators have been saying, and the entire nation would be outraged enough to demand some changes.

Since the Nixon administration seems to be concerned more about "crime in the streets" than eliminating poverty and hunger in America, the least President Nixon could do is effect some personnel changes to mollify the situation. Like making Vice President Spiro Agnew head of the poverty program. Poor folks would still be hungry, of course, but at least their appetites would be spoiled.

But America continues to be interested more in taking pot shots at the moon than in shooting down hunger. America is concerned more with the *possibility* of moon folks than with the *reality* of hungry poor folks. That priority doesn't even make sense scientifically. It ought to be easier to place food in a man's stomach than to place a man on the moon. At least in the feeding process you have gravity working on your side. Food digests and is expelled from the body in accord with the law of gravity. With moon shots it is an uphill struggle all the way.

Just think of the insult to poor folks watching their government spend $24 billion to go to the moon to collect a few pounds of rocks, only to see those rocks ground up and fed to some white mice. Not only were there no black astronauts, but NASA didn't even have sense enough to get those mice from a ghetto dweller. The black ghetto can supply the NASA laboratories with any kind of rats or mice they need—black, brown, white, albino, or queer.

But getting back to the lessons of history, I suppose we could say that Miles Standish started the whole ugly process—stealing food from the mouths of Indians to keep the colonizers alive. And America has been living off the oppressed ever since. The Puritan Pilgrims themselves were in great need of purification.

BIBLES AND BULLETS

Or maybe decontamination would be a better choice of words. The plague that wiped out nearly half the New England Indian population was undoubtedly a disease introduced by white Europeans. Modern authorities are reluctant to try to diagnose the disease, since historical scraps of evidence are both vague and contradictory. There is general agreement on what it was not: yellow fever, smallpox, jaundice, or typhoid fever. It could have been measles, bubonic plague, or perhaps even a combination of diseases that hit various tribes of Indians simultaneously. At any rate, the Pilgrims seemed to be immune, though they were probably carriers. Yet the Pilgrims saw themselves as carrying the gospel of Jesus Christ rather than disease. The plague, they felt, was divine action, showing that clearly God was making room for his people.

The general attitude of the Pilgrims toward the Indians was that they were heathens who needed to be saved. Popular mythology of the time saw the Indians in America as descended from the ten lost tribes of Israel, and therefore in special need of conversion. The Reverend Thomas Thorowgood, for example, argued this opinion in his *Jewes in America, or Probabilities that the Americans are of that Race,* published in London in 1650. He offered as evidence similarities between Jews and Indians in speech, customs, and ease of childbirth. Pushing the conversion and missionary idea, Cotton Mather wrote in his *Magnalia Christi Americana* in 1702: "Though we know not when or how these Indians first became inhabitants of this mighty continent, yet we may guess that probably the devil decoyed those miserable savages hither in hopes that the gospel of the Lord Jesus Christ would never come here to destroy or disturb his absolute empire over them."

So once again the Bible was used to cover up the "discovery" of a land that was already occupied. Not only occupied, but being *used* at the time. The Pilgrims felt they had "spiritual" benefits to offer the Indians—the gospel of Jesus Christ—and the Indians had certain "temporal" benefits to offer them, namely land. The Pilgrims seemed to feel that was a fair exchange.

But the Bible has always been cleverly used in colonization efforts. In fact, the history of the performance of white Christian missionaries in Africa first aroused my own personal curiosity about the strange power of the Bible. When the white Christian missionaries went to Africa, the white folks had the bibles and the natives had the land. When the missionaries pulled out, they had the land, and the natives had the bibles. Now that's a pretty good trick if you can pull it off. I've often wondered if I could try the same pattern with the Board of Directors of General Motors. I'd walk into the board meeting with my Bible under my arm. If I could find the magic formula that worked so well for the missionaries, when I left the meeting, I'd own the corporation and each director would have a Bible.

Of course, the magic formula that worked so well for the Pilgrim fathers was guns and gunpower. Genocide became the substitute for conversion. Folks in America today, both black and white, who say it looks like this country is getting ready to *start* practicing genocide simply do not know their American history, as any Indian can tell you. America is just now getting ready to expand her *group*.

When the Indians first decided to pay a visit to the Plymouth Plantation at the end of that first winter, the first to come calling was an Indian named Samoset who had learned some English from fishermen on the coast and was inclined to be friendly. He came with words of welcome. He was later followed by Chief Massasoit, accompanied by a group of feathered and painted warriors. The Chief and the Governor smoked the pipe of peace, while Miles Standish and a half-dozen musketeers stood by just in case.

Later on when the Chief of the Narragansett Indians, Canonicus, decided to check the Pilgrims out by issuing a challenge, gunpowder again proved to be the answer, though it was not fired. Canonicus sent a messenger to Governor Bradford with a bundle of arrows wrapped in snakeskin. Bradford sent back the same snakeskin wrapped around some gunpowder and bullets. Canonicus could have mustered two thousand warriors, but the bluff worked, giving the Pilgrims a little more time. The Indians didn't know what the stuff was and carried it gingerly out of camp. Considering their experience with white folks to date, I'm not surprised they were suspicious. After all, it might have been plague powder.

It is hard to imagine what America might have developed into had there been no guns from the very beginning. The Pilgrim fathers would have had to approach the Indians from the standpoint of pure morality, rather than from a standpoint of puritanism, which always had in the background thoughts of acquisition, colonization, and profit. Just as it would be difficult to imagine what a nonviolent army could accomplish today. If thousands of American troops appeared on the battlefields of the world totally unarmed. Or if America gave up the space and arms races and instead began *really* feeding starving peoples the world over, sending out technical and medical teams to wipe out disease everywhere rather than military supplies and assistance. A new kind of race among nations could be initiated. America could stand proudly before the eyes of the world and say to Russia, "Instead of matching us rocket for rocket, or missile for missile, let's see you match us in morality, humanitarian act for humanitarian act."

But the Pilgrim fathers chose instead to bring and use their guns. And the severity of that usage shocked the Plymouth Pilgrims' dearest friend and spiritual leader, John Robinson, who had been pastor of the church in Leyden, Holland, but remained behind when the congregation sailed for America. He received a report of the Pilgrims' retaliatory attack upon the Indians, after an earlier Indian attack caused by the wrongdoings of another Englishman in the area, Andrew Weston. In a letter to Governor Bradford, Robinson wrote:

Concerning the killing of those poor Indians, of which we heard at first by report, and since by more certain relation. Oh, how happy a thing had it been, if you had converted some before you had killed any! Besides, where blood is once begun to be shed, it is seldom staunched of a long time after. You will say they deserved it. I grant it; but upon what provocations and invitements by those heathenish Christians [Mr. Weston's men]. Besides, you being no magistrates over them were to consider not what they deserved but what you were by necessity constrained to inflict. Necessity of this, especially of killing so many (and many more, it seems, they would, if they could) I see not. Methinks one or two principals should have been full enough, according to that approved rule, The punishment to a few, and the fear to many. Upon this occasion let me be bold to exhort you seriously to consider of the disposition of your Captain, whom I love, and am persuaded the Lord in great mercy and for much good hath sent you him, if you use him aright. He is a man humble and meek amongst you, and towards all in ordinary course. But now if this be merely from an humane spirit, there is cause to fear that by occasion, especially of provocation, there may be wanting that tenderness of the life of man (made after God's image) which is meet. It is also a thing more glorious, in men's eyes, than pleasing in God's or convenient for Christians, to be a terrour to poor barbarous people. And indeed I am afraid lest, by these occasions, others whould be drawn to affect a kind of ruffling course in the world.

Robinson's words remain a healthy reminder today. The "staunch" fouls the air we breathe more than any industrial form of air pollution. As America sends her troops all over the world to make it "safe for democracy," who is going to guarantee the Indian at home that he is safe from his neighbors?

Samuel Sewall saw well what was happening back in 1700, and suggested a better approach in a letter to Sir William Ashhurst:

I should think it requisite that convenient Tracts of Land should be set out to them; and that by plain and natural Boundaries, as much as may be; as Lakes, Rivers, Mountains, Rocks, Upon which for any English man to encourach, should be accounted a Crime. Except this be done, I fear their own Jealousies, and the French Friers will persuade them, that the English, as they encrease, and think they want more room, will never leave till they have crouded them quite out of all their Lands. And it will be a vain attempt for us to offer Heaven to them, if they take up prejudices against us, as if we did grudge them a Living upon their own Earth.

Those boundaries became "reservations," as the Indians were "crowded quite out of all their lands." And the reservations remain shameful pockets of squalor, hunger, poverty, and disease. The Pilgrim fathers, and their English sponsors, were indeed out to acquire land and goods, and guns were essential to such acquisition.

THE COMPACT MAYFLOWER CABINET

While the *Mayflower* was anchored in Cape Cod, the free adult males gathered in the ship's cabin and drew up what was known as the "Mayflower Compact." Since the Plymouth Rock settlers did not have a charter, it was to govern them until other provisions were made. Said the compact:

IN YE NAME OF GOD, AMEN! We whose names are underwritten, the loyall subjects of our dread soveraigne Lord, King James, by ye grace of God, of Great Britaine, Franc & Ireland, king, defender of ye faith, &c., haveing undertaken, for ye glorie of God and advancement of ye Christian faith and honour of our king and countrie, a voyage to plant ye first colonie in ye Northerne parts of Virginia, doe by these presents solemnly and mutually in ye presence of God, and one of another, covenant and combine our selves together into a civill body politick, for our better ordering and preservation and furtherance of ye ends aforesaid; and *by vertue hearof* to enacte, constitute, and frame such just and equall lawes, ordinances, acts, constitutions, and offices, from time to time, as shall be thought most meete and convenient for ye general good of ye Colonie, unto which we promise all due submission and obedience.

The document was signed by forty-one men.

Historians have said this Mayflower Compact of 1620 "stands with the Virginia Assembly of 1619 as the foundation stones of American institutions. Nothing like these happened anywhere else in the world for almost two centuries." That historical observation is probably true.

Governor Bradford, of course, would not have claimed to be setting any democratic standards. It was his belief that men are elected to office to govern, and that their decisions should not be subjected to public review. With such a belief, he would fit in well with the modern-day Presidents. Having been elected to office, Bradford could say with conviction that his decisions "will in no way whatsoever be affected" by demonstrations of the populace.

The little group who met in the ship's cabin to sign the Mayflower Compact symbolizes the exclusiveness that continues to mark American institutions. They were free, adult males. That excludes women, youth, and poor folks (or servants). In fact, Governor Bradford had to write back to his capitalist backers in England, the Adventurers, to assure them that such exclusion was indeed being practiced. Such wild rumors of the kind of democracy being allowed in the colony were circulating in England that, in 1623, Bradford sent personal word that women and children were not voting. I guess it was just assumed that servants had no say, but the Adventurers seemed to be worried that a women's liberation and a youth movement were taking root in their colony.

Thus the symbolic foundation for institutional racism and exclusion today. Basically, black folks in America do not hate white folks. Of course, you have some black folks who hate turnips. What blacks folks in America hate and resent are the stinking white racist institutions.

I suppose white folks' arrogance makes them think they are black folks' problem. But, really, individual white folks are insignificant. Individual expressions of racism never hurt me. A man has a constitutional right to call me a "nigger," under the Bill of Rights. That's freedom of speech. But that man better not spit in my face while he's saying it. Institutional racism in America continues to spit in the face of black folks and choke us to death.

Let me give an example of the insignificance of individual white folks. If all the white folks in America disappeared overnight, leaving no one but blacks, Puerto Ricans, Indians, Chicanos, and Orientals, and we continued to have to take those college entrance exams in white educational institutions, we *still* couldn't get in. And it would have nothing to do with the presence of individual white folks. The American system has compressed black folks into condensed, overcrowded urban areas called ghettos, and in such an atmosphere, black folks have had to develop their own culture in order to survive. Yet when a black kid takes the college entrance exam, he does not find one question relating to that black culture. What does a black ghetto kid know or care about the Eiffel Tower or the governments of Europe? But ask him about the failure of the poverty program or if the model cities program has eliminated rats and roaches, and I'll bet he knows the answer. An Indian youth will not be asked any questions on his college entrance exam about life on the Indian reservation where America has forced him to live. He will be asked a question like "What was Abraham Lincoln's mother's name?" If we really wanted to find out how dumb the rest of Americans are, we should let the Indian write the college entrance exam. "What was Sitting Bull's grandma's name?"

I meet so many black folks who say, "I just don't understand these black students today. When I was in college, we fought to integrate the dormitories. Now these black students say they want separate facilities." I can understand such black folks because they were in the same bag I was in when I went to a predominantly white college. I didn't have to take the entrance exam. I happened to be the third fastest half-miler in the country, so the coach didn't want to take any chances on my passing a racist exam. Every time I would try to get into the line waiting to take the entrance exam, they'd snatch me out of line saying, "We already took the exam for you." I didn't know what they meant until I saw my entrance application one day with the notation, "The boy runs good."

Even the menu of the cafeteria of my college reflected institutional racism. The first time I went into the cafeteria I felt like Colonel Sanders at a vegetarian convention. I began to look for something I was used to eating. There was no watermelon in sight. Instead of liver and onions, I found steak and mushrooms. And the steak was so rare the blood was running out. That's white folks' food. Down in the black ghetto, the meat we get is so bad we cook it done-er than well.

Of course, if some white colleges knew how unhealthy soul food is, and how many years it is cutting off the lives of black folks, soul food would be "required eating" for all black students.

But I was so glad to get into a white college that I didn't mind all those "coon" notes the white students used to stick under my door, or those little "nigger" signs they used to leave on the wall. But the young black students today have a different attitude. They are struggling for dignity and manhood. And they are saying, "Before we take all these damn insults, let us live by ourselves." These young black kids have decided they are not going to be America's niggers any more, so they are demanding to be taught who they are. They are sure their history goes back further than slavery. If the average white student knew the true history of black folks, he would discover that his own momma comes closer to being that "nigger" than black folks. Black students are realizing that a man without knowledge of himself and his heritage is like a tree without roots.

In the process black folks are being called racists themselves. So many interviewers these days ask me, "Mr. Gregory, what do you think about separatism in the black community?" When white folks get so concerned about separatism, let them get the Indian off the reservation. That is a pure example of separatism, but it seems to be all right with white folks as long as the white system is doing it.

It would be an entirely different matter if the Indian were advocating separatism. If the Indians held a press conference and announced on national television, "We like the reservation and don't want any more white folks on it," white folks would call out the army.

Institutional white racism permits some Jews to get upset because they found out that black anti-Semitism exists in the black ghetto. Every Jew in America over fifteen years old knows another Jew who doesn't like "niggers." Now they find out some black folks don't like Jews, why are they so upset? Because in a white racist system the underdog is never permitted to do the same things the man on top does.

Anti-Semitism has always existed in the black community. Many black folks in America who were raised in a large urban area heard their own momma unconsciously make an anti-Semitic statement. Now it is out in the open, and I am personally glad it has been exposed. Such exposure is the only way to begin to solve the problem. If I had cancer, I would want to know it. That's the first step in trying to find a cure. I hope everything we are doing wrong in the black ghetto reaches the level of public exposure. It is the only sane and sensible way to begin to solve the problem.

The institutional racism of the transportation industry is illustrated by the fact that for many years the only job opportunity on railroad trains open to black folks was the category of pullman porters. As long as we've had trains in this country, black folks have never been permitted to drive them. I know some white folks think black folks are dumb, but you really don't need much sense to drive a train. All you have to do is follow the tracks. Yet if all pullman porters got together one day and made a public announcement saying, "We don't want to drive your old white trains, or take up your white tickets," the whole country would be upset and would be saying such an announcement was "reverse racism."

Since I travel a lot, I am reminded of this country's institutional racism every time I open my passport. Listed in the passport are the communist countries prohibited for American travel by the United States government—Red China, North Vietnam, and Cuba. Do you think it is an accident that they just happen to be non-white communist countries? Americans are permitted by their government to travel to Moscow. Yet every American boy who is killed in Vietnam dies from a bullet supplied by Russia. Every pilot shot down over North Vietnam is the victim of Russian-supplied weaponry. But Russian communists are white.

So black folks do not hate individual white folks. But they do hold white folks individually responsible for the system. A simple illustration will clarify the distinction. Suppose you came by my house with your little daughter, and while you were visiting me, my dog jumped on your daughter and bit her. Who are you going to sue—my dog or me? Of course you would sue me, even though I didn't bite your daughter. But I would be responsible for the actions of my dog. In like manner white folks are responsible for white racist institutions. Not that all white folks are racists, but all white folks are responsible for the system because it is theirs.

Now suppose you brought your daughter by my house, and my dog jumped up on the couch and bit both your daughter and mine. You would not be so angry with me, because you would realize we both have a similar problem. Then if my dog jumped at your daughter and I reached out to grab the dog and in the process was severely bitten myself, you wouldn't be mad at all. That is what black folks are saying to white America. Black folks are very upset about being continually bitten by this mad-dog-racist system. And they will stay upset with white folks until they either change the dog's habits or put themselves in a position where the dog will bite them, too.

Institutional racism and exclusion dwells deep within the soul of America. Though cries for true freedom have echoed in the wilderness throughout American history, *democracy* continues to be used as a cover for human *liberation*. Perhaps it is because those who came to these shores claiming to seek God mistakenly believed that God had already found them. As God's supposedly special *elect,* they felt free to trust their own impulses. They did not seem to realize that where human life is truly celebrated, where men and women are respected for their humanity, there God finds fit company for divine companionship and is pleased to dwell.

PROPERTY RIGHTS VERSUS HUMAN RIGHTS

Edward Potts Cheyney sums up the colonization motives this way:

The propriety companies of Virginia, Massachusetts, New Netherland, Canada, and other colonies were primarily commercial bodies seeking dividends, and only secondarily colonization societies sending over settlers. This distinction, and the gradual predominance of the latter over the former, is the clew to much of the early history of settlement in America. The commercial object could only be carried out by employing the plan of colonization, but new motives were soon added. The patriotic and religious conditions of the times created an interest in the American settlements as places where men could begin life anew with new possibilities. Hence the company, the home government, dissatisfied religious bodies, and many individuals, looked to the settlements in America with other than a commercial interest.

But commercial preoccupation, having been the initial stimulus for colonization, was too deeply entrenched in the American psyche to be replaced by pure humanitarian motives. Some early forms of colonial democracy, for example, gave voting status only to property holders. Profit motives and the dollar wove their way into the American fabric, and the thread can be traced up to the present moment in American history. Americans continue to display more allegiance to the Jolly Green Jesus than to the Lord of the Church.

Perhaps the Bible itself first indicated this trend. The book of Joel says that young men shall prophesy and the old men will dream dreams. That is precisely the situation in America today. The youth have become the prophets and their parents are dreaming—of money.

Wherever the dollar is held supreme and capitalistic interests dominate, a higher value will always be placed upon property rights than upon human rights. I do not advocate destroying the capitalistic system, but I do say that all Americans should work like hell to put the capitalists into their proper place under the United States Constitution and not on top of it. This country is not governed by the United States Constitution, nor does it function under the democratic process. As long as the capitalists are in control, we will always give *property* the priority over *humanity*.

The cigarette industry is a good example. The cigarette industry has been told that there is strong evidence of a direct link between smoking and cancer; yet they fight the FCC to keep their commercials on television and radio. A little kid watching a cigarette commercial sees a cowboy riding a horse stop against the background of a beautiful western sunset, light up a cigarette, and say, "I always smokes me a Marlboro." Imagine the effect upon that young mind. The kid knows he can never have a horse, but he can get the cigarette. It wouldn't be so bad if the cowboy rode his horse to a stop right in the middle of a cemetery, lighted up his cigarette, looked around and said, "This is Marlboro country."

Mayor Daley of Chicago once illustrated his preference for property over humanity. During a tense period of ghetto rebellion he ordered his police to shoot all looters to kill. He never said shoot murderers to kill or shoot dope pushers to kill: murderers and dope pushers deal with human life; looters deal with property.

But to be honest with you, that statement was one of the few statements by Mayor Daley I could agree with. In fact, I sent him a telegram. It read: "Dear Mayor: Your statement pertaining to shooting all looters to kill I agree with wholeheartedly if you make one stipulation. Let's make it retroactive and let's first put the gun in the Indian's hand."

The dollar gets more respect than human beings. If you lived in the state of Illinois and decided to drive your car down South, there are certain sections where some "Yankee-hater" might shoot you driving down the highway because you had "Land of Lincoln" on your license plate. Yet that same "Yankee-hater" would not burn a five-dollar bill which has both Lincoln's name and his picture on it.

Even our legal system illustrates the worship of the dollar. If a man kills another man and goes into court accused of first degree murder, he can enter a plea of temporary insanity. But if a man forges a check or embezzles some money, he could never go into court and plead temporary insanity. The man who takes human life might be judged insane. The man who tampers with money or property will never get off that easy.

The national furor over a series of bombings and bomb threats, attributed to militants of the left wing, is another good example of the higher value placed upon property than upon human life. A quick analysis of such bombing incidents reveals that bombs were placed in buildings, triggered to go off at night when the buildings were empty. In many instances warning calls were placed to make *sure* the buildings were emptied. Newspapers all over America ran editorials saying how vicious and irrational such bombings were.

At about the same time, in Danbury, Connecticut, some bank robbers held up a bank and set off a series of bombs to occupy the attention of the police, thereby enhancing the chances of a clean getaway. They blew up an automobile, during the day, parked in the middle of a crowded shopping center where mothers were shopping with their little babies. Not only was human life threatened but the innocent, defenseless lives of little children. Yet there were no newspaper editorials deploring that act. Most Americans could understand the rationale behind the Danbury bombing. The thugs were after some money, and they would do anything to make sure they got it.

Worship of the dollar produces some strange reactions. If two men broke into an old lady's house, killed the old lady, and found out she only had a nickel, most people would place a higher value on the lady's life than the nickel and would say, "It was awful for those inhumane beasts to kill that old woman for a nickel. They ought to get the electric chair." But if the same two men broke into the old woman's house, killed her, and found ten million dollars, everybody would say, "She didn't have any business having that much money in the house."

So money and property continue to take precedence over pure religious interests in America. The church has become a wealthy property holder, and every time Americans spend their money they are reminded "In God We Trust."

THE MARKS OF COLONIZATION

The marks of colonization, whether in the Third World or the American colonies, are aggrandizement and slavery or servitude. As many as two-thirds of the original labor force of the English colonies in America were white indentured servants. Under the indenture system a man made a contract with the shipping company for free passage, agreeing to let the ship's captain sell his services for a number of years to the highest bidder. Hundreds of thousands of white men from England, some religious dissenters, some paupers and prisoners came to the New World in this manner. After the period of service was up—two to seven years—the law required that a man be given a suit of clothes, a little plot of land, some light subsistence, and the status of freedman.

Beyond indenture, the cold, hard capitalistic fact of a

land-rich but labor-scarce economy brought with it, from the very beginning, the institution of slavery. Colonists in the New World had three categories of slaves. First, Indians were taken as prisoners of war. English colonists followed a sort of international law of the time that Indians were free men. They could be exploited but not enslaved, except Indians taken in combat or convicted of some other crime. Second were Moors, Turks, and some Jews whose slavery was justified on the grounds that they were all non-Christians. Black folk constituted the third category of slaves. Colonists saw a lot of things wrong with black folks. They were non-Christians and therefore heathens, but black folks were also considered savages, set apart from the rest of humanity, doomed by the curse of Noah to a life of perpetual slavery.

American mythology states that originally black folks were treated the same as white indentured servants; that slavery did not appear until certain colonial statutes of the 1660's; and that the good colonial church folks would have practiced racial equality if they had been left alone to pursue their better instincts. Some very early legal statutes indicate that black folks were the victims of racial discrimination at the outset of colonization. In Virginia, between 1630 and 1646, statutes and resolutions appear: (1) accusing a white man of defiling his body and dishonoring himself because he had intercourse with a black woman; (2) prohibiting black men and no one else from carrying guns; and (3) wording the text in such a way as to indicate that the black man was in the same category as an object and not as a human being. The 1646 Virginia Treaty with the Indians requires that Chief Necotowance "bring in the English prisoners, And all such negroes and guns

which are yet remaining either in the possession of him-
selfe or any Indians."

The real clincher comes in a 1652 Rhode Island
statute which begins, "Whereas, there is a common
course practised amongst Englishmen to buy negers, to
the end that they may have them for service or slaves
forever. . . ." The statute goes on to insist that "no
blacke mankind or white" could be made to serve
"longer than ten yeares." Any man violating that statute
was to "forfeit to the collonie forty pounds."

Not that slavery was accepted unchallenged, of
course. Men of compassion will always raise their voices
in protest. The Germantown Mennonite Resolution
Against Slavery of 1688 represents an early voice of
protest in colonial America. It said in part:

In Europe there are many oppressed for conscience-
sake; and here there are those oppressed which are of a
black colour. And we who know that men must not commit adultery—some do commit adultery *in* others, separating wives from their husbands, and giving them to
others: and some sell the children of these poor cretures
to other men. Ah! do consider well this thing, you who
do it, if you would be done at this manner—and if it is
done according to Christianity! You surpass Holland and
Germany in this thing. This makes an ill report in all
those countries of Europe, where they hear of [it], that
the Quakers do here handel men as they handel there the
cattle. And for that reason some have no mind of inclination to come hither. And who shall maintain this your
cause, or plead for it? Truly, we cannot do so, except you
shall inform us better hereof, viz.: that Christians have
liberty to practice these things. Pray, what thing in the
world can be done worse towards us, than if men should
rob or steal us away, and sell us for slaves to strange
countries; separating husbands from their wives and chil-

dren. Being now this is not done in the manner we would
be done at; therefore, we contradict, and are against this
traffic of men-body. And we who profess that it is not
lawful to steal, must, likewise, avoid to purchase such
things as are stolen, but rather help to stop this robbing
and stealing, if possible. And such men ought to be delivered out of the hands of the robbers, and set free as in
Europe. Then is Pennsylvania to have a good report, instead, it hath now a bad one, for this sake, in other countries; Especially whereas the Europeans are desirous to
know in what manner *the Quakers* do rule in *their* province; and most of them do look upon us with an envious
eye. But if this is done well, what shall we say is done evil?

If once these slaves (which they say are so wicked and
stubborn men,) should join themselves—fight for their
freedom, and handel their masters and mistresses, as they
did handel them before; wil these masters and mistresses
take the sword at hand and war against these poor slaves,
like, as we are able to believe, some will not refuse to do?
Or, have these poor negers not as much right to fight for
their freedom, as you have to keep them slaves? . . .

Judge Samuel Sewall, who wrote the first abolitionist
tract in America, is remembered in the history books,
but not for his denunciation of slavery. Rather, he is
remembered as one of the presiding judges at the Salem
witch trials. Perhaps that is America's way of getting
back at Judge Sewall for his defense of black folks. In
The Selling of Joseph (1700), Judge Sewall demolished
the existing proslavery arguments by insisting that the
inherent immorality of slavery outweighed any possible
benefits derived from a system of bondage. Incidentally,
for those inclined to want to see Judge Sewall as the first
hip white man, he still felt blacks were not the equal of
whites. Against the argument that black folks were the
descendants of Ham and therefore under the curse of
slavery, Sewall said they were really descended from

Cush. To those who said black folks were brought out of a pagan country to a place where they could hear the gospel of Jesus Christ, Judge Sewall replied that "evil must not be done that good may come of it."

Another proslavery argument insisted that African tribes wage war upon one another and that slave ships bring lawful captives taken in such wars. Sewall brought down that argument with a hometown illustration. Said the judge:

An unlawful war can't make lawful captives. . . . I am sure if some gentlemen should go down to the Brewsters to take air, and fish, and a stronger party from Hull should surprise them and sell them for slaves to a ship outward bound, they would think themselves unjustly dealt with, both by sellers and buyers. And yet it is to be feared, we have no other kind of title to our Negroes.

One man who saw the inherent hypocrisy undergirding English colonization and said so publicly was Roger Williams. Williams arrived in the New World with his wife Mary on February 5, 1631, landing at Nantasket, outside Boston. A religious purist through and through, Williams turned down a good job as teacher at a Boston church because he "durst not officiate to unseparated people." After a short time at the Plymouth Plantation as a pastor's assistant, Roger Williams became minister to a Salem church.

Governor Bradford and other Pilgrim officials held Williams in high regard when he first came. In a short time they were trying to run him out of the colony. Bradford made the mistake of asking Roger Williams to do some writing for him. Williams prepared a treatise extended by King Charles I was no good. Roger Williams correctly believed that the land belonged to the Indians. No kings, wrote Williams, including Charles,

were "invested with Right by virtue of their Christian-
itie to take and give away the Lands and Countries of
other men." Needless to say, it was an unpopular view.
It placed the Pilgrim fathers in the category of invading
land grabbers rather than free religious spirits. Popular
opinion held that all land "discovered" in the name of
European monarchs automatically became their property.

Such a view is like my wife and me walking down the
street and coming across you and your wife parked in
your brand-new automobile. My wife says to me, "That
sure is a beautiful car. I sure would like to have one."
So I answer, "Well, Lillian, let's discover it." The feeling you would have as we took over your car gives some
idea of how the Indians must have felt.

So Roger Williams insisted that the Plymouth colonists had no right to be there, that their title from the
King was no good, and that the only legitimate claim
they could ever have would have to be worked out in a
deal with the Indians. Having dropped his bombshell,
Williams went back to Salem. In a short time, Roger
Williams was in hot water with the officials of the
Massachusetts Bay Colony. It seems they didn't like his
treatise any more than Governor Bradford did. Three
passages especially irked the Massachusetts officials. In
one passage Williams called King James a liar, "because
in his patent he blessed God that he was the first Christian Prince that had discovered this land." Then he
charged King James with "blasphemy for calling Europe
Christendom, or the Christian world." Finally, Williams
used some particularly uncomplimentary passages from
the Book of Revelation to apply personally to King
Charles.

The Massachusetts Bay officials tried to get Williams
to reject what he had said and take a loyalty oath, but

of course he refused. Williams said he had written the treatise for Governor Bradford's personal use, and that the Governor could burn the paper up if he wanted to. So in 1635 Roger Williams was sentenced to "dep(ar)te out of this jurisdiccòn within six weekes" because he had "broached & dyvulged dyvers newe & dangerous opinions, against the authorities of magistrates & yet maintaineth the same without retraccòn."

Roger Williams was banished, and he went out to found the colony of Rhode Island. The Pilgrim fathers refused to admit their guilt in dealing with the Indians —a guilt which should haunt Thanksgiving Day school assemblies today. The Indian kept the little *Mayflower* group alive. The Plymouth Plantation's own "house Indian," Squanto, who came to visit in the company of Chief Massasoit and stayed, taught the pilgrims how to plant, where to fish and hunt, and how to fertilize the ground.

When the fall harvest yielded a bountiful supply of blessings, the Indians, whose religion was rooted in a gratitude for nature's provisions, taught the pilgrims to give thanks with a feast of celebration. Americans have continued that feast ever since, but even as Thanksgiving dinners are consumed, the Indians starve on reservations.

If there is a garbage can in heaven, it must be reserved for American Thanksgiving Day prayers.

II

THE MYTH OF THE SAVAGE

or "Where Have All the Buffalo Gone?"

In Chicago, Illinois, during April 1968, President Johnson spoke these words to a group assembled at a fund-raising dinner: "I ask you if there is anybody in this room tonight who would trade where you are for where you were when you discovered this land?"

Shouts of "No, no, no" swept through the audience, and I could not help feeling that there must not have been any Indians in attendance that evening! When the President's ancestors "discovered" America, the Indians were occupying their own land, governing their own affairs, and enjoying the natural endowments of an unspoiled environment.

If President Johnson had been greeted by a group of young Indian militants, he might have heard some unfamiliar rhetoric from the mouths of Indians. The cover story of *Time* magazine (February 10, 1970) includes the following not-so-reserved quotes from the Indian reservation:

> The next time whites try to illegally clear our land, perhaps we should get out and shoot the people in the bulldozers.

> It's time that Indians got off their goddam asses and stopped letting white people lead them around by their noses. Even the name Indian is not ours. It was given to us by some dumb honky who got lost and thought he'd landed in India.

> We weren't meant to be tourist attractions for the master race.

> Someday you're going to feel like Custer, baby.

Undoubtedly there are some older Uncle Tom-Tom Indians who would insist such rhetoric does not represent true Indian sentiment; that it is just the opinion of a few young Indian radicals—the "Stokely" Running Horses and the "Rap" Black Clouds. But the conditions of Indian reservations in America today seem designed to produce more and more militant Indian rhetoric, just as the traditional myth of American history concerning the Indian is a continuing and deeply entrenched insult to Indian heritage and culture.

THE MYTH

The traditional myth of the Indian in American history has produced at least three different images in the minds of most Americans. First, there is the image of the noble savage, wild, undomesticated, living close to nature in spiritual communion with the natural elements. Jean Jacques Rousseau helped the noble savage concept along as explorers brought back word of their new "discoveries" inhabited by those who exemplified the "natural man." In his *Discourse on the Origin and Foundation of Inequality Among Men* (1755), Rousseau wrote:

nothing can be more gentle than him [Man] in his primitive State, when placed by Nature at an equal Distance from the Stupidity of Brutes, and the pernicious good Sense of civilized Man; and equally confined by Instinct and Reason to the Care of providing against the Mischief which threatens him, he is withheld by natural Compassion from doing any Injury to others, so far from being ever so little prone even to return that which he has received. For according to the Axiom of the wise Locke, *Where there is no Property, there can be no Injury*. . . . The more we reflect on this State, the more convinced we shall be, that it was the least subject of any to Revolutions, the best for Man, and that nothing could have drawn him out of it but some fatal Accident, which, for the public good, should never have happened. The Example of the Savages, most of whom have been found in this Condition, seems to confirm that Mankind was formed ever to remain in it, that this Condition is the real Youth of the World, and that all ulterior Improvements have been so many Steps, in Appearance towards the Perfection of Individuals, but in Fact towards the Decrepitness of the Species.

Rousseau also cited the example of a North American Indian chief who was brought before the Court of London, where efforts were made to impress him with the relics of European "civilization." Said Rousseau:

Our Arms appeared heavy and inconvenient to him; our Shoes pinched his Feet; our Cloaths incombered his Body; he would accept of nothing; at length, he was observed to take up a Blanket, and seemed to take great Pleasure in wrapping himself up in it. You must allow, said the

Europeans about him, that this, at least, is an useful Piece of Furniture? Yes, answered the *Indian*, I think it almost as good as the Skin of a Beast.

The noble savage image lingers in America's memory today as a quaint stage in the American experience, as good material for folklore, children's stories, and sometimes adult novels; the wild innocence of the noble savage has been corrupted by a thousand stories into the stupidity of one, for example, who sells Manhattan Island for a few trinkets. This aspect of the traditional American myth sees the Indian as essentially ungrateful, reacting with hostility to the New World Settlers who came with all the benefits of European civilization, instead of being wise enough to assimilate with them.

The second image of the Indian is the ignoble savage —the fierce, ferocious, heartless, and relentless warrior who tortured his victims mercilessly, had a real fetish for scalping, and seemed to take special sadistic delight in massacring the women and children of lonely frontier settlers.

John Gorham Palfrey's *History of New England* (1858–1890) provides an excellent example of the image of the ignoble savage. Speaking of King Philip's war in which he led the Wampanoag Indians against the Plymouth pilgrims, Palfrey wrote:

And now, without provocation and without warning, they [the Indians] had given full sway to the inhuman passions of their savage nature. They had broken out into wild riot of pillage, arson, and massacre. By night they had crept up, with murderous intent, to the doors of dwellings familiar to them by the experience of old hospitality. They had torn away wives and mothers from ministrations to dying men, and children from their mothers' arms, for death in cruel forms. They had tortured their prisoners with atrocious ingenuity. Repeatedly, after they rose in arms, overtures of friendship had been made to them. But whether they disregarded such proposals or professed to close with them, it was all the same. The work of massacre and ravage still went on. The ferocious creature had tasted blood, and could not restrain himself till he should be surfeited.

Palfrey's words "wild riot of pillage" and "arson" have a very familiar ring to black folks. When oppressed people in America react to their oppression, American mythology always responds by calling them "rioters, looters and arsonists."

But at least America has come to anticipate a reaction from black folks: America has even designated a riot season for the black community—July through August. During the summer of 1969 black folks failed to show up for their riot season, and all America got upset. White America asked, "Where were you? We had the tanks waiting." I understand George Wallace was asked to comment on the lack of rioting in the black community during that summer, and he said, "Oh, you know those colored folks are lazy and shiftless. They just got tired!" Radio and television interviewers were always asking me the same question. Of course I didn't really know the reason why black folks failed to show up for their riot season, but I always had an answer. I said, "The reason why there were so few riots in the black community during the summer of 1969 is that all our black leaders were in Northern Ireland serving as technical advisers."

Personally, I think the reason for a lack of rioting was that black folks got tired of stealing all those bad, no-good products. During the summer of 1969 black folks decided to go underground—to study the consumer reports.

The third image of the Indian appears in the *Time* magazine cover story, in these words:

Then there is a recent image, often seen through air-conditioned automobile windows. Grinning shyly, the fat squaw hawks her woven baskets along the reservation highway, the dusty landscape littered with rusting cars, crumbling wickiups and bony cattle. In the bleak villages, the only signs of cheer are romping, round-faced children and the invariably dirty, crowded bar, noisy with the shouts and laughter of drunkenness.

Thus the image of the Indian as tourist attraction, a quaint but grim piece of Americana, and an obsessive consumer of "fire water." Advertising agencies continue to perpetuate the latter image. A large distillery ran an ad with a picture of an Indian saying, "If I had whiskey this smooth I never would have called it fire water."

Perhaps traditional American mythology is best answered by an excerpt from Indian mythology. Whereas American mythology is used to perpetuate the lie, Indian mythology (like all true mythology) is an ancient way of articulating the deep truths of life. The Cherokees tell the following story of "The Pretty Colored Snake":

A long time ago there was a famous hunter who used to go all around hunting and always brought something good to eat when he came home. One day he was going home with some birds that he had shot, and he saw a little snake by the side of the trail. It was a beautifully colored snake with all pretty colors all over it, and it looked friendly too. The hunter stopped and watched it for a while. He thought it might be hungry, so he threw it one of his birds before he went home.

A few weeks later he was coming by the same place with some rabbits he had shot, and he saw the snake again. It was still very beautiful and seemed friendly, but it had grown quite a bit. He threw it a rabbit and said "hello" as he went on home.

Some time after that the hunter saw the snake again. It had grown very big, but it was still friendly and seemed to be hungry. The hunter was taking some turkeys home with him, so he stopped and gave the snake a turkey gobbler.

Then one time the hunter was going home that way with two buck deer on his back. By this time that pretty colored snake was very big and looked so hungry that the hunter felt sorry for him and give him a whole buck to eat. When he got home he heard that the people were going to have a stomp dance. All the Nighthawks came, and that night they were going around the fire, dancing and singing the old songs, when the snake came and started going around too, outside of where the people were dancing. That snake was so big and long that he stretched all around the people and the people were penned up. The snake was covered all over with all pretty colors and he seemed friendly; but he looked hungry too, and the people began to be afraid.

They told some of the boys to get their bows and arrows and shoot the snake. Then the boys got their bows. They all shot together and they hit the snake all right. That snake was hurt. He thrashed his tail all around and killed a lot of people.

They say that snake was just like the white man.

The late Senator Robert F. Kennedy visited the Fort Hall, Idaho, Reservation with other members of the Indian Education Subcommittee. Two days after the visit, a sixteen-year-old Indian youth with whom the Senator had been chatting committed suicide. He had been confined in the county jail without a hearing and without his parents' knowledge, because he had been accused of drinking during school hours. The Indian lad hanged himself from a pipe extending across the cell. Two other Indians from the same reservation had committed suicide in the same cell, using the same pipe, during the preceding year. One was a seventeen-year-old Indian girl from the same school.

Life on the Indian reservation is so disoriented from a future of hope and promise that the suicide rate among Indian teen-agers reaches as high as ten times the national average. Those Indian teen-agers who survive suicidal impulses can look forward to dying some twenty-five years before other Americans, as the average Indian dies at age forty-four. The life expectancy of white Americans is now seventy-one. Alaskan natives die on the average by age thirty-five.

Ninety per cent of housing on the Indian reservations is considered substandard by government guidelines. Some 70 per cent of Indians on reservations haul water a mile or more from its source. The average Indian family income in America is $1,500 a year. Yet if the money spent annually for the Bureau of Indian Affairs and governmental agencies working with Indians were divided up among Indians themselves, every Indian would receive $4,000 or more.

Unemployment runs as high as 80 per cent on some Indian reservations. And government often perpetuates that unemployment. A few years ago I joined the Nisqualy Indians in the state of Washington in a "fish-in" demonstration. Indians who were once prosperous fishermen now go hungry because the state will not allow them to fish. The state of Washington spends up to $2,000 per salmon to protect these fish for sportsmen and commercial fisheries, which catch over 90 per cent of them. Indians catch less than 10 per cent. Even though the right to fish forever was promised to the

Indians in exchange for taking away their land, the state of Washington refuses to permit Indians to enjoy this right.

Indians have 12.2 times the chance of alcohol-related arrests as the average white American. Disease on the Indian reservations is appalling. The lack of medical personnel and facilities is even more appalling. That pestilence mentioned earlier still plagues the Indian reservations. Infant mortality among Indians is the highest in the nation. Of every 1,000 babies born on the Indian reservations, the death rate is 32.2 (compared with 23.7 nationally), and on some reservations the rate reaches a staggering 100 deaths per 1,000 births. That's about twice the infant mortality rate in the worst black ghettos of America and four times the death rate among white babies.

The Indian mortality rate for influenza and pneumonia is double the national average. The tuberculosis death rate for Indians is 500 per cent higher than the national average. Indians whose ancestors taught the Pilgrims how to plant food suffer today from hunger and malnutrition more than any other group of Americans now occupying their land. Yet there is one doctor to every 900 Indians on the reservations and one dentist to every 2,900. Many Indians must travel some 100 miles to a clinic, only to find a line of 300 people waiting ahead of them, and leave at the end of the day without seeing a doctor or receiving medical attention.

Then there is the matter of education on the Indian reservations. The dropout rate among Indians is 60 per cent, more than twice the national average. The average years of schooling among reservation Indians is 5.5 years. The Bureau of Indian Affairs spends about $18 per year per child on textbooks and supplies, compared with a national average of $40. Over and over again it is proved that allowing the current Bureau of Indian Affairs to be in charge of the "Indian problem" is like giving the Ku Klux Klan the authority to implement the Civil Rights Acts.

Why do Indian children fail to take advantage of the white man's educational offerings? Look in on a Chippewa reservation classroom in the Northwest. The children are busily writing a composition. Their topic is scrawled out in chalk on the blackboard: "Why we are all happy the Pilgrims landed."

A WAY-OUT VIEW

Perhaps the best way to uncover the reality of white-Indian relations in this country is to imagine a visitor coming to America from another planet. I hesitate to employ that image because of the way America handled her first lunar landing. I happened to be watching the first moon shot on television on an Indian reservation. You can imagine the reaction among Indians when the astronauts came out of their module and planted a sign reading "We come in peace."

Then the astronauts had only been on the surface of the moon for five minutes when they decided there was no life there. They called for full speed ahead on scientific testing, including the shooting of the laser beam. Suppose the situation had been reversed and some moononauts had landed on earth. Only they landed in the middle of the desert in Arizona. Since they didn't know anything about the rest of the planet earth, they would assume the desert was pretty typical.

Can't you just hear the conversation between the moononauts and Tranquility Central Control? MOONONAUTS: "Earth to Moon. We've landed safely." CONTROL: "What's it like?" MOONONAUTS: "Well, we can't use our regular kangaroo leap. We have to walk slue-footed and pigeontoed." CONTROL: "Is there any life on earth?" MOONONAUTS: "No, we can't see any signs of life. Go ahead and shoot the laser beam." And right away the beam would wipe out New York City.

Now suppose that just the week before the earth landing at the same spot in the desert the Shriners had just held their annual picnic. And that a little farther away the army had been testing some of their nerve gas. And that just a little bit beyond that point the Ku Klux Klan had just held a membership rally.

So the moononauts would start picking up specimens of the earth's crust. They'd pick up an empty whisky bottle or beer can left over from the Shriners' picnic. Can't you just hear them saying, "Isn't that strange? You can see right through the earth's crust." Walking a few more steps, the moononauts would pick up an empty nerve gas canister, still thinking it was part of the earth's crust. Finally they'd find a Ku Klux Klan membership card and put it in the sack.

When the moononauts got back home, they would give their specimens of the earth's crust to some brilliant moon scientists. The scientists would take the beer can, the whisky bottle, the nerve gas canister, and the Ku Klux Klan membership card, grind them up into earth dust and feed it to a black mouse. And the mouse would die.

The moon scientists would hold a press conference and announce: "Yes, we've found that the earth is definitely contaminated and not fit for human habitation." And you know they wouldn't be far off?

But suppose a visitor came to America from another planet and was given a fresh look at American history as a neutral observer. Suppose also that our other planetary outside illuminator was given a definition of the word "savage": "*adj.* Of or pertaining to the forests; in a state of nature; *n.* A brutal person; also, one lacking in civility or manners; *v.t.* To attack savagely; to treat with savagery." Suppose finally that the visitor were asked to look at two groups of people—the settlers who came to America and the Indians who were already here—and to decide which group best embodied the definition of the word "savage."

The visitor would see that the Indian was a deeply religious and mystical person. His religion was a worship of and communion with nature itself. The Narrative of Black Elk states: "Is not the sky a father and the earth a mother and are not all living things, with feet and wings or roots their children?" Respect for nature and nature's processes was a religious duty for the Indian. The thought of defiling nature is abhorrent to Indian culture, as reflected in an Indian proverb:

> The frog does not
> Drink up
> The pond in which
> He lives.

Perhaps the visitor would interview Paul Bernal, a Pueblo Indian, who would explain:

It is said, years ago, many years ago, when the Indian was alone in his country, he cherished every little thing. He cherished the auger, the bow, the stones, the buffalo hide, the deerskin to make moccasins with. He cherished the corn, the kernel of corn that he planted with his hands to make his flour, his bread. He cherished the trees. He believed the trees had a heart, like a human being. He never cut down a living tree. A tree was a living thing. It was not to be cut, or hurt, or burned.

Every living thing that grew from the green earth of nature, he cherished.

In the skies he cherished the king of the flying species—

the eagle. He cherished the little birds as well. He cherished the skies and stars as well.

He cherished human beings, all people, most of all. He cherished himself.

The visitor would also see that the white settler was religious in a quite different way. His religion was Christianity which in practice did not seem to respect either nature itself or human life as profoundly as did the Indian's religion. The white Christian came bringing his cross. He cut down the forests, the Indian's church, to make both the cross and his own church. It is obvious that the Indian would feel the same way seeing his trees cut down as a modern-day preacher would feel seeing his church blown up or burned to the ground.

I have had personal experience with the contradictions of white Christianity. I got my first taste of such contradictions when I was very young. A white Christian minister came up to me one day and said, "Boy"— that's how I knew he was a white Christian—"what do you want to do when you grow up?" I said, "Oh, Mr. White Christian, I wants to go to Africa and visit my ancestors!" With a look of pious horror, Mr. White Christian said, "Why would you want to have anything to do with those uncivilized people? Your ancestors are cannibals."

Reflecting my childhood innocence, I said, "Canni— who?"

"Cannibals, boy. Your ancestors eat folks."

"Oooee! You mean they eat real live people?"

I was so shocked and ashamed that I followed Mr. White Christian into his church to pray. I fell on my knees and asked God to forgive my ancestors. "Please, God," I prayed, "forgive my ancestors for being so uncivilized that they eat people."

Mr. White Christian heard my prayer and came over

to me. "We don't usually let colored boys in this church," he said. "But I like the way you pray. I want you to stay and have communion with us." "Thank you, Mr. White Christian," I said. "But what's communion?" "Just get down on your knees and I'll show you," Mr. White Christian replied.

So I got down on my knees at the altar rail with the other folks, and Mr. White Christian rubbed my head for luck and handed me a piece of bread and a cup of grape juice and said, "This is his *body* and this is his *blood*." So I decided then and there I would have to add Mr. White Christian to my prayer!

And the visitor would see that the white settlers went further than just cutting down trees in their disrespect for nature. They also polluted the waters, the rivers, lakes, and streams, even the air they breathed. The visitor could not help noticing a disrespect for human life. He would see that as the white population in the United States had multiplied over and over again, the Indian population had dwindled to far less than half its number when the settlers arrived.

The visitor would notice further the continuing stockpiling of munitions for war and killing; the billions of dollars being spent for bombs and dynamite while Indians and other minorities in America continued to starve.

Analyzing such information, any neutral observer would have to decide that the Indian fits the definition of simple nobility. Guess who would be cited as a brutal savage?

THE MARKS OF SAVAGERY

One of the marks of pure savagery is a tendency to desecrate temples and willfully destroy places of worship. Hebrew leaders felt that the Roman emperors were treacherous and savage when they descrated Jewish temples, just as decent-thinking people in America viewed the bombing of a black church in Birmingham, Alabama, as a ferociously savage act. Yet desecration of Indian temples continues today with government approval.

Paul Bernal, of Taos Pueblo, had always trusted the white man to look out for the Indian's continuing fight for survival. The Taos Pueblo Indians were struggling to protect their religious shrine, Blue Lake, and the lands surrounding it. Bernal tells of a conversation he had with Senator Clinton Anderson, one of the white men he had trusted.

I said to Senator Anderson: "I know little white men and medium-sized white men and big white men. I know the biggest white man of all. But that does not frighten me."

I said to Senator Anderson: "Just because you are a big white man and I am a little, merely an Indian, does not mean that I will do what you say. No!" I said: "My people will not sell our Blue Lake that is our church, for $10 million, and accept three thousand acres, when we know that fifty thousand acres is ours. We cannot sell what is sacred. It is not ours to sell."

I said to Senator Anderson: "Only God can take it away from us. Washington is not God. The U. S. Senate is not God."

I said to Senator Anderson: "Why do you want to steal our sacred land?"

Senator Anderson said: "Paul, I like you. But there is timber on that land, millions of dollars of timber."

I said to Senator Anderson: "It is our sacred land. We will wait."

Even if the myth of the pure religious intentions and the good faith of the white settlers of America is given credibility, when those white settlers have to run the Indians out to enact their religious program, or force and trick the Indians into going along with it, the pure religious intentions are already corrupted. And the childhood play song sung by millions of children in America—"ten little, nine little, eight little Indians"—is a continuing reminder of the genocidal policy of extermination enacted against the Indians.

One hundred years after the signing of the Declaration of Independence, the *New York Times* reported, July 7, 1876, that there were "high officers" in the War Department who advocated "the policy of extermination of the Indians and think the speedier, the better, its accomplishment." Indian wars were "wars of annihilation" to these officers according to the *Times.*

Indian testimony indicates that once again the War Department got its way:

Once we were happy in our own country and we were seldom hungry, for then the two-leggeds and the four-leggeds lived together like relatives, and there was plenty for them and for us. But the *Wasichus* [white man] came, and they have made little islands for us and other little islands for the four-leggeds, and always these islands are becoming smaller, for around them surges the gnawing flood of the *Wasichu;* and it is dirty with lies and greed.

Writing about the same time as John Gorham Palfrey, 1860, Peter Oliver held a different view of the Wampanoag Indians, King Philip, and their relationship to the Plymouth Pilgrims. He saw the Indians as victims of their own hospitality. Oliver wrote:

Though "even like lions" to the rest of their neighbors, yet to the starving, feeble band of Independents, who intruded upon their shores, the Wampanoags had been *"like lambs, so kind, so submissive and trusty, as a man may*

truly say many Christians are not so kind or so sincere."
But how were they requited? Suffice it that Massasoit,
though called an "enemy to Christianity," continued a
firm friend of the Plymouth settlers until his death; that
his eldest son and successor, Wamsutta, renewed the league
of amity, which existed between his father and Plymouth;
and, as if to seal the friendly compact, accepted from the
governor of that colony the name of Alexander, which he
retained during his brief career; that, a few years after,
Alexander died of a broken heart, on account of his
ignominious treatment by that colony, which, without
cause, suspected his fidelity; that his brother, Metacom,
who also had accepted the name of Philip, pardoning this
outrage, ratified a compact, which was fast ruining the
wild glory of his race; and that these leagues or treaties
were entirely of an *ex parte* nature, enuring favorably to
the English, and being of no manner of benefit to the
Indians. For, in what position did Philip find his people,
when called upon to direct their affairs? Their lands,
formerly extending from the easterly boundary of the Nar-
ragansetts to the westerly limits of what is now the county
of Plymouth, in Massachusetts, and comprehending generally the present county of Bristol, were, for the most
part, in the hands of the English, and the native proprietors
were confined to a few tongues of land, jutting out into
the sea, the chief of which is now known as Bristol, in
Rhode Island. These necks of land were alone, of all their
possessions, rendered by the Plymouth laws inalienable by
the Indians; partly, it was said, *because they were "more
suitable and convenient" for them, and partly because
the English were of a "covetous disposition," and the
natives, when in need, were "easily prevailed upon to part
with their lands."* Here, then, Philip found his people
huddled together, by the insidious policy of the Plymouth
Colony, surrounded on three sides by the ocean, and, on
the fourth, hemmed in by the ever-advancing tide of civilization. And this was all that forty years of friendship
with "the Pilgrims" had benefited the Wampanoags.

Another mark of savagery, of course, is the practice of scalping. Most Americans think that Indians invented the practice. It is difficult to pin down its precise origin, but it is clear that scalping and practices close to it were not unfamiliar to Europeans before their arrival in America. Poachers in England were punished by having their ears cut off. Certainly the European settlers introduced the practice of scalping to some tribes of Indians who had never scalped before.

The white settlers must take credit for the practice of paying for scalps, however. Bounties were set on dead Indians, and the scalp was proof of the deed. Governor Kieft of New Netherland is generally credited with originating the idea. He felt scalps were easier to handle than the whole Indian head. The going Dutch price was so high for scalps that they virtually cleared southern New York and New Jersey of Indians before the English got there.

By 1703 the colony of Massachusetts was paying the equivalent of about $60 for every Indian scalp. Pennsylvania's scalp rate by the mid-eighteenth century was $134 for males and only $50 for females. It is said that some entrepreneurs with an eye for making a buck simply hatcheted any old Indians who still survived and sold their scalps.

Today black folks are said to be preoccupied with cutting. But the white man at war with the Indian surpassed any Saturday night cutting on a ghetto street corner. Lieutenant James D. Connor, of the New Mexico Volunteers, described before the United States Senate what happened to Cheyenne at the Battle of Sand Creek:

In going over the battlefield the next day I did not see a body of [an Indian] man, woman, or child but was scalped, and in many instances the bodies were mutilated in the most horrible manner—men, women, and children's privates cut out, etc. One man [said] he had cut out a woman's private parts and had them for exhibition on a stick . . .

I heard of numerous instances in which men had cut out the private parts of females and stretched them over the saddlebows, and wore them in their hats while riding in the ranks. . . .

General George Custer justified such acts of savagery because he felt the Indians themselves were savages. His motto seemed to be, "Do unto the savage as you think the savage might want to do unto you." Custer believed that the Indian was "savage in every sense of the word," having "a cruel and ferocious nature [that] far exceeds that of any wild beast of the desert." Custer rejected the image of the noble savage by saying that the "beautiful romance [of] the noble red man" who was a "simple-minded son of nature" was "equally erroneous with that which regards the Indian as a creature possessing human form." So Custer felt that such "wild beasts" should not be "judged by rules or laws [of warfare] applicable to any other race of men."

So rules of warfare were suspended, and Indians were given blankets, for example, infected with smallpox, thus establishing a precedent for germ warfare. Folk hero Kit Carson was really given his name by the Indians. Indians called him "Kid" Carson because he killed more Indian children than any other white man. Carson's fighting companions were known by the Indians as the "Long Knives of Kit Carson," because of their bayonets. The "Long Knives" would cut off the breasts of Navajo girls and then toss the severed breasts back and forth like baseballs. These are the Wild West heroes American history remembers, and there was even a Boy

Scout troop on the Navajo reservation named after Kit Carson.

The true savage can be expected to bite the hand that feeds him and kill the man who keeps him alive. Whereas the white settlers brought disease to the New World, the Indian has given at least fifty-nine drugs to modern medicine, including coca (for cocaine and novocaine), curare (a muscle relaxant), cinchona bark (the source of quinine), cascara sagrada (a laxative), datura (a pain reliever), and ephedrine (a nasal remedy). In return the white man has given the Indians millions of Excedrin headaches. The Indian introduced tobacco; the white man learned to inhale it and get cancer. The Indian produced cotton; the white man got some slaves to pick it. The Indian has influenced fashion (jewelry, clothing and blanket designs, moccasins) and relaxation (smoking pipes, hammocks, canoes, snowshoes, toboggans) and provided the names for countless towns, cities, states, lakes, mountains, rivers, and other geographical sites. Whereas the Indian taught the white settlers how to survive, the white man attacks the Indian's very source of life. Indians remember the now extinct bison:

That fall [1883], they say, the last of the bison herd was slaughtered by *Wasichus*. I can remember when the bison were so many that they could not be counted, but more and more *Wasichus* came to kill them until there were only heaps of bones scattered where they used to be. The *Wasichus* did not kill them to eat; they killed them for the metal that makes them crazy, and they took only the hides to sell. Sometimes they did not even take the hides, only the tongues; and I have heard that fireboats came down the Missouri loaded with dried bison tongues. You can see that the men who did this were crazy.

The Indian observed that white America was crazy. Money made white folks do crazy things. The Indian had medicinal drugs, but he didn't have a dope problem. Nor did he have a drinking problem until the white man introduced him to "fire water" and made life so unbearable that the Indian had to drink as a form of escape.

But that practice is not new to America. Alcoholic beverages were brought to America at least by 1607 with the settling of Virginia. Twelve years later the good religious folks of Virginia Colony were experiencing a booze problem. A law was passed decreeing that any person found drunk for the first time was to be reproved privately by the minister; the second time publicly; and the third time to "lye in halter" for twelve hours and pay a fine. The very same year, however, the Virginia Assembly passed other legislation encouraging the production of wines and distilled spirits in the colony.

When a person is sick, and the doctor comes to examine the patient, the doctor usually insists, "You've got to get a lot of rest. You've got to take off from work. You've got to go to bed early, and most of all you must quit drinking." The person who is really sick has no business fooling around with alcohol. That is the biggest problem in this nation today. Sick Americans refuse to stop drinking.

Perhaps if American parents would put down their cocktail glasses for a moment and take a sober look at the narcotics problem, they would understand what is happening in America today. Governmental response to dope traffic is nothing less than savage. That savagery is best represented by the Nixon administration's Operation Intercept. In 1969, taking a leaf from his Vietnam notebook, President Nixon began dealing with the Mexican government to shut off the flow of marijuana from

Mexico into the United States. Just as the United States teamed up with the government of South Vietnam to spray napalm on the villages of North Vietnam, the federal government spearheaded the spraying of marijuana fields in Mexico.

A stop-and-search campaign was begun at the Mexican border to cut off the flow of any pot (marijuana) that survived the spraying. Tourists were annoyed as traffic jams at the border backed up for miles, and businessmen were annoyed because the tourists were annoyed. But Operation Intercept was successful, as any pot smoker in a large urban area could testify.

Marijuana became very scarce, and the price skyrocketed. But there was a curious accompanying phenomenon to the pot depletion. Hard narcotics, such as heroin, became cheaper and more available. A teen-ager from New York City's Lower East Side, unable to obtain marijuana and fast becoming a heroin user, told me that bags of heroin formerly costing five or six dollars were suddenly available for two or three dollars.

His statistics were substantiated in official places. Dr. Michael Braden, New York City's associate medical examiner and a specialist in addiction problems, testified before hearings of the Joint Legislative Committee (New York) on Protection of Children and Youth and Drug Abuse, saying that Operation Intercept had helped to drive the price of marijuana so high that it had become competitive with heroin. Speaking of the rise of the use of hard narcotics among youth, Dr. Braden estimated that of New York City's 100,000 addicts, 25,000 were below the age of twenty. He said that 250 teenagers would die from the use of heroin by the end of the year—a new record. At the time of Dr. Braden's testimony in 1969 the total number of deaths related to heroin use thus far for the year in New York was 700.

One would think that a real narcotics crackdown would *begin* with heroin and work down to the lighter stuff. Doesn't it seem strange that an administration that fought so hard for an antiballistic system to save our country from destruction does not fight equally hard for an antinarcotics system to prevent the slow destruction of our nation's youth? Since hard narcotics, such as heroin, are controlled by organized crime, one can only assume that Russia is the Nixon administration's enemy and the Cosa Nostra its friend. How else can one explain the maintenance of a watchful eye on Russia and overlooking the continuing activities of the Mafia in smuggling hard narcotics?

Not long after Operation Intercept, President Pompidou of France came to pay President Nixon a visit. President Pompidou also visited other cities in America, where he was met by protest demonstrations, calling for peace in the Middle East. President Nixon was so upset by such demonstrations (though even Mayor Daley of Chicago complimented demonstrators in his city for "the orderly manner in which they exercised their rights as American citizens") that he flew to the Waldorf Astoria hotel in New York City, substituting for Vice President Spiro Agnew, to offer personal apologies to President Pompidou for the actions of antiwar protestors.

President Nixon should have apologized to grief-stricken American mothers and fathers whose sons and daughters have died from overdoses of heroin. President Nixon knows the route of heroin traffic into America. About 80 per cent of the heroin entering this country illegally is the end product of the opium harvest in Turkey. The traffic starts with the Turkish farmer who diverts part of his crop to smugglers. They either get it out of the country or arrange to extract the morphine base from the opium while it is still in Turkey. Morphine base is a crude brown heroin that has to be bleached and further refined; since ten kilos of opium reduces to one kilo of morphine base, it is in the interest of the narcotics traffickers to get it reduced if they can for more profitable smuggling.

Then the morphine base is taken to the clandestine heroin laboratories of southern France for further refining. President Pompidou's country thus aids in the conversion of a product whose value starts at $8 and ends up in America in the millions. One wonders if President Nixon mentioned that issue to President Pompidou while they were extolling the virtues of French-American friendship.

Could it be that the Nixon administration would rather see the youth of America hooked on heroin than using marijuana? It is not uncommon for the use of marijuana, being "turned on" to pot, to accompany social and political awareness. Not so with the use of heroin and other hard drugs. A hard narcotics user's main concern is with keeping his needle supplied. The pot smoker may want to change the system. The hard narcotics user will destroy himself. Even Hitler in all his madness did not encourage the flower of his nation, Germany's youth, to shoot anything but guns!

I can never accept the rationalization that law enforcement cannot find the narcotics man. I could go into any city in America where heroin is being used, and fifteen minutes after my arrival I could have made a contact to purchase some dope. Fifteen minutes after making that contact I could have the heroin running through my veins. If it is that easy for a newcomer to a city, why is it the police, who work there every day, many of whom have lived there all their lives, can never seem to be able to find the narcotics suppliers? If the police sincerely cannot find them, perhaps we should make the users the police because they never have any trouble recognizing a pusher!

Once again an Indian comment is the best summation. Janet McCloud, speaking at the Law Day ceremonies of the University of Washington Law School, May 1, 1969, said:

> You have a very complicated legal system. It is not that way with my people. I have always thought that you had so many laws because you were a lawless people. Why else would you need so many laws? After all, Europe opened all prisons and penitentiaries and sent all their criminals to this country. Perhaps that is why you need so many laws. I hope we never have to reach such an advanced state of civilization.

PILGRIMS AND STATESMEN

The key to exploding the myth of the savage is to destroy the "discovery hoax." If Americans, white or black, can believe that their ancestors "discovered" the New World, the door is left open for understanding if not justifying all that went along with occupying their "discovery." It is true that black men were numbered among the early explorers the same as whites. Black participation in exploration and so many other facets of American life are forgotten pages in American history and will be dealt with in subsequent chapters. But the Indian was the pure pilgrim in America. The white man is a newcomer to the American experience, whereas the Indian's roots go back twenty-five thousand years.

The Indian's ancestors apparently abandoned their home in what is now the Gobi Desert, traveled across the Bering Strait into Alaska, and from that initial arrival eventually settled the New World. They found an unmolested, beautiful reservoir of natural resources and developed a mystical religion and high culture in deep communion with nature itself. So the pure pilgrims, the Indian ancestors, exemplified a true reverence for life and a worship of nature itself rather than imposing a religious standard upon native occupants.

Vine Deloria, Jr., sums it up in his book *Custer Died for Your Sins* by saying that the Western Hemisphere or the land of the Indians produced wisdom, whereas Western Europe produced knowledge. That crucial distinction continues to plague life in America today. Wisdom is understanding how to live. Knowledge is used to make a living. The distinction is apparent in the colleges and universities of America today, and it is one of the reasons for student unrest. When I was in college, my fellow students and I were so busy trying to learn how to make a living that we forgot to learn how to live. If a student uses his college years to truly learn how to live, making a living will be the easiest thing in the world for him.

I hear so many people say, "I'm going to college to learn how to be somebody." But every man is *born* somebody. If he lets someone teach him to be somebody else, that makes him two people. Check and see what Sigmund Freud says happens to a man when he becomes two folks. It doesn't make sense to go away to college for four years and pay top money to be taught to be crazy!

Then people say, "You have to eat to live. I'm going to college so I can get a good job and eat." A gorilla eats more food in one meal than most people eat all week. Have you ever known a gorilla to go to college to get a job? When you were shopping in a supermarket, have you ever bumped into a gorilla? When is the last time you read where a gorilla starved to death? You will never read about a gorilla starving as long as he knows how to live. But the first time a gorilla decides he wants to make a living, there will be colleges for gorillas too.

A man is born with all the wisdom he needs for life. The Indian understands this. All a college or a university can do is bring out the wisdom nature has already implanted. The Indian understands the power and wisdom of nature and man's relationship to nature. Each man is the universe. Each man is nature. There are nine planets to the universe, and each person has nine holes in his body. That is no accident.

Let me illustrate how strong nature is. Very few people reading this book will understand Chinese. Yet at this very moment, dogs in China understand Chinese, and they have never been to college. Dogs in Russia understand Russian, and dogs in Germany understand German. Yet many people graduate from college understanding only their native tongue, which a dog knows instinctively.

Colleges and universities in America are so disoriented from nature that emphasis is placed upon *indoctrination* rather than *education*. Education means to bring out wisdom. Indoctrination means to push in knowledge. The transcript of grades is used as a measure of how well the indoctrination process has succeeded. But nature is not interested in college transcripts. If a student leaves college, falls in love and decides to get married, a husband or a wife will not ask to see the college transcript nor will either sexual partner want that transcript in bed.

The Indian respected nature and learned how to live, and that wisdom informed all of his actions. Even his speech, as Thomas Jefferson recognized. Jefferson wished that the men of Congress could orate half as well as the Indian. In his *Notes on the State of Virginia,* Jefferson offered an example of Indian eloquence:

I may challenge the whole orations of Demosthenes and Cicero, and of any more eminent orator, if Europe has furnished more eminent, to produce a single passage, superior to the speech of Logan, a Mingo chief, to Lord Dunmore, when governor of this state. And, as a testimony of their talents in this line, I beg leave to introduce it, first stating the incidents necessary for understanding it. In the spring of the year 1774, a robbery was committed by some Indians on certain land-adventurers on the river Ohio. The whites in that quarter, according to their custom, undertook to punish this outrage in a summary way. Captain Michael Cresap, and a certain Daniel Greathouse, leading on these parties, surprized, at different times, travelling and hunting parties of the Indians, having their women and children with them, and murdered many. Among these were unfortunately the family of Logan, a chief celebrated in peace and war, and long distinguished as the friend of the whites. This unworthy return provoked his vengeance. He accordingly signalized himself in the war which ensued. In the autumn of the same year a decisive battle was fought at the mouth of the Great Kanhaway, between the collected forces of the Shawanese, Mingoes, and Delewares, and a detachment of the Virginia militia. The Indians were defeated, and sued for peace. Logan however disdained to be seen among the suppliants. But lest the sincereity of a treaty should be distrusted, from which so distinguished a chief absented himself, he sent by a messenger the following speech to be delivered to Lord Dunmore.

"I appeal to any white man to say, if ever he entered Logan's cabin hungry, and he gave him not meat; if ever he came cold and naked, and he clothed him not. During the course of the last long and bloody war, Logan remained idle in his cabin, an advocate for peace. Such was my love for the whites, that my countrymen pointed as they passed, and said, 'Logan is the friend of white men.' I had even thought to have lived with you, but for the injuries of one man. Col. Cresap, the last spring, in cold blood, and unprovoked, murdered all the relations of Logan, not sparing even my women and children. There runs not a drop of my blood in the veins of any living creature. This called on me for revenge. I have sought it: I have killed many: I have fully glutted my vengeance. For my country, I rejoice at the beams of peace. But do not harbour a thought that mine is the joy of fear. Logan never felt fear. He will not turn on his heel to save his life. Who is there to mourn for Logan?—Not one."

The wisdom of the Indian produced statesmanship and a better form of government than that later developed by the knowledge of European politicians. Vine Deloria, Jr., reminds us that true democracy was more prevalent among the Indian tribes before Columbus came to America than it has been since. "Despotic power," says Deloria, "was abhorred by tribes that were loose combinations of hunting parties rather than political entities." Some of America's favorite statesmen marveled at the Indian form of government. Benjamin Franklin, in his *Poor Richard's Almanack,* in 1775, spoke of the "great order and decency" in tribal life. And Franklin put his finger on the source of that order and decency. "The Savages," wrote Franklin, had a society where "There is no force, there are no prisons, no officers to compel obedience or inflict punishment."

So the Indians without mayors, governors, congressmen, or presidents were able to live happily in the present borders of the United States. Perhaps it is because they believed in and practiced community control. Community pressure, approval or disapproval of the members of the community, was relied upon more than vindictive punishment.

Eskimos in Alaska today use community approval or disapproval as a means of settling disputes. All disputes except murder are settled by the song duel, which seems to be a musical version of the longstanding ghetto game "dozens." The parties in a dispute sing insults and obscenities at each other much to the delight of the audience. The audience decides who wins the song duel, and the loser receives community disapproval which is painful punishment in a group as small as that of the Eskimo.

Statesmen are wise men of uncompromising truth and honesty. Politicians are students of the art of compromise. Being statesmen, the Indians signed treaties with the white man in good faith. Being politicians, the white settlers and their ancestors have yet to honor a single Indian treaty. Yet all the while America continues to justify her current actions in Vietnam on the grounds that "the North Vietnamese have repeatedly violated the 1954 Geneva Accords." America did not even sign the Geneva treaty. Yet she will send her troops ten thousand miles away to defend a treaty she *didn't* sign while she violates Indian treaties at home.

Deloria reminds our government that the last Indian treaty to be broken, the Pickering Treaty of 1794 with the Seneca tribe of the Iroquois nation, was violated at the very time America's bloody action in Vietnam was being justified as a commitment-keeping responsibility.

White America's signing treaties with the Indians was pure politics from the very beginning. Self-interest is a more accurate description of America's true motives than fidelity to commitments. Indian treaties were originally made either to keep peace on the frontier or to acquire land for white settlers. Both reflect strong self-interest motives. When foreign conquest appeared to be an imminent possibility, the United States was quick to sign agreements with the Indians to make sure they were on the right side.

"During the darkest days of the Revolution," says Vine Deloria, Jr., "in order to keep the Indians from siding with the British and completely crushing the new little nation, the United States held out equality and statehood to the Delawares and any other tribes they could muster to support the United States. But when the shooting was all over the Delawares were forgotten in the rush to steal their land."

The same thing happened during the War of 1812, when the United States government was eager to make sure Indians would not side with Great Britain. A treaty was signed with the Wyandots, the Delawares, the Shawnees, the Senecas, and the Miamis engaging them "to give their aid to the United States in prosecuting the war against Great Britain, and such of the Indian tribes as still continue hostile." What was the final result of such honorable treaty commitment? Deloria gives the answer in these words: "Within a generation these same tribes that fought and died for the United States against Great Britain were to be marched to the dusty plains of Oklahoma, dropped in an alien and disease-ridden land, and left to disappear."

Indians are still denied hunting and fishing rights, rights guaranteed by original treaties, but not honored by government. And they remain the long-suffering victims of outright land thefts, frequently for construction and transportation interests, again in violation of treaties made in good faith.

America's commitment to treaties any place in the world cannot be taken seriously until full commitment to treaty obligations is faced at home. And America's dealings with Indians display to the world her true motives. "America has always been a militantly imperialistic world power," observes Deloria, "eagerly grasping for economic control over weaker nations." America's dealings with Indian tribes are a superb illustration of such motives.

WHO'LL BE THE INDIAN?

America's basic sickness is illustrated by the fact that she has always chosen to play a game of cowboys and Indians. Every now and then America goes off to fight a war, but she always comes back home to resume playing cowboys and Indians.

America—Uncle Sam—has always been the cowboy, but the Indian role has changed over and over again. The Indian himself was the original Indian, of course. Then one day the Indian came to Uncle Sam and said, "Hey, Great White Father. Me don't want to be your Indian no more. Me can't play this game with you. You something else." Uncle Sam said, "What's the matter, redskin, can't you take it?" The Indian answered, "No, white man, it's not that. I can take all the punishment you lay on me except that one final insult. When you commit all the atrocities you do, and you display your sick degeneracy, and then you tell the world I'm the savage—no, white man, I can't take that. Nobody is scared of death, white man, but you. So regardless of what you may do to me, I'm not going to play with you no more."

Uncle Sam got very upset. He cried for a while, and he told the Indian he was being very unfair. Uncle Sam said resentfully, "Who do you think you are, telling me you won't be the Indian any more. I'll just lock you up on a reservation." The Indian answered, "Do anything you want. You can wipe me out if you want to, but it won't be in the game we used to play."

After a little while Uncle Sam missed the Indian. He longed to play another game of cowboys and Indians, so he had to find himself a new Indian. Uncle Sam looked around and saw the Jew, and he decided the Jew would make a good Indian. So the Jew became the Indian and went along with the game for a while. Then one day the Jew came up to Uncle Sam and said, "Boss, I can't be your Indian any more. You play too rough." And again Uncle Same got very uptight. He started calling the Jew some dirty names: "You long-nose Jew bastard. What do you mean telling me you're not going to be the Indian any more? Just after I trained you how to be a good Indian!"

But the Jew held firm. He said, "Call me anything you want to, I still won't be your Indian any more. But I'll tell you what I will do. I'll join up with you, and we'll find somebody else to be the Indian." The original Indian was too morally pure to ever make that offer. He would rather suffer the indignity of life on the reservation than participate in the sick, oppressive games America was playing.

So Uncle Sam looked around for a new Indian, and his eye fell upon the Irishman. Uncle Sam thought the Irishman was pretty ignorant and he might need a lot of training, but even so the Irishman would make a good Indian. So the Irishman became the Indian. But after a while the Irishman also came to Uncle Sam and said, "Boss, I can't be your Indian any more. This game is no fun any more. But I'll tell you what I will do. I'll be your cop. You fix some bad laws and I'll enforce them for you."

Uncle Sam got upset again. He called the Irishman a dirty, doublecrossing, shanty bastard. And the Irishman said, "You can call me anything you want to call me. Just give me my uniform, my badge, my gun and a big stick, and I'll deal with those names."

Once more Uncle Sam needed a new Indian. He

searched for a while and finally came across the Italian. Uncle Sam was very pleased because he could tell immediately that the Italian would make a good Indian. There was something about him. Uncle Sam didn't know that in the earlier days of history Hannibal had put some black soul in the Italian.

So the Italian became the Indian, and Uncle Sam played the game very hard. Uncle Sam found two Italians who just didn't act like good Indians, Nicola Sacco and Bartolomeo Vanzetti, so he accused them of murder, placed them on trial, and condemned them to die. People all over the country, as well as in Latin America and Europe, were convinced Sacco and Vanzetti were innocent, and came out into the streets to protest their execution. Even the prosecuting attorney who had tried Sacco and Vanzetti went to the Governor on their behalf, saying he felt there was insubstantial evidence, but the Governor knew what Uncle Sam wanted and said, "Kill them damn 'Indians,' boy."

Bartolomeo Vanzetti's final words before the court that convicted him stand today as a classic reminder of the price Uncle Sam demands for refusing to be the Indian:

I have talk a great deal of myself but I even forgot to name Sacco. Sacco too is a worker from his boyhood, a skilled worker lover of work, with a good job and pay, a good and lovely wife, two beautiful children and a neat little home at the verge of a wood, near a brook. Sacco is a heart, a faith, a character, a man; a man lover of nature and of mankind. A man who gave all, who sacrifice all to the cause of Liberty and to his love of mankind; money, rest, mundane ambitions, his own wife, his children, himself and his own life. Sacco has never dreamt to steal, never to assassinate. He and I have never brought a morsel of bread to our mouths, from our childhood to today—which has not been gained by the sweat of our brows. Never.

Oh, yes, I may be more witful, as some have put it, I am a better babbler than he is, but many, many times in hearing his heartful voice ringing a faith sublime, in considering his supreme sacrifice, remembering his heroism I felt small small at the presence of his greatness and found myself compelled to fight back from my throat to not weep before him—this man called thief and assassin and doomed. But Sacco's name will live in the hearts of the people and in their gratitude when Katzmann's and your bones will be dispersed by time, when your name, his name, your laws, institutions, and your false god are but a dim rememoring of a cursed past in which man was wolf to man. . . .

If it had not been for these things, I might have live out my life talking at street corners to scorning men. I might have die, unmarked, unknown, a failure. Now we are not a failure. This is our career and our triumph. Never in our full life could we hope to do such work for tolerance, for justice, for man's understanding of man as now we do by accident. Our words—our lives—our pains—nothing! The taking of our lives—lives of a good shoemaker and a poor fishpeddler—all! That last moment belongs to us—that agony is our triumph.

One day the Italian came to Uncle Sam and said, "I just can't be your Indian any more. You'll have to get off my back." Uncle Sam said, "What do you want to do?" The Italian said, "I'll push a little dope for you. I'll pull a little policy. As a matter of fact, I'll do better than that. I'll be your scapegoat and cover up for the real criminals in America, the wealthy families and the rich corporations."

Just as Uncle Sam was looking for a new Indian to replace the Italian, black folks came to him and said, "Hey, white man, how come you don't use us for the

Indian?" And Uncle Sam said, "Boy, you're already the nigger. You can't be the Indian." So black folks said, "That's all right. We'll be the Indian too." Uncle Sam thought for a while and said, "Well, I don't know what we can do in this game if you're the Indian. With our Indians we usually rape the women and misuse the children and we've already done that to you."

So black folks said, "The reason we want to be the Indian is that according to the rules of the game, you have to give us a little piece of land and some guns, because the Indian gets to shoot back. We'd be better off being the Indian than the slave." Uncle Sam's eyes lit up and he said, "You know you boys are right. We haven't got anybody to shoot at."

So black folks became the Indian, and they almost out-Indianed the Indian. Finally black folks also decided they didn't want to be the Indian any more. But there was a sad difference in telling Uncle Sam. With all the other groups who had been the Indian, the adults went to Uncle Sam and said they didn't want to play any more. With black folks, our kids carried that message. Some of the older black folks didn't want to stop being the nigger or the Indian. So the young black kids said to Uncle Sam, "We're not going to be your Indian any more. A few black folks still want to be your Indian, but don't make the mistake of getting your Indians mixed up."

In the early 1960's black folks began to say, "No more Indian games with us." We said it with a new kind of rhetoric. We said it with Martin Luther King and Malcolm X and Medgar Evers and Father Groppi and the Black Panthers and the NAACP and the Urban League. But Uncle Sam didn't want to let black folks stop being the Indian. He went back to all the other groups who had been the Indian before and said, "If black folks aren't the Indians any more, you all might be in trouble." Black folks were the first group that Uncle Sam decided to force to continue to be the Indian.

Before the 1960's were over, however, there was no doubt in Uncle Sam's mind that black folks were not going to be the Indian any more, due to the efforts of Stokely Carmichael and Rap Brown. Stokely and Rap said, "If you just stop looking like the Indian, Uncle Sam will understand. You can't come up to him wearing all the war paint that makes you the Indian and say you aren't going to be the Indian any more. Let your hair grow out the way nature gave it to you. Be yourself, black, beautiful and proud."

So young black folks told Uncle Sam, "Not only are we not going to be your Indian any more, but we aren't going to look like your Indian and we may decide to deal with you." Of course there were some black folks who wanted to join Uncle Sam like the other groups had done, but Uncle Sam wouldn't let them in. He said, "Get back over there, nigger. You might not be the Indian any more, but you're still going to be the nigger—nigger!"

There were only two groups that didn't join Uncle Sam's posse: the original beautiful Indian because he didn't want to join, and black folks because Uncle Sam wouldn't let us join. Still some black folks kept trying to join. They are over in Vietnam today killing folks. When they come back home and realize their own momma needs to be liberated, they wouldn't dare raise their guns.

One day in 1970, Uncle Sam got itching for another Indian. He said to himself, "Who'll be the Indian? There's nobody left but my own kids." So Uncle Sam made his own white youth both the Indian and the new nigger. Uncle Sam never makes distinctions with his

"Indians" and "niggers." There are no distinctions between good and bad, right wing or left wing. All niggers
and Indians look alike.

Abraham Lincoln once said that if America ever dies,
it will be because she has committed suicide. By attacking her own kids, America has finally given full sway to
her suicidal tendencies. What a man does to his own
kids, he will do to everybody else.

If you follow me home one day and you see mē grab
my twelve-year-old daughter and hit her over the head
with a stick and throw tear gas and Mace on her and
stick her with a bayonet, you would say, "Brother Greg
has gone crazy." Even if I told you my daughter had just
killed my wife, it wouldn't make any difference. Nothing
could justify my treating my own daughter in such a
way. And America can never expect to shoot down her
youth on the campus of Kent State University and hope
to justify that act in the eyes of the world.

> "The tree of liberty must be refreshed from time to time with the blood of patriots and tyrants. It is their natural manure."
>
> THOMAS JEFFERSON, 1787

III

THE MYTH OF THE FOUNDING FATHERS

or The True Spirit of '76

Back in 1761, James Otis, noted Boston lawyer, observed that government need not make hobbyhorses, asses, and slaves of its subjects, for nature had made enough of the first two "from the harmless peasant in the field to the most refined politician in the cabinet; but none of the last, which infallibly proves they are unnecessary." Otis was credited by John Adams as being the real founding father of American independence. In that same year Otis had rendered a brilliant plea against writs of assistance (arbitrary search warrants), which Adams declared was "a flame of fire," causing every hearer to depart to take up arms against the writs. Even though Otis lost his case, John Adams said, "Then and there the child Independence was born."

Always outspoken against oppressive forms of government, Otis launched an abusive newspaper attack in 1769 against a commissioner of customs. As a result, he was severely beaten in a coffeehouse with a cane wielded by the commissioner. Some folks felt that Brother Otis was not quite right after that, and said that he was "fiery and feverous . . . liable to great inequalities of temper"; and they attributed his radical behavior to the injuries he had received in the beating. One enemy of Otis said he was "the first who broke down the barriers of government to let in the hydra of Rebellion."

But Otis seems to have been very much on the ball when he made his observation about asinine behavior in high levels of government as well as among the common folks. For a contemporary example, consider the November 1969 Moratorium Day demonstrations in America. President Nixon asked all the good "patriots" who agreed with his Vietnam policy to drive around with their automobile headlights turned on in the daytime. James Otis' words were recalled by the fact that many drivers did it! Such "pariots" should have realized that turning on their automobile headlights would not kill any Vietcong. At best such an act would only sell a whole lot of batteries. Rather than turning on their headlights, supporters of the President's Vietnam policy should have turned their cars around and headed for the nearest military induction center to enlist.

The myth of the founding fathers reveres the revolutionary words and deeds of folk heroes of the American Revolution, yet fosters an attitude that condemns those who try to re-enact the spirit of those founding fathers today. The early patriots, those who led the Revolution and founded the United States, always seemed to be on the side of the oppressed. Americans who call themselves patriots today always end up siding with the oppressor. There is more to that contradiction than what James Otis called man's natural affinity to "hobbyhorses and asses." His reference to "slavery" is more at the heart of the matter. When slavery was at stake, most of the founding fathers overlooked their opposition to oppression.

THE MYTH

The myth of the founding fathers portrays men of courage and moral dedication who were opposed to governmental oppression and denials of freedom. They felt tyranny must be opposed at all costs. It is better to die than live under governmental tyranny. Thus, Patrick Henry testified, "Give me liberty or give me death." Some two hundred years later Judge Julius Hoffman, presiding judge of the 1969 Chicago conspiracy trial, appears to be a judge who would have taken Patrick Henry up on the *second* part of his statement.

A unique romanticism surrounds the founding fathers meeting in the back rooms of taverns and coffeehouses to plot their revolution—a romanticism conspicuously absent in contemporary newspaper accounts of gatherings of Black Panthers or Students for a Democratic Society. Though King George III of England emerges in the myth as the "enemy" and "tyrant," the real gripe of the founding fathers was with the British Parliament. They felt that colonial legislatures should be free to act on their own, and that the only link with the government of England should be through the crown. Thus, Benjamin Franklin asserted, "The sovereignty of the Crown I understand, the sovereignty of Britain I do not understand. . . . We have the same King, but not the same legislature." But King George chose to support the rights of Parliament over the colonial legislatures, caus-

ing the founding fathers to accuse the King of supporting the claims of "subjects in one part of the King's
dominions to be sovereigns over their fellow-subjects in
another part of his dominions."

A series of acts passed by Parliament imposing duties
and taxes on the colonies caused the founding fathers
to raise their voices in colonial assemblies saying that
"taxation without representation" was tyranny. Of
course not all colonials were radicalized, and the American colonies had their share of white Uncle Toms.
Thomas Hutchinson, descendant of Anne Hutchinson
and Lieutenant-Governor (later Governor) of Massachusetts, wrote to a friend in England:

The colonists claim a power of making laws, and a
privelege of exemption from taxes, unless voted by their
own representatives. . . . Not one tenth of the people of
Great Britain have a voice in the elections to Parliament;
and, therefore, the colonies can have no claim to it; but
every man of property in England may have his voice, if
he will. Besides, acts of Parliament do not generally affect
individuals, and every interest is represented. But the
colonies have an interest distinct from the interest of the
nation; and shall the Parliament be at once party and
judge? . . .
The nation treats her colonies as a father who should
sell the services of his sons to reimburse what they had
cost him, but without the same reason; for none of the
colonies, except Georgia and Halifax, occasioned any
charge to the Crown or kingdom in the settlement of
them. The people of New England fled for the sake of
civil and religious liberty; multitudes flocked to America
with this dependence, that their liberties should be safe.
They and their posterity have enjoyed them to their content, and therefore have endured with greater cheerfulness
all the hardships of settling new countries. No ill use has
been made of these priveleges; but the domain and wealth

of Great Britain have received amazing addition. Surely the services we have rendered the nation have not subjected us to any forfeitures?

Thus Thomas Hutchinson and others sought to reason with England and call attention to the British Constitution and the special conditions prevailing in America—that is, to avoid the revolutionary route. Those who urge such a course upon black and white radicals in America today should remember that in 1765 those in agreement with the revolutionary-minded founding fathers sacked and burned Thomas Hutchinson's mansion and dumped his precious historical manuscripts into the street when he tried to enforce the Stamp Act.

Benjamin Franklin read everything he could get his hands on, pro and con, regarding the respective rights and prerogatives of British and colonial legislatures and came up with a different conclusion. In 1768, Franklin wrote:

I am not yet master of the idea these . . . writers have of the relation between Britain and her colonies. I know not what the Boston people mean by the "Subordination" they acknowledge in their Assembly to Parliament, while they deny its power to make laws for them, nor what bounds the Farmer sets to the power he acknowledges in Parliament to "regulate the trade of the colonies," it being difficult to draw lines between duties for regulation and those for revenue; and, if the Parliament is to be the judge, it seems to me that establishing such a principle of distinction will amount to little. The more I thought and read on the subject, the more I find myself confirmed in opinion, that no middle ground can be well maintained, I mean not clearly with intelligible arguments. Something might be made of either of the extremes: that Parliament has a power to make *all laws* for us, or that it has a power to make *no laws* for us; and I think the arguments for the latter more numerous and weighty, than those for

the former. Supposing that doctrine established
nies would then be so many separate states, or
to the same king, as England and Scotland we ....ore
the union.

As more and more taxes were levied, more and more
colonials became radicalized, and Franklin's "no laws"
role for Parliament gained wide popularity. Especially
insulting and upsetting to American colonials were the
taxes levied on tea. When I first read the American history book, I just could not believe that George Washington and his ragged band of guerrillas took on the
whole British army over a tax on some *tea!* I thought
surely the Revolution must have been fought over some
issue like civil rights, or fair housing, or jobs. But it
really was a tax on tea. In 1970 most Americans don't
even drink tea, yet they will accept and admire the
courageous spirits who would fight a revolutionary war
over a tea tax. Isn't it strange those same Americans
find it so hard to understand today's revolutionaries,
who are concerned with much deeper issues?

In 1770 the New York Sons of Liberty said that the
tax on tea remained "as a test of the parliamentary
right to tax us." In a move to bail the East India Company out of near bankruptcy, Parliament removed all
duties, except the colonial tea tax, from the company's
surplus tea exported to the colonies. Though the East
India Company was able to undersell both legitimate
importers and smugglers, the tax made tea drinking a
political issue in the colonies, and a boycott was called
as a form of protest.

A tea boycott was not an easy thing to pull off in the
American colonies. The Whigs complained that tea was
the "Idol of America" and that tea drinkers were lost
to reason. The Swedish traveler, Peter Kalm, observed
that there was "hardly a farmer's wife or a poor woman,

who does not drink tea in the morning," and he felt that tea addiction was the reason that American girls often lost their teeth before they were twenty years old. An estimated minimum of a million Americans were tea drinkers; and in Philadelphia, it was said that "the women are such slaves to it, that they would rather go without their dinners than without a *dish of tea.*"

Ever since the Townshend Acts of 1767, when tea was first taxed, tea drinking was condemned in the colonies as a dangerous, unpatriotic habit. Physicians testified that tea caused spleen and weakened "the tone of the stomach, and therefore of the whole system, inducing tremors and spasmodic affections." Tea drinkers were warned that they were in danger of becoming "weak, effeminate and valetudinarian for life." So tea was harmful to both the body and civil liberties. A colonist admonished, "Do not suffer yourself to sip the accursed, dutied STUFF; for if you do, the devil will immediately enter into you, and you will instantly become a traitor to your country."

So tea was the "baneful weed" of American revolutionary sentiment, and many Sons of Liberty were fearful that their wives and daughters were too addicted to give it up. One indignant patriot accused British Prime Minister Lord North of attempting "to damn half mankind by tempting *female weakness* with *empoisoned* TEA." And Englishmen believed that American patriots would be conquered by their wives "for the New England husbands however they may intimidate British merchants and the British administration, are, in their own houses, too much on the hen-pecked establishment, to be able to carry such a measure against the Sovereign and absolute authority of their fair helpmates."

But the women exploded all the myths concerning female weakness, and they led the boycott. The women began drinking home-grown "Labradore" instead of the taxed tea, and said the new brew was "vastly more agreeable" than anything out of China. The grateful Whigs realized how important women were to the struggle and said, "With the Ladies on our Side, we can make every Tory tremble." An early example of the power of Women's Liberation was the tea addict in Bedford, Massachusetts, who was found guilty of possession. The patriots gave him a choice of either surrendering his tea or being turned over to the ladies for punishment. The man promptly and wisely gave up his tea, for which he received "three cheers from the sons and a glass of American wine from the daughters of liberty."

The tempest in the teapot culminated on the night of December 16, 1773, when three companies of fifty men, in blackface and wearing Indian blankets and feathers, boarded the three tea ships in Boston Harbor and heaved the cargo of tea overboard. Though none of the rioters and looters was apprehended, it was rumored that the tea was destroyed by "King Hancock, and the damn'd sons of liberty." The "violent" rebellion, known as the Boston Tea Party, ended any possibilities that the colonies and Parliament might reach a compromise. The harbor riot launched a course that led to full-scale revolution; and on July 4, 1776, the adoption of the Declaration of Independence made America's rejection of tyranny and oppression official. The myth was born.

PATERNAL INTEGRATION

During the 1969 Chicago conspiracy trial (see Chapter XI), defendant Bobbly Seale objected to the display of portraits of certain founding fathers in the courtroom

on the grounds that they were slaveholders. George
Washington was cited as an example. In an interview in
Look magazine, March 18, 1969, the noted historian
Arnold Toynbee implied that George Washington was
not only a slaveholder but that he engaged in the usual
relationships between master and slaves. Commenting
on present-day interracial relations, Mr. Toynbee said:

After all, a man in Virginia will not object to having
sexual relations with a Negro woman as long as he doesn't
marry her; if she's his prostitute or his mistress, that's all
right. She's still in an inferior position. But it shows there
isn't really a physical antipathy.

The planters had illegitimate children by Negroes.
George Washington caught a cold while visiting Negro
quarters on his estate for this purpose. It is never put into
the official biographies, but this was the cause of his death.
After all, it was a normal thing for a gentleman to do.

Drawing upon this example, Mr. Toynbee suggested
that the only "radical cure" for racism in America is
"fusion," and that the only "radical way of fusing is to
intermarry."

Perhaps Toynbee's revelation explains some of the
sentiment behind George Washington's dying wish in
1799, contained in his last will and testament: ". . .
Upon the decease of my wife, it is my Will & desire that
all the Slaves which I hold in *my own right*, shall receive
their freedom." The conclusion of Washington's will
indicates a curious fondness for a particular man born
of white and black sexual intercourse:

. . . And to my Mulatto man William (calling himself
William Lee) I give immediate freedom; or if he should
prefer it (on account of the accidents which have befallen
him, and which have rendered him incapable of walking
or of any active employment) to remain in the situation
he now is, it shall be optional in him to do so: In either

case however, I allow him an annuity of thirty dollars during his natural life, which shall be independent of the victuals and cloaths he has been accustomed to receive, if he chuses the last alternative; but in full, with his freedom, if he prefers the first;—& this I give him as a testimony of my sense of his attachment to me, and for his faithful services during the Revolutionary War.

But during his lifetime, George Washington had the same callous attitude toward slaves as property as had any other slaveholder. Two days before the Declaration of Independence, the father of our country sent a black slave to Barbados to be exchanged for a hogshed of molasses, a cask of rum and "other good old spirits." On July 2, 1776, George Washington wrote from Mt. Vernon to Capt. Joh. Thompson:

Sir: With this letter comes a Negro (Tom) which I beg the favor of you to sell in any of the islands you may go to for whatever he will fetch and bring me in return from him:

> One hhd. of best molasses
> One ditto of best rum etc., etc.

Many of the founding fathers who receive greatest visibility in the traditional story of American history were "Virginia gentlemen"—including George Washington, Thomas Jefferson, Patrick Henry, James Madison, and James Monroe. Four of the first five Presidents of the United States were from Virginia, and are usually referred to as the "Virginia Dynasty." Thus the tradition of families of wealth and privilege occupying a prominent place in American politics began with the birth of the nation.

Life in the Virginia countryside was far removed from such ugly urban events as harbor riots. Young Thomas Jefferson revealed his wealthy playboy instincts to a friend named Fleming. "Dear Will," wrote Jefferson, "I have thought of the cleverest plan of life that can be imagined. You exchange your land for Edgehill, or mine for Fairfields, you marry Suckey Potter, I marry Rebecca Burwell, and get a pole chair and a pair of keen horses, pactice the law in the same courts, and drive about to all the dances in the country together. How do you like it?"

Life in mid-eighteenth-century Virginia was cozy for the landholding aristocrats who did the voting and made the laws. A few wealthy families ran almost everything. They owned the largest tobacco plantations and the most slaves, and tobacco was the foundation for everything else. Families of the tobacco aristocracy usually intermarried. So the same founding fathers from Virginia who played together as children, partied together as young men, ended up running the new government together when they grew up.

Election day in Virginia, when members were elected to the House of Burgesses (legislature), was like a family picnic. To be a voter, a man had to be a "freeholder" —to own land of a certain value. Technically any Virginian who was qualified to vote could run for office, but no one who was not a member of the tobacco aristocracy would dare try it. There were no political parties or campaign speeches, because the voters were all old friends and neighbors of the candidates. So candidates threw parties, serving large quantities of barbecued beef and pork, rum punch and ginger cakes. Such persuasion was expensive, although not by present standards of campaign spending. Each time George Washington ran for the House of Burgesses, he spent at least £25, and once his bill came to £50 (which was several times what it cost a man to buy the house and land qualifying him as a voter).

Voting was a sporting affair, and in good weather an

election was held in the open air on the courthouse lawn. Voting was not at all secret, and there were no paper ballots. At a table sat the sheriff and the clerks who counted the votes. Also at the table sat the candidates. There was little chance of a "dark horse" candidate running away with the vote, because the sheriff was chosen by the wealthy aristocracy and he managed the elections. The sheriff decided when the voting should begin and when it should end. If the sheriff's favored candidate was running ahead, he could close the voting during the early afternoon. On the other hand, if the sheriff's candidate was running behind, he could keep the voting going into the following day.

So the voters came up to the table and announced their vote aloud. When a candidate seated at the table received a vote, he would arise and thank the voter personally. Addressing the voter by name, the candidate would say, "I shall treasure that vote in my memory. It will be regarded as a feather in my cap forever." When George Washington ran for the House of Burgesses in 1758, he was away commanding the militia, but he appointed a personal representative, the most influential man in the county, to sit at the polling table and thank each voter for him.

Landholders could vote in every county in which they held enough land. Likewise, a landholder could run for office in any county where he could vote. Thus, any founding father with a Virginia background had a rather limited concept of practical democracy. And wealthy aristocrats who were so used to controlling affairs in their own colony would quite naturally have a rather strong aversion to the outside control of the British Parliament.

But even with money and power, life for the wealthy Virginia aristocrats was sometimes lonely and monotonous. George Washington used to get so bored seeing the same folks day after day that he would send a slave to the nearest crossroad to waylay a passing traveler, with instructions to bring him back to Mount Vernon for dinner and to spend the night. Without radio and television, it was the only way Brother George could keep in touch.

The myth of the founding fathers features only those white folks whose wealth and privilege allowed them the benefit of education, and therefore they spoke and wrote the inspiring words of the American Revolution. The reality of American independence requires some paternal integration. While the now-famous white patriots were articulating the spirit of independence, some little-known black folks were taking care of business. Not all black folks were running errands for George Washington. Some were placing their lives on the battle line to give him a country of which he could be father.

Some three years before the Boston Tea Party, a street confrontation took place on the Boston Common which really began the radicalization process in the colonies. Two regiments of British troops, who had been sent to Boston at the request of the Governor, arrived aboard the warship *Romney* in 1768. Troops were felt to be necessary to preserve law and order because of popular resentment against the Townshend Acts. But the Boston citizenry resented even more the necessity of quartering British soldiers in their town against their will.

Resentment reached a boiling point on the cold and snowy night of March 5, 1770. A crowd of demonstrators assembled before the Custom House on King Street to protest the presence of British soldiers. As tension mounted with the angry demonstrators on one side and a company of nervous British soldiers on the other, fire bells rang out summoning Crispus Attucks and other men and youths of Boston. Crispus Attucks was a black man, and he was soon to shed his blood in an event about which Daniel Webster would later declare: "From that moment we may date the severance of the British Empire."

Crispus Attucks was a big man, six feet two inches tall, described by at least one eyewitness as "stout." He was forty-seven years old, and his "knees were nearer together than common." Brother Attucks was a runaway slave who had made a successful escape from Framingham in 1750. The Tuesday, October 12, 1750, edition of the *Boston Gazette* ran the following advertisement: "Ran away from his master William Brown of Framingham, on the 30th of September last, a Mollato Fellow, about 27 Years of Age, named Crispas. . . . Whoever shall take up said Run-away and convey him to his abovesaid master, shall have ten pounds." No one collected the reward, as Crispus Attucks became a seaman, and the Boston newspapers were writing about him again twenty years later—this time on the editorial pages.

Many of the British soldiers were young and inexperienced, but they held loaded muskets. The demonstrators felt the soldiers would never use their weapons; that they were under orders not to fire. Though the term "pigs" was not yet in use, the demonstrators on the Boston Common were shouting, "The wretches dare not fire." Other favorite epithets for British soldiers were "Lobster" and "Bloody-backs." The crowd began to pelt the soldiers with snowballs and other missiles. Suddenly shots rang out, and two bullets from a British private's musket crashed into Cripus Attucks' chest, killing him instantly. Moments later, three of his companions fell, fatally wounded, to the ground. Before the volley of shooting was over, five more people were seriously injured, and several others were wounded slightly.

The event was seized upon by the founding fathers and called the "Boston Massacre." Samuel Adams went immediately to Acting Governor Hutchinson's house and successfully demanded the immediate removal of the soldiers from the town. Samuel Adams was one of the founding fathers who had been writing the rhetoric of the Revolution. When the British troops first landed in Boston in 1768, Adams wrote: "Military power is by no means calculated to convince the understandings of men. It may in another part of the world affright women and children, and perhaps some weak men, out of their senses, but will never awe a sensible American tamely to surrend his liberty." Concerning the continuing presence of troops in Boston, Adams went on:

Are we a garrisoned town, or are we not? If we are, let us know by whose authority and by whose influence we are made so. If not—and I take it for granted we are not —let us then assert and maintain the honor, the dignity, of free citizens, and place the military where all other men are, and where they ought always and will be placed in every free country,—at the foot of the common law of the land! To submit to the civil magistrate in the legal exercise of power, is forever the part of a good subject; and to answer the watchmen of the town in the night, may be the part of a good citizen, as well as to afford them all necessary countenance and support. But to be called to account by a common soldier, or any soldier, is a badge of slavery, which none but a slave will wear.

So it took a slave to translate Sam Adams' words into deeds. A few days after Crispus Attucks was killed, the right-wing press took over, and the Boston *Transcript* denounced Brother Attucks as a "firebrand of disorder and sedition" who, "if he had not fallen a martyr, would richly have deserved hanging as an incendiary." But the founding fathers saw the Boston Massacre in a different light. Such men as Sam Adams and John Hancock continually lifted the bloody relics of the Boston Massacre to public view, and they used a liberally embellished version of the gory scene on the Boston Common to fan the fires of revolution. March 5, 1770, became a national day of mourning and remained such until July 4, 1776, replaced it as a national day of celebration. When the real fighting began in the Revolutionary War, George Washington exhorted his troops in battle with the cry, "Remember the Boston Massacre." To the founding fathers, Brother Attucks and his compatriots were "martyrs," not "rioters," and many white folks who had been straddling the fence regarding opposition to the British government became radicalized when they realized that a black man escaped from slavery was willing to shed his blood and give his life to champion the cause of freedom. They weren't radicalized enough to end slavery, of course, but they were moved to do something about their own oppression.

Two hundred years and two months after the Boston Massacre, a group of student demonstrators gathered on the campus of Kent State (Ohio) University to protest the presence of National Guard troops. Many of the Guardsmen were young and inexperienced, but they held loaded rifles. The students felt that the soldiers would not use their weapons; that they were under orders not to fire. Epithets were hurled at the Guardsmen, along with stones and other missiles. Suddenly shots rang out, and four students lay dead, and several others were wounded. Echoing the words of Sam Adams, the faculty of Kent State said: ". . . We deplore the prolonged and unduly provocative military presence on the campus not only because we regard the use of massive military force against unarmed students as inappropriate in itself, but because it symbolizes the rule of force in our society and international life. We regard student protest against this rule of force as their moral prerogative."

Throughout the country a day of mourning was declared to reflect upon the meaning of the Kent State deaths. Many people, young and old, who had been straddling the fence with regard to joining revolutionary sentiment in America crossed over when they saw young women being fired upon and killed on a college campus in their country. After the Boston Massacre, the "King's Friends" in Parliament condemned Acting Governor Hutchinson for his "cowardly surrender" to mob spirit. After the Kent State Massacre, President Nixon held a press conference on national television during which he stated that he had studied American history, and there would be no revolution in this country. President Nixon would probably have said the same thing had he been alive in 1770. No doubt he would have called Crispus Attucks and his companions "bums." And Vice President Spiro Agnew would probably have said that the Boston mob exacerbated a volatile situation making the end result of killing inevitable.

But if President Nixon had studied the reality rather than the myth of American history he would know that Great Britain misread the signs of the times. Little did the "King's Friends" know what six years would bring. The British government's attempts to conciliate the colonies were followed by deeper insults. And as the cry, "Remember the Kent State Massacre," becomes more and more sustained in America, an old and familiar pattern seems to be emerging.

Another slave from Framingham heard the white

founding fathers' call to take up arms against oppression. His name was Peter Salem and he was the property of Major Lawson Buckminster. Brother Salem was enrolled in Captain Simon Edgehill's company of seventy-five minutemen, all from Framingham. The company roll shows that he served four days with Edgehill's company, from April 19 through April 23, 1775. Those were important days for the American Revolution.

Late at night on April 18, English General Thomas Gage sent a military force under Lieutenant Colonel Francis Smith to arrest colonial leaders and seize their cache of supplies and ammunition hidden at Concord. Paul Revere and William Dawes warned of the advancing redcoats in their famous midnight ride. Some seventy minutemen met an advance party led by Major John Pitcairn at Lexington. Major Pitcairn ordered the ragged band of "rebels" to disperse. A shot was fired, and the subsequent volley of British shots left eight minutemen dead. At least one black man, Prince Estabrook of West Lexington, was among the minutemen assembled on the Lexington common.

Two Framingham companies of minutemen, Captain Edgehill's and Captain Micajah Gleason's, hurried some fifteen miles north to Concord, covering the distance in two hours. When Pitcairn's men got to the Concord bridge, they were met and turned back by the "embattled farmers." A black minister, Lemuel Haynes, was among those who fought at Concord, as were other black men including Cuff Whittemore, Cato Wood, Pomp Blackman, Samuel Craft, and Caesar Ferritt with his son John. Prince Estabrook was a casualty in the battle of Concord. Little is known of Peter Salem's role in the Concord battle, but he was to make quite a name for himself in the later Battle of Bunker Hill.

A few weeks after Lexington and Concord, Ethan

Allen and his "Green Mountain Boys" captured the British fort at Ticonderoga on Lake Champlain. Among the "Boys" were such black men as Lemuel Haynes, Primas Black, and Epheram Blackman.

On June 16, 1775, a force of 1,200 Americans decided upon a countermove against General Gage's plans to occupy Dorchester Heights, southeast of Boston. The American commander, General Artemus Ward, ordered several Massachusetts regiments to enter Charlestown Peninsula and fortify Bunker Hill. Colonel William Prescott was in charge. Some officers insisted that Breed's Hill should be fortified since it was closer to Boston. Finally it was decided to fortify Breed's Hill and build a second line of defense for reinforcements and for a retreat to Bunker Hill.

The British tried to drive the Americans off Breed's Hill by a bombardment from warships. But the attempt failed. So about one o'clock on the afternoon of June 17, the British forces, under the command of General Howe, landed at Moulton's Point on the Charlestown Peninsula. While the British troops were landing, reinforcements were arriving to support the 1,200 Americans who had fortified the hill. Among the reinforcements was the 5th Massachusetts Regiment, which Peter Salem had joined after serving Captain Edgehill at Concord. Brother Salem's regiment was commanded by a man named Nixon (Colonel John). The British redcoats stormed the hill two times, but they were driven off by the deadly fire of the Americans just before reaching the trenches. The third time the British soldiers raced up the hill, the Americans were out of gunpowder and were finally driven from their position with bayonets.

During that last charge up Breed's Hill, Peter Salem's old Concord adversary Major John Pitcairn raced up the hill shouting, "The day is ours!" in an attempt to rally his British soldiers. Brother Salem took careful aim and shot "the gallant Pitcairn" dead.

Concerning the Battle of Bunker Hill, historian Samuel Swett wrote:

Young Richardson of the royal Irish, was the first to mount the works, and was instantly shot down; the front rank which succeeded shared the same fate. Among these . . . Major Pitcairn, who exultingly cried "The day is ours," when a black soldier named Salem shot him and he fell. His agonized son received him in his arms and tenderly bore him to the boats.

Swett also recorded: "A contribution was made in the army for this soldier [Peter Salem], and he was presented to Washington, as having performed this feat."

Josiah H. Temple of Framingham left this record of Peter Salem's part in the battle:

During the action, he [Salem] with others, was sent from Capt. Drury's company, as a support to Col. Prescott in the redoubt. He reached the redoubt just as Prescott's men had spent their last powder; and with a single charge in his gun, and perhaps another in his powder horn. Just then, in the language of Judge Maynard, "I saw a British officer . . . come up with some pomp, and he cried out, "Surrender, you . . . rebels!" But Prescott . . . made a little motion with his hand, and that was the last word the Briton spoke; he fell at once . . . this shot was fired by Peter Salem.

Another black patriot, Salem Poor, was singled out for special commendation by Colonel William Prescott (who earlier in the Battle of Bunker Hill had shouted the now immortal words, "Don't fire until you see the whites of their eyes!"). Prescott, with thirteen other officers, commended: "A Negro man named Salem Poor," who "behaved like an experienced officer, as well as an excellent soldier."

So today the Peter Salem musket is preserved at the Bunker Hill Monument in Boston, even though George Washington and others had sought to keep black trigger fingers out of the Revolutionary Army. Slaves had served in state militia and had fought in the earliest battles of the American Revolution when the Continental Army was formed in June 1775, with George Washington as commander, but many white folks in America thought it was not a good idea to arm slaves. Slaves might be tempted to insurrection or at least get the idea that the words of the Declaration of Independence applied to them, too.

Washington held a council of war on July 9, 1775, and issued an order instructing recruiting officers not to sign up "any stroller, Negro, or vagabond." Those blacks who were already in the army were allowed to stay, but no additional black patriots could enlist. In September, Edward Rutledge of South Carolina introduced a resolution at the Continental Congress to drop blacks already in the service. The resolution was defeated. Two weeks later George Washington's council of war voted unanimously to exclude slaves and, by a majority vote, to reject free blacks. On October 31 the quartermaster general was instructed not to permit blacks to re-enlist, though those already enlisted could remain, at the direct insistence of George Washington himself.

But the policy began to produce complications. The British began to recruit blacks, promising freedom to slaves who enlisted in their forces. Lord Dunmore, Governor of Virginia, issued a proclamation to that effect on November 7, 1775. Washington became alarmed, as he had visions of black slaves flocking to the side of the British. George Washington listened to his fears, even though he had a tendency not to listen to black folks. Two weeks before the order was issued excluding blacks from military service, black poetess Phillis Wheatley, from Massachusetts, sent Washington a poem praising him as commander. Washington sent her a thank-you note, saying that only possible accusations of vanity on his part prohibited him from having the poem published, and told her to drop by if she was ever in the neighborhood.

Washington wrote another note, this time to John Hancock, President of the Continental Congress, telling him that free black soldiers were quite riled at being excluded. Washington said that he was going ahead and re-enlisting them, but he would stop the practice if Congress so ordered. On January 16, 1776, Congress approved the re-enlistment of free blacks but upheld the ruling that no new blacks could be taken into the Continental Army. State militia followed the same course in both the North and the South.

In the end, at least five thousand black men served in the Continental Army. Blacks were present at every major battle. Blacks froze with white patriots at Valley Forge, and they watched their commander George Washington accept Cornwallis' surrender at Yorktown in 1781. Black slaves and former slaves did not have the education to write the stirring words of freedom and independence enshrined in the history book account of the American Revolution. But they had the strength and the courage to implement those words, even though their ancestors remain excluded from that American Dream to this day.

DECLARATIONS AND DEEDS

Not all blacks were lacking in education, however. One of the most brilliant men in all the colonies was a black man named Benjamin Banneker. Born in 1731 near Ellicott's Mill (now Ellicott City), Maryland, Banneker's formal education was limited to attending a Quaker school near Joppa, Maryland. Benjamin Banneker's mother, Mary, was the oldest daughter of a white indentured servant, Molly Welsh, and an African prince named Bannaky, whom Molly had purchased and later married. So Brother Ben was born free, following the status of his mother rather than that of his freedman father, Robert. Robert took his wife's name, which had been Anglicized to Banneker.

Benjamin was a favorite of his grandmother and, long before the days of Head Start programs for black folks, learned to read the Bible at her knee at the age of four. He became an avid reader and a self-educated genius. Brother Banneker has an impressive list of accomplishments to his credit. He made the first clock in America while he was still a youth—a wooden clock which struck the hours. He published one of the first and most complete almanacs in this country, containing tidal information, astronomical observations, including the successful predictions of eclipses, and medicinal formulas. And Banneker was the chief engineer who laid out the blueprints for the new capital of his fledgling nation, Washington, D.C. Little did Brother Banneker realize he was laying plans for the future Resurrection City.

One writer has suggested, "Color Benjamin Franklin black and you get Banneker." It would probably be more accurate to say, "Color Ben Franklin black and you would get quite an argument from Ben Franklin." But there is no doubt that Banneker's genius as scientist, astronomer, and mathematician greatly impressed Thomas Jefferson. Jefferson found Benjamin Banneker's annual almanacs every bit as helpful as Benjamin Franklin's *Poor Richard's Almanack*.

In 1791, Banneker sent the manuscript of his new almanac to fellow scientist and admirer Secretary of State Thomas Jefferson. In sending his gift, Brother Banneker took the opportunity to suggest that, if the Secretary of State admired his (Banneker's) work so much, he might also be interested in freeing black folks. Long before singer James Brown, Banneker was saying, "I'm black and I'm proud," though using a vocabulary which reflected the language patterns of his own era. "I freely and cheerfully acknowledge," said Banneker in his letter to Thomas Jefferson, "that I am of the African race, and in that color whch is natural to them of the deepest dye; and it is under a sense of the most profound gratitude to the Supreme Ruler of the Universe, that I now confess to you, that I am not under that state of tyrannical thralldom, and inhuman captivity, to which too many of my brethren are doomed."

Banneker also reminded Jefferson of the words he had written to be issued on the first Fourth of July. Said Banneker:

This, Sir, was a time when you clearly saw into the injustice of a state of slavery, and in which you had just apprehensions of the horror of its condition . . . your abhorrence thereof was so excited, that you publicly held forth this true and invaluable doctrine, which is worthy to be recorded and remembered in all succeeding ages: "We hold these truths to be self-evident, that all men are created equal, that they are endowed by their Creator with certain unalienable rights, and that among these are life, liberty and the pursuit of happiness."

. . . Tender feeling for yourselves had engaged you

thus to declare, you were then impressed with proper ideas of the great violation of liberty, and the free possession of those blessings, to which you were entitled by nature; but, Sir, how pitiable is it to reflect, that although you were so fully convinced of the benevolence of the Father of Mankind, and of his equal and impartial distribution of these rights and priveleges, which he hath conferred upon them, that you should at the same time counteract his mercies, in detaining by fraud and violence so numerous a part of my brethren, under groaning captivity, and cruel oppression, that you should at the same time be found guilty of that most criminal act, which you professedly detested in others, with respect to yourselves.

Benjamin Banneker received a reply from Secretary of State Jefferson.

I thank you sincerely [said Thomas Jefferson] for your letter of the 19th instant, and for the Almanac it contained. Nobody wishes more than I do to see such proofs as you exhibit, that nature has given to our black brethren talents equal to those of the other colours of men, and that the appearance of a want of them is owing only to the degraded condition of their existence both in Africa and America. I can add with truth that no one wishes more ardently to see a good system commenced for raising the condition both of their body and mind to what it ought to be, as fast as the imbecility of their present existence, and other circumstances which cannot be neglected, will admit.

Jefferson then informed Banneker that he had sent the Almanac to Monsieur de Condorcet, Secretary of the Academy of Sciences in Paris.

Things haven't changed much in the past 170-odd years. Translated into a twentieth-century idiom, Banneker asked Jefferson: "How can you white folks be so hypocritical to insist upon freedom and democracy for yourselves, and broadcast that insistence all over the world, while you still keep my black brothers under the thumb of oppression at home?"

And retaining the same idiom, Jefferson's answer: "If they were all like you, Ben, things would be different. Black folks just aren't ready. Education is the problem. You've got to be more patient."

Is it any wonder that black folks are finally laying down their pens and picking up other instruments of liberation?

Benjamin Banneker's letter to Thomas Jefferson aroused an old dilemma in Jefferson's mind. Jefferson believed in the inferiority of blacks *and* the immorality of slavery. Concerning the inferiority of blacks, Jefferson wrote in a reply to a questionnaire from the Secretary to the French legation in 1731:

The first difference which strikes us is that of color. Whether the black of the negro resides in the reticular membrane between the skin, and scarf-skin, or in the scarf-skin itself; whether it proceeds from the color of the blood, the color of the bile, or from that of some other secretion, the difference is fixed in nature, and is as real as if its seat and cause were better known to us. And is this difference of no importance? Is it not the foundation of a greater or less share of beauty in the two races? . . . The circumstance of superior beauty, is thought worthy attention in the propagation of our horses, dogs, and other domestic animals; why not in that of man? Besides those of color, figure, and hair, there are other physical distinctions proving a difference of race. They have less hair on the face and body. They secrete less by the kidneys, and more by the glands of the skin, which gives them a very strong and disagreeable odor. This greater degree of transpiration, renders them more tolerant of heat, and less so of cold than the whites. . . . They seem to require less sleep. A black after hard labor through the day, will be induced by the slightest amusements to sit up till midnight, or later, though knowing he must be out with the first dawn of the morning.

They are at least as brave, and more adventuresome. But this may perhaps proceed from a want of forethought which prevents their seeing a danger till it be present. When present, they do not go through it with more coolness or steadiness than the whites. They are more ardent after their female; but love seems with them to be more an eager desire, than a tender delicate mixture of sentiment and sensation. Their griefs are transient. Those numberless afflictions which render it doubtful whether heaven has given life to us in mercy or in wrath, are less felt, and sooner forgotten with them. In general, their existence appears to participate more of sensation than reflection. To this must be ascribed their disposition to sleep when abstracted from their diversions, and unemployed in labor. An animal whose body is at rest, and who does not reflect, must be disposed to sleep of course. Comparing them by their faculties of memory, reason, and imagination, it appears to me that in memory they are equal to the whites; in reason much inferior, as I think one could scarcely be found capable of tracing and comprehending the investigations of Euclid; and that in imagination they are dull, tasteless, and anomalous. It would be unfair to follow them to Africa for this investigation. We will consider them here, on the same stage with the whites, and where the facts are not aprocryphal on which a judgment is to be formed. It will be right to make great allowances for the difference of condition, of education, of conversation, of the sphere in which they move. Many millions of them have been brought to, and born in America. Most of them, indeed, have been confined to tillage, to their own homes, and their own society; yet many have been so situated, that they might have availed themselves of the conversation of their masters; many have been brought up to the handicraft arts, and from that circumstance have always been associated with the whites. Some have been liberally educated, and all have lived in countries where the arts and sciences are cultivated to a considerable degree, and all have had before their eyes samples of the best works from abroad. . . .

But never yet could I find that a black had uttered a thought above the level of plain narration; never saw even an elementary trait of painting or sculpture. In music they are more generally gifted than the whites with accurate ears for tune and time, and they have been found capable of imagining a small catch. Whether they will be equal to the composition of a more extensive run of melody, or of complicated harmony, is yet to be proved. . . .

It is not their condition then, but nature, which has produced the distinction. Whether further observation will or will not verify the conjecture, that nature has been less bountiful to them in the endowments of the head, I believe that in those of the heart she will be found to have done them justice. That disposition to theft with which they have been branded, must be ascribed to their situation, and not to any depravity of the moral sense. . . .

I advance it, therefore, as a suspicion only, that the blacks, whether originally a distinct race, or made distinct by time and circumstances, are inferior to the whites in the endowments both of body and mind. . . .

In his *Notes on the State of Virginia,* written in 1781–1782, Jefferson commented upon how white racism was transmitted from parents to their offspring and indicated his hope that slavery would end:

There must doubtless be an unhappy influence on the manners of our people produced by the existence of slavery among us. The whole commerce between master and slave is a perpetual exercise of the most boisterous passions, the most unremitting despotism on the one part, and degrading submissions on the other. Our children see this, and learn to imitate it; for man is an imitative animal. This quality is the germ of all education in him. From his cradle to his grave he is learning to do what he sees others do. If a parent could find not motive either in his philanthropy or his self-love, for restraining the intemperance of passion towards his slave, it should always be a sufficient one that his child is present. But generally it is not sufficient. The parent storms, the child looks on, catches the lineaments of wrath, puts on the airs in the circle of smaller slaves, gives a loose to the worst of passions, and thus nursed, educated, and daily exercised in tyranny, cannot but be stamped by it with odious peculiarities. The man must be a prodigy who can retain his manners and morals undepraved by such circumstances. And with what execration should the statesman be loaded, who, permitting one half the citizens thus to trample on the rights of the other, transforms those into despots, and these into enemies, destroys the morals of the one part, and the *amor patriae* of the other. For if a slave can have a country in this world, it must be any other in preference to that in which he is born to live and labor for another; in which he must lock up the faculties of his nature, contribute as far as depends on his individual endeavors to the evanishment of the human race, or entail his own miserable condition on the endless generations proceeding from him. With the morals of the people, their industry also is destroyed. For in a warm climate, no man will labor for himself who can make another labor for him. This is so true, that of the proprietors of slaves a very small proportion indeed are ever seen to labor.

And can the liberties of a nation be thought secure when we have removed their only firm basis, a conviction in the minds of the people that these liberties are the gift of God? That they are not to be violated but with his wrath? Indeed I tremble for my country when I reflect that God is just; that his justice cannot sleep forever; that considering numbers, nature and natural means only, a revolution of the wheel of fortune, and exchange of situation is among possible events; that it may become probable by supernatural interference! The Almighty has no attribute which can side with us in such a contest. But it is impossible to be temperate and to pursue this subject through the various considerations of policy, of morals, of history natural and civil. We must be contented to hope they will force their way into every one's mind. I think a change is already perceptible, since the origin of the present revolution. The spirit of the master is abating, that of the slave rising from the dust, his condition mollifying, the way I hope preparing, under the auspices of heaven, for a total emancipation, and that this is disposed, in the order of events, to be with the consent of the masters, rather than by their extirpation.

Even in 1776, Thomas Jefferson had tried to slip his antislavery sentiments into the Declaration of Independence. Two years earlier Jefferson had written the brilliant and widely read pamphlet *A Summary View of the Rights of America*, so his fellow members of the Continental Congress commissioned Jefferson to write their Declaration. Actually a five-member committee including Jefferson was appointed: John Adams, representing Massachusetts; Robert R. Livingston, representing New York; Roger Sherman, representing Connecticut; and Benjamin Franklin, representing Pennsylvania. The others served as editors, deleting or altering words and phrases, but the basic text was the work of Jefferson.

Jefferson did his writing in the upstairs parlor of a German bricklayer, in whose home he was lodging during the session of the Continental Congress in Philadelphia. Working at a portable desk he had designed and brought with him, Jefferson wrote and rewrote the Declaration. On June 28 the committee submitted the final draft of the Declaration of Independence to the Continental Congress. For the next two days delegates became an editorial board and went to work on the

Declaration. When they got to one paragraph, they struck it out completely:

He [King George III] has waged cruel war against human nature itself. Violating its most sacred rights of life and liberty in the persons of a distant people, who never offended him, captivating and carrying them into slavery in another hemisphere, or to incur miserable death in their transportation thither, this piratical warfare, the opprobrium of *infidel* powers, is the warfare of the *Christian* King of Great Britain. Determined to keep open a market where MEN should be bought and sold, he has prostituted his negative for suppressing every legislative attempt to prohibit or restrain this execrable commerce.

So the delegates to the Continental Congress said "Right On!" to Jefferson's other enumerations of tyrannies and oppressions, but they felt he went a little too far in condemning slavery. That particular oppression hit a little too close to home. Later, when writing his *Autobiography,* Thomas Jefferson explained that the deletion of the slavery clause was part of the "southern strategy" of Congress:

The Clause . . . reprobating the enslaving of the inhabitants of Africa was struck out in complaisance to South Carolina and Georgia, who have never attempted to restrain the importation of slaves, and who on the contrary still wished to continue it.

Our Northern brethren also I believe felt a little tender under these censures; for tho their people have very few slaves themselves yet they had been pretty considerable carriers of them to others.

That "tenderness" was to remain a point of contention up to the Civil War period. Northerners controlled the ships that were used to bring black folks to these shores from Africa. We were sold by a northern white man to a southern white man. Then the northern white man got slick one day and turned to his southern brother, after he had pocketed the money, and said, "Get rid of your slaves." The southerner had every right to say, "Do I get a refund?" The storekeeper will give you two cents back on a Coke bottle, if the bottle belongs to you! But with slavery it was strictly "No refund, no return."

On February 25, 1861, Congressman Joseph Jonas spoke to that issue:

Who entailed upon us the curse of slavery? The answer is, Northern men and Northern ships. Who continues this horrid trade? Echo says, Northern men and Northern ships. Yes, gentlemen, the descendants of the pilgrim Fathers, hypocrites as they are, after rolling in wealth and luxury from this illegal trade, after entailing on the South this curse, they would abolish slavery, and deprive them of their property, and leaving the negro at large, plunge their victims into irremediable ruin.

Anthony Benezet, French-born Quaker philanthropist, pamphleteer, and teacher, best summed up the hypocrisy in the slavery clause's omission from the Declaration of Independence:

If these solemn truths uttered in such an awful crisis, are *self-evident:* unless we can show that the African race are not *men,* words can hardly express the amazement which naturally arises on reflecting that the very people who make these pompous declarations are slave holders, and, by their legislation, tell us, that these blessings were only meant to be the *rights of white men,* not of all *men;* and would seem to verify the observation of an eminent writer: "When men talk of liberty, they mean their own liberty, and seldom suffer their thoughts on that point to stray."

Though the founding fathers had a peculiar blindness to the oppression of slavery, they were very clear in arti-

culating the right of revolution. The rioting and looting
of the Boston Tea Party was described by John Adams:

This is the most magnificent Movement of all, there is
a dignity, a Majesty, a Sublimity, in this last effort of the
Patriots that I greatly admire. The people should never
rise, without doing something to be remembered, something notable and striking. This Destruction of the TEA
is so bold, so daring, so firm, intrepid and inflexible, and
it must have so important consequences, and so lasting,
that I can't but consider it an Epoch in History.

And though John Adams was not able, with his revolutionary fervor, to rid the new nation of the awful institution of slavery, he passed a revolutionary heritage
on to his son, John Quincy Adams, which surfaced in
the latter days of his life, causing certain fellow members of Congress to call the son of John Adams a traitor.

John Quincy Adams as a boy saw his father being
hunted as a traitor by government soldiers and Tories.
He saw the Declaration of Independence issued by the
Continental Congress and a new nation being born. And
John Quincy Adams rose to the highest offices the new
nation had to offer: first, Secretary of State under James
Monroe and finally, President of the United States.

When he left the presidency, John Quincy Adams did
not settle down quietly to the life of elder statesman. He
ran for the House of Representatives and served seventeen years until the time of his death. While in Congress, John Quincy Adams saw slavery and racism
slowly defiling and mocking the great promises of the
revolution his father had been so instrumental in making. He stood on the floor of Congress, now a shaking,
feeble old man, but able to spew forth the most stinging,
biting, withering attacks against slavery that the slaveholders in Congress had ever heard. When John Quincy

Adams rose to speak, large groups of slaveholding Congressmen stalked out of the room.

In 1842, John Quincy Adams was accused of high treason. In that year he had presented a petition to Congress signed by Benjamin Emerson and forty-five other citizens of Haverhill, Massachusetts. It was a petition to dissolve the Union. The Southerners thought they had caught John Quincy Adams, on the grounds that calling on Congress to break its oath to preserve the Union with a proposition to dissolve it was an act of high treason. But Adams, remembering the revolutionary training he had received at his father's knee, proclaimed it was his revolutionary right, guaranteed by the Declaration of Independence. The following exchange on the floor of Congress is taken from the *Congressional Globe* for the second session of the Twenty-seventh Congress of 1842:

MR. ADAMS: I am not surprised at the charge that has been brought against me of high treason. What is high treason? The Constitution defines what high treason is, and it is not for him, or his puny mind, to define what high treason is and confound it with what I have done. Sir, the first volume of the laws of the United States will show what it is. I desire the clerk to read the first paragraph of the Declaration of Independence. (Raising his voice.) The first Paragraph of the Declaration of Independence. (Raising his voice to a still higher pitch.) The first Paragraph of the Declaration of Independence!
The CLERK read as follows:

"We hold these truths to be self-evident, that all men are created equal, that they are endowed by their Creator with certain unalienable Rights, that among these are Life, Liberty and the pursuit of Happiness. That to secure these rights, Governments are instituted among Men deriving their just powers from the consent of the governed. That whenever any Form of Government becomes destructive of these ends, it is the Right of the People to alter or to abolish it, and to institute new Government, laying its foundation on such principles, and organizing its powers in such form, as to them shall seem most likely to effect their Safety and Happiness. Prudence, indeed, will dictate that Governments long established should not be changed for light and transient causes; and accordingly all experience hath shewn, that mankind are more disposed to suffer, while evils are sufferable, than to right themselves by abolishing the forms to which they are accustomed. But when a long train of abuses and usurpations, pursuing invariably the same Object evinces a design to reduce them under absolute Despotism, it is their Right, it is their Duty, to throw off such Government, and to provide new Guards for their future security."

MR. ADAMS: (repeating after the Clerk) "the Right of the People to alter or to abolish it." Now Sir, if there is a principle sacred on earth and established by the instrument just read, it is the right of the people to alter, to change, to destroy the Government, if it becomes oppressive to them. There would be no such right existing, if the people had not the power, in pursuance of that right, to petition for it.

Sir, if my attachment to this Union and this Constitution could be questioned, that provision would be sufficient to refute any slanderous attacks that might be made on me. I rest that petition on the Declaration of Independence and let me tell the gentleman, and let me tell this house that they are not the only persons to whom these sentiments are familiar.

When I come to make my defense before the House, I shall show other oppressions, not only actual, but intended. I shall show that the portion of the country from which the gentleman comes are endeavoring to destroy the right of habeas corpus, the right of trial by jury, and all the rights of which the liberty of this country exists . . . and that there is a continued system and purpose to destroy all the principle of civil liberty in the free States, not for the purpose of preserving their institutions within their own limits, but to force their detested principles of slavery into all the free States. I will show that measures are systematically pursued or projected to force this country into a war. This is the state of things that exists and it is provided in the Declaration of Independence; and if there is no other remedy for it, it is the right and duty of the people of that portion of the Union to take that remedy.

A PAINE-FUL REMINDER

If any one man can be said to have kept the American Revolution alive with words, that man was Thomas Paine. Yet Thomas Paine's life is a tragic reminder of how quickly men turn against their former heroes and of the price one must pay for being consistently dedicated to his beliefs.

In January 1776, Thomas Paine published his little pamphlet *Common Sense*. Six months later the Continental Congress took the very course Thomas Paine recommended in his pamphlet. Said Paine:

The sun never shined on a cause of greater worth. 'Tis not the affair of a City, a County, a Province or a Kingdom; but of a continent—at least one-eighth part of the habitable globe. 'Tis not the concern of a day, a year, or an age; posterity are virtually involved in the contest, and will be more or less affected even to the end of time, by the proceedings now. Now is the seed-time of Continental union, faith and honor. The least fracture now will be like a name engraved with the point of a pin on the tender rind of a young oak; the wound would enlarge with the tree, and posterity read it in full grown letters. . . .

O! Ye that love mankind! Ye that dare oppose not only the tyranny but the tyrant, stand forth! Every spot of the old world is overrun with oppression. Freedom hath been hunted round the Globe. Asia and Africa have long expelled her. Europe regards her like a stranger, and England hath given her warning to depart. O! receive the fugitive, and prepare in time an asylum for mankind.

Thomas Paine sought to put his body where his words were, so in the summer of 1776 he joined General Roberdeau's division of the Pennsylvania troops as a volunteer. He seems to have been in the thick of some of the worst defeats the American army suffered. In the autumn and winter of 1776, George Washington suffered a series of shattering defeats at the hands of the British army. A succession of calamities followed defeat in the battle of Long Island: the abandonment of New York on the twenty-eighth of October, the surrender of Fort Washington on the sixteenth of November, the stampede from Fort Lee on the eighteenth of November, the retreat through New Jersey, and, on the eighth of December, Washington's escape across the Delaware. A British letter writer among the enemy troops says that "the rebels fled like scared rabbits" from Fort Lee, leaving behind "some poor pork, a few greasy proclamations, and some of that scoundrel *Common Sense* man's letters, which we can read at our leisure, now that we have got one of the 'impregnable redoubts' of Mr. Washington's to quarter in."

Washington's troops were haggard, morale was down, the weather was cold, defeat was bitter, and the spirit of the revolution needed encouragement. Thomas Paine wrote the words of much-needed encouragement:

These are times that try men's souls. The summer soldier and the sunshine patriot will, in this crisis, shrink from the service of their country; but he that stands it *now*, deserves the love and thanks of man and woman. Tyranny, like hell, is not easily conquered; yet we have this consolation with us, that the harder the conflict, the more glorious the triumph. What we obtain too cheap, we esteem too lightly. If there be trouble, let it be in my day that my children may have peace. It is dearness only that gives everything its value. Heaven knows how to put a proper price upon its goods; and it would be strange indeed if so celestial an article as *freedom* should not be highly rated.

Then Paine issued such a call to battle that would almost bring slain patriots back to life:

Up and help us; lay your shoulders to the wheel; better have too much force than too little, when so great an object is at stake. Let it be told to the future world, that in the depth of winter, when nothing but hope and virtue could survive, the city and country, alarmed at one common danger, came forth to meet and repulse it. . . . It matters not where you live, or what rank of life you hold, the evil or the blessing will reach you all . . . The heart that feels not now, is dead. The blood of his children will curse his cowardice, who shrinks back at a time when a little might have saved the whole, and made them happy. I love the man that can smile in trouble, that can gather strength from distress, and grow brave by reflection. 'Tis the business of little minds to shrink; but he whose heart is firm, and whose conscience approves his conduct, will pursue his principles unto death. . . . It is the madness of folly to expect mercy from those who have refused to do justice. . . . By perseverance and fortitude, we have the prospect of a glorious issue; by cowardice and submission, the sad choice of a variety of evils,—a ravaged country, a depopulated city, habitations without safety, and slavery without hope, our homes turned into barracks and bawdy-houses for Hessians, and a future race to provide for, whose fathers we shall doubt of. Look on this picture and weep over it; and if there yet remains one thoughtless wretch who believes it not, let him suffer it unlamented.

Thomas Paine would never accept defeat, nor would he tolerate anyone else among his fellow patriots becoming discouraged after losing a battle. Once after a defeat in battle, Paine exhorted:

Those who expect to reap the blessings of freedom, must like men undergo the fatigues of supporting it. The event of yesterday was one of those kind alarms which are just sufficient to rouse us to duty, without being of consequence enough to depress our fortitude. It is not a field of a few acres of ground, but a cause, that we are defending; and whether we defeat the enemy in one battle, or by degrees, the consequence will be the same. . . . We have always been masters of the past push, and always shall be while we do our duty. . . . Shall a band of ten or twelve thousand robbers, who are this day fifteen hundred or two thousand men less in strength than they were yesterday, conquer America, or subdue even a single State? The thing cannot be done, unless we sit down and suffer them to do it. Another such brush, notwithstanding we lost the ground, would, by still reducing the enemy, put them in a condition to be afterwards totally defeated. . . . It is distressing to see an enemy advancing into a country, but it is the only place in which we can beat them, and in which we have always beaten them, whenever they have made the attempt. . . . You have too much at stake to hesitate. You ought not to think an hour upon the matter, but to spring to action at once. Other States have been invaded; have likewise driven off the invaders. Now our time and turn is come, and perhaps the finishing stroke is reserved for us. When we look back on the dangers we have been saved from, and reflect on the success we have been blessed with, it would be sinful either to be idle or to despair.

When the final victory was won in the American Revolution, Thomas Paine again used his pen to celebrate the successful revolution and to caution of the dangers that lay ahead in making a new government work:

The times that tried men's souls are over—and the greatest and completest Revolution the world ever knew, gloriously and happily accomplished. But to pass from the extremes of danger to safety—from the tumult of war to the tranquility of peace—though sweet in contemplation, requires a gradual composure of the senses to receive it. Even calmness has the power of stunning, when it opens too instantly upon us. . . . In the present case, the mighty magnitude of the object, the various uncertainties of fate which it has undergone, the numerous and complicated dangers we have suffered or escaped, the eminence we now stand on, and the vast prospect before us, must all conspire to impress us with contemplation. To see it in our power to make a world happy, to teach mankind the art of being so, to exhibit on the theatre of the universe a character hitherto unknown, and to have, as it were, a new creation intrusted to our hands, are honors that command reflection, and can neither be too highly estimated, nor too gratefully received. In this pause, then, of reflection, while the storm is ceasing, and the long-agitated mind vibrating to a rest, let us look back on the scenes we have passed, and learn from experience what is yet to be done. . . .

But that which must more forcibly strike a thoughtful, penetrating mind, and which includes and renders easy all inferior concerns, is the union of the States. On this, our great national character depends. It is this which must give us importance abroad and security at home. . . . In short, we have no other national sovereignty than as United States. . . . Individuals, or individual States, may call themselves what they please; but the world, and especially the world of enemies, is not to be held in awe by the whistling of a name. Sovereignty must have power to protect all the parts that compose and constitute it; and as the United States, we are equal to the importance of the title, but otherwise we are not. Our union, well and wisely regulated and cemented, is the cheapest way of being great—the easiest way of being powerful, and the happiest invention in government which the circumstances of America can admit of. . . . I ever feel myself hurt when I hear the union, that great palladium of our liberty and safety, the least irreverently spoken of. It is the most sacred thing in the constitution of America, and that which every man should be most proud and tender of. Our citizenship in the United States is our national character. Our citizenship in any particular State is only our local distinction. By the latter we are known at home, but the former to the world. Our great title is AMERICANS.

The revolution in America was over, but another revolution was brewing in France, and it stirred Paine's passions. He went to England, where he wrote an essay, *The Rights of Man,* directed against Edmund Burke and those opposing the French revolutionists. His attack on English institutions forced him to flee to Paris. Paine was made a citizen of the Republic, was elected to the Legislative Assembly, became allied with the moderates, and was jailed during the Terror of 1793. While in jail Paine wrote *The Age of Reason,* which was seen as an attack on the Bible by many religious folks in America. Paine lost all favor with George Washington when he wrote a letter to him ending, "As to you, Sir, treacherous in private friendship and a hypocrite in public life, the world will be puzzled to decide, whether you are an APOSTATE or an IMPOSTOR, whether you have abandoned good principles, or whether you ever had any."

Washington was a slaveholder, and Paine had always hated the "infernal traffic in negroes." He had kept quiet on the subject during the Revolution in America for fear of ruining everything. But since then he wrote, "We must push that matter [abolition] further on your side of the water. I wish that a few well-instructed negroes could be sent among their brethren in bondage; for until they are enabled to take their own part nothing will be done." Tom Paine had no admiration for the father of *our* country as a political leader and said, "The disposition of Washington was apathy itself, and nothing could kindle a fire in his bosom—neither friendship, fame, nor country."

Paine was released from jail through the intervention of James Monroe, and in 1802 he returned to the United States. But Thomas Paine found no hero's welcome in the nation where his words had kept the Revolution alive. Two decades had passed and America was becoming a settled government of parties and factions. Paine's radical freethinking was feared by politicians and considered dangerous. Thus he was accused of atheism, cowardice, adultery, and drunkenness.

Paine settled down on a farm near New Rochelle, New York, whch had been given to him by Congress when the Revolution was over. But it was a bad place for Paine, now a weary, sick, nearly broken old man, to settle. New Rochelle was Tory country during the American Revolution, and was now anti-President Jefferson, as was most of Westchester County. The villagers had not fought the war and had given all the aid they could to the British and the Tory counterrevolutionaries called "Roger's Rangers." Thomas Paine became the object of village ridicule and harassment. Whenever he went out, little children would follow him down the street, throwing rocks and mud at him, shouting: "Damned old devil! Damned old devil!"

The crowning blow came when Thomas Paine ventured into town to vote in the 1806 election. Thomas Paine, the brilliant orator of the American Revolution, shuffled into town with the taunting children following at his heels. When the election officials saw him coming, they smiled at one another; and when he announced his name, he was told he was not a citizen of the United States and could not vote. Thomas Paine protested, saying that Congress gave citizenship to all soldiers of the Revolution. But the election officials said that he was never a soldier in the Revolution, that he was a foreigner, and that he could not vote. Such was the price Thomas Paine was forced to pay for being a freethinker in America.

The insult was not over. Thomas Paine died June 8, 1809. He was buried on his farm in unhallowed ground. The good people of New Rochelle invaded the farm, ripped branches from trees that had been planted at the grave, and sold them as souvenirs. They broke chips off the tombstone and pulled up any flowers. Ten years later a man named William Cobbett dug up Paine's bones with the intention of taking them to England to be exhibited in various cities. But the British government foiled Cobbett's scheme, and Paine's remains disappeared somewhere in England.

So today Paine's resting place is unknown. But Thomas Paine is actually buried deep in the hearts and minds of all decent-thinking people everywhere—this courageous freethinker who once said, "Where freedom is not, there is my country."

"The only weapon of self defense I could use successfully was that of deception."

HENRY BIBB, AN AMERICAN SLAVE

"I fooled Old Master seven years, Fooled the overseer three. Hand me down my banjo, and I'll tickle your bel-lee."

SLAVE JINGLE

"They think because they hold us in infernal chains of slavery that we wish to be white, or of their color but they are dreadfully deceived—we wish to be just as it pleased our creator to have made us."

DAVID WALKER, BLACK ABOLITIONIST, 1828

IV

THE MYTH OF BLACK CONTENT
or Black Is Beautiful

Southern folklore of the mid-1800's is rich in tales of slave cleverness and wit. Typical are Joel Chandler Harris' tales of Uncle Remus—immortalized in the Walt Disney film *Song of the South*—where Br'er Rabbit uses his wit and ingenuity to get himself out of numerous impossible situations. Many slave folk heroes emerged out of such stories. One of these was Old John, the symbol of a slave's use of cunning to outwit his master and turn an impossible situation to his own advantage.

One tale tells how Old John's master made a wager of a few thousand dollars that Old John could whip the most powerful black man on a neighboring plantation. On the day of combat, Old John arrived at the battle site to find his opponent chained to an iron stake. He was scratching and pawing the ground, snorting through his nostrils, a bull in human form ready to tear Old John apart.

Old John sized up the situation, walked over to his master's wife and slapped her across the face. His opponent pulled up his stake and ran away as fast as he could. Of course, Old John's master was outraged and demanded an explanation of such impudent behavior. Old John coolly replied: "Well, Jim knowed if I'd slap a white lady, I'd kill him, so he ran." John's master picked up his money and his lady and split.

Black slaves were so totally at the mercy of their white owners that every ounce of wit and ingenuity that could be mustered was necessary for survival. And it is not at all surprising that black folks were able to develop such a survival kit, since the greatest storyteller and artist of creative ingenuity in all history was a black man named Aesop. Aesop's fables have been learned by children the world over for many centuries, and they were born of the survival necessities of this black slave.

Aesop was born in a town called Amorium in Phrygia and he lived in the sixth century B.C. He had a keen mind, a deformed body, and a far from handsome face. One writer described him in detail: "His head was long and pendant, a hump back and complexion dark, from which he contracted his name, large belly, and bow legs; but his greatest infirmity was that his speech was slow, inarticulate, and very obscure."

An early story of Aesop's ingenuity tells of a time when his stuttering and stammering almost did him in. Aesop was sent by his master to work in the fields. While Aesop was out in the fields, a peasant came by and gave his master some figs. The master thought the figs so good that he had his butler, Agathopus, put them away, intending to finish them after he had his bath. While the master was bathing, Agathopus got into the figs and also shared them with some of his friends. Just at the inopportune time, Aesop came into the house, and when the master discovered the missing figs, Agathopus made Aesop the scapegoat, accusing him of the theft.

Aesop threw himself at his master's feet and stammered for mercy. Curious, the master stayed punishment until Aesop could make his point. Aesop got himself some warm water, drank it down, put his finger down his throat and vomited. Then he made signs suggesting that the others in the room do the same thing. Agathopus and his friends took the warm water treatment, and when they vomited, the condemning evidence of undigested figs came up.

Legend has it that Aesop was miraculously cured of his stammering by the goddess Fortune shortly thereafter. Another story tells of Aesop's cleverness when he became the property of a merchant on his way to Ephesus to sell some slaves. All the equipment needed for the trip was carried on the backs of the slaves. As a newcomer, Aesop was given his choice of the burden he was to carry. Everyone was amazed when Aesop picked up the bread basket, which was the heaviest burden of all. The other slaves thought Aesop must be slightly stupid. But at dinner time Aesop's burden became lighter when some of the bread was removed for the meal. The same thing happened the next day and each succeeding day during the trip. So by the end of the journey, Aesop was carrying nothing but the empty basket, while the other slaves still had their original loads.

Two of Aesop's fables could be said to have particular contemporary meaning, with regard to both the black struggle and world politics. Aesop's most famous fable is probably that of the hare and the tortoise. There was a hare who was always making fun of the tortoise for being so slow, while at the same time bragging about his own speed. Finally the tortoise had enough, and he said: "All right, let's have a race and settle this thing once and for all. I'll race you for five miles and I bet I'll win."

The hare was quite amused and took the tortoise up on the bet. So they picked the fox as the judge, and the race began. The hare took off like the wind and was soon so far out in front that he stopped and laughed and laughed while he waited for the slow-moving tortoise to come into sight. He waited for a long time, and he was so far out in front that the hare said: "I'll just lie down and take a quick nap." He lay down in the grass, and it was so soft and comfortable that he fell into a deep sleep. The tortoise, meanwhile, kept moving along at his slow, steady pace. When the hare awoke, he jumped up with a start and ran down the road, but he was too late. The tortoise was just crossing the finish line. The hare's arrogance had defeated him. Moral: Slow but steady wins the race.

Finally there is the story of the frogs in the pond. Finding their pond too quiet and lacking in excitement, the frogs prayed to Jupiter for a king. Jupiter threw them down a log, which after the first splash, lay still in the pond. The frogs felt that their king was not noisy or spectacular enough, and they jumped upon him in contempt. They begged Jupiter for another king. This time Jupiter sent a beautiful stork. King stork was not lacking in spectacle and made life in the pond exciting by eating up the frogs.

Perhaps Brother Aesop best spoke for all black slaves when he was on the auction block at Ephesus.

Aesop was standing between an orator and a singer. A prospective buyer was the Lydian philosopher Xantus. Xantus asked the orator what he could do. "Anything," was the answer. He asked the same question of the singer. "Everything," came the reply. Finally Xantus got around to Aesop and asked him what he could do. "Nothing," said Aesop.

"Nothing?" Xantus repeated disbelievingly.

"One of my companions," said Aesop, "says he can do anything and the other says he can do everything. That leaves me nothing."

Xantus liked Aesop's answer and asked, "If I buy you, will you promise to be good and honest?"

"I'll be that whether you buy me or not," said Aesop.

"Will you promise not to run away?"

"Did you ever hear a bird in a cage tell his master that he intended to escape?" was Aesop's reply.

THE MYTH

The myth of black content sees life in the Old South through the rose-colored glasses of the slaveholder. It portrays black slaves as a happy, carefree lot, good singers, dancers, storytellers and musicians, taken from the uncivilized existence of Africa to the utopia of Southern culture. Black slaves were cared for by the white folks, the myth says, given food and clothing, and some blacks even made it up to the big house, where they cooked, took care of the master's kids, and became almost part of the family.

Edna McGuire offers this version of slavery in her sixth-grade text entitled *America Then and Now*: "When the master was kind, those black people lived very happy lives. They were provided with food, clothing, shelter and were cared for when they were old and sick." In another of her works, *A Full Grown Nation,* the sixth grade visits a cotton plantation in 1858 and meets a "busy [white] woman [who] finds that each new slave adds something to her cares." In one cabin she finds a lame old "Negro" whose black face lights up when he sees "Missus" striding across the threshold of his abode. Then a few pages later the sixth graders meet a banjo-strumming kid whose black feet pound the earth in rhythmic accompaniment to his own music.

George Fitzhugh of Virginia, an apologist for the South's "peculiar institution" of slavery, wrote:

The Negro slaves of the South are the happiest, and, in some sense, the freest people in the world. The children and the aged and infirm work not at all, and yet have all the comforts and necessities of life provided for them. They enjoy liberty, because they are oppressed neither by care nor labor.

After quoting Fitzhugh's observation, Robert Goldston, in *The Negro Revolution,* comments further on the myth of the contented slave:

This viewpoint was most useful to the South's ruling class of large plantation owners; it is familiar even today. The vision has been celebrated in story and song and cinema with insistent banality. There stands the old plantation house, white-pillared, a Greek revival mansion surrounded by gently sloping green lawns, gracefully bowing willow trees: " 'tis summer, the darkies are gay." The sun always shines in azure skies, and the white-goateed "Ole Marse" sips his mint julep on the long veranda, while his beautiful daughters prepare themselves for yet another ball and "Young Marse" prances around on a thoroughbred horse like some knight out of the age of chivalry. From the fields comes the happy laughter of carefree slaves, bending over the white acres of cotton plants, while from within the mansion can be heard the shrill scolding of "Mammy" as she tells off the naughty scions of "Ole Missy" for dipping their fingers in the ever-present pancake batter. "Ole Missy" herself is feeling poorly, affects a touch of pallor to her languid face, and is generally napping. She is exhausted from caring for sick slaves in the cheerful row of cabins behind the Big House.

Oh what does "Ole Missy" dream during her nap? What vision does "Ole Marse" glimpse through the bourbon haze of his julep? Why, of a world that never changes, of a life devoted to graceful indulgence in pleasure, to the appreciation of art, to ennobling sentiments; a life from which the need for work has been largely banished; a life in which women devote themselves only to their own beauty and men devote themselves to high politics and the noble arts of war. It has been observed of ruling classes before and since that the more precarious their position becomes, the more imminent becomes their downfall, the more they retreat from reality, thereby contributing to their own destruction.

So black music and smiles are held up by the myth as proof of black content. And white folks love to hear and sing "Negro" spirituals to this day. But if white folks ever analyzed the words of those songs, they would stop singing them overnight. Listen to the words of the slave songs, the "Negro" spirituals, and you will find they were death songs. "I've got shoes; you've got shoes; all God's chillun got shoes. When *I get to heaven,* I'm gonna put on my shoes." In heaven, the slaves were singing, white and black will be equal. But how do you get to heaven? You have to *die* first. So the "contented" slaves were offering their natural rhythmic version of how they planned to kill white folks, even as "Old Massa" sat on the porch, tapping his foot while sipping a mint julep.

The great black statesman and abolitionist, Frederick Douglass, writes of the slave songs in his *Narrative*:

I did not, when a slave, understand the deep meaning of those rude and apparently incoherent songs. I was myself within the circle; so that I neither saw nor heard as those without might see and hear. They told a tale of woe which was then altogether beyond my feeble comprehension; they were tones loud, long, and deep; they breathed the prayer and complaint of souls boiling over with the bitterest anguish. Every tone was a testimony against slavery, and a prayer to God for deliverance from chains. The hearing of those wild notes always depressed my spirit, and filled me with ineffable sadness. I have frequently found myself in tears while hearing them. The mere recurrence to those songs, even now, afflicts me; and while I am writing these lines, an expression of feeling has already found its way down my cheek. To those songs I trace my first glimmering conception of the dehumanizing character of slavery. I can never get rid of that conception. Those songs still follow me, to deepen my hatred of slavery, and quicken my sympathies for my brethren in bonds. If any one wishes to be impressed with the soul-killing effects of slavery, let him go to Colonel Lloyd's plantation, and, on allowance-day, place himself in the deep pine woods, and there let him, in silence, analyze the sounds that shall pass through the chambers of his soul,—and if he is not thus impressed, it will only be because "there is no flesh in his obdurate heart."

I have often been utterly astonished, since I came to the north, to find persons who could speak of the singing, among slaves, as evidence of their contentment and happiness. It is impossible to conceive of a greater mistake. Slaves sing most when they are most unhappy. The songs of the slave represent the sorrows of his heart; and he is relieved by them, only as an aching heart is relieved by its tears. At least, such is my experience. I have often sung to drown my sorrow, but seldom to express my happiness. Crying for joy, and singing for joy, were alike uncommon to me while in the jaws of slavery. The singing of a man cast away upon a desolate island might be as appropriately considered as evidence of contentment and happiness, as the singing of a slave; the songs of the one and the other are prompted by the same emotion.

CONTENTMENT REVISITED

Rather than smiles and songs, chains and cunning are better indicators of the real slave mood. The most liberal versions of American history tend to see slavery through another kind of idyllic vision. Blacks are portrayed as the *passive and docile victims* of slavery. It must be admitted that black folks were first and foremost Africans in chains. Black folks were warriors, stolen from their tribal existence in their native land. So black folks, though they were called slaves, never really fitted that definition. The slave is one who recognizes and accepts his status. The real slave does not need to be chained. Black folks never accepted their lot, thus chains were necessary. If you kidnap a warrior and call him a slave, you *must* put him in chains. Then you must watch him constantly, lest the warrior in him break forth and reclaim his free existence. James H. Hammond spoke for his fellow slaveholders when he explained the necessity for using chains and irons: "You will admit that if we pretend to own slaves, they must not be permitted to abscond whenever they see fit; and that if nothing else will prevent it these means must be resorted to." Three entries in Hammond's diary in 1844 indicate his commitment to this iron-clad philosophy: July 17: "Alonzo runaway with his irons on." July 30: "Alonzo came in with his irons off." July 31: ". . . re-ironed Alonzo."

Not all black folks who came to America were kidnaped Africans, however, nor were such stolen treasures the first. Black Africans accompanied Spanish explorers and *conquistadores* on their journeys to the New World. When Christopher Columbus sailed the ocean blue in 1492, a black man, Pedro Alonzo Niño, was navigator of one of the ships, the *Niña*. Neflo de Olaña was one of the thirty blacks with Balboa when he sighted the Pacific Ocean in 1513. Six years later, three hundred blacks accompanied the expedition of Cortez through Mexico. One black member of that expedition planted the first wheat crop grown and harvested in the New World. Some two hundred blacks joined Alvarado in his exploration through equatorial South America. Blacks accompanied Pizarro to Peru, Coronado to New Mexico, Narváez and Cabeza de Vaca in their explorations of what is now Arizona and New Mexico.

In 1940 the Southwest celebrated a quattrocentennial. The celebration remembered that it had been four hundred years since the last of the *conquistadores,* Don Francisco Vásquez de Coronado, had marched his little army from Mexico and opened up Texas, New Mexico, Arizona, and eastern regions to Spanish settlement. But the celebration did not mention the true "discoverer" of Arizona (the state of Barry Goldwater) and New Mexico. The man was known variously as Estevan, Estevanico, "Little Stephen," and Esteban de Dorantes. He was an African, a slave, a black man.

Esteban came to the New World on a voyage organized by Pánfilo de Narváez ("the One-Eyed") in 1527 to conquere and govern Florida and the Gulf Coast and to grab any excess gold that might be lying around. There were five ships and six hundred men. When the expedition was over, there were to be four survivors, including Esteban, the personal slave of Andres Dorantes de Carranca. One-fourth of the men deserted at the first port, San Domingo. Two of the ships were then lost in a hurricane. The rest were lost in a storm off Florida. When the four hundred remaining men landed in what is probably Sarasota Bay in April 1528, they split into two groups and fanned out, one group heading inland and the other going north in search of Apalachen, a city filled with gold.

The Florida Indians quickly got rid of the party heading inland. The gold seekers also fell victim to Indians, starvation, and disease. When they ran out of food, they ate their horses, then each other. A small party with Narváez in charge found Apalachen, but no gold, only about forty clay huts. Of course they were disappointed, but no more so than Captain John Smith a hundred years later who was sailing up Virginia rivers in search of a route to the Orient. All but four of the Narváez party were killed trying to cross the Mississippi. The four survivors were Esteban, his master Dorantes, Alonzo de Castillo Maldonado, and Cabeza de Vaca.

The survivors made it for a while with the Indians because they were thought to be medicine men. But the Indians made slaves out of the Spaniards, which was nothing new for Esteban, and he spent his time learning the Indian languages, dialects, sign languages, ways, and mores. He became quite an Indian expert during a six-year period. Finally the four escaped, and made their way across Texas and the Southwest, walking clear to the Gulf of California and effecting the first transcontinental crossing of the United States. On this journey they picked up tales of the fabulous Seven Cities of Cibola, a site reputed to be a fantastic store of jewels, gold, and buried treasures.

When the four travelers got to Mexico, they told the stories of the Seven Cities. Two Spanish expeditions set out at the same time to gather the riches. In 1529, Hernando de Soto set out from Cuba and made his way across the southern portion of the Mississippi and its tributaries. In Mexico, Antonio de Mendoza became fascinated by the four explorers' golden accounts. Mendoza tried to buy Esteban from Dorantes, but Dorantes refused to sell. Finally a deal was worked out to *lease* Esteban. Friar Marco de Niza was chosen by Mendoza to lead the expedition to the Seven Cities of Cibola. Esteban was the guide and translator and general go-between with the Indians.

One member of the traveling party described the indispensable role Esteban played in the expedition: "It was the Negro who talked to [the Indians] . . . all the time: he inquired about the roads we should follow, the villages: in short about everything we wished to know."

Friar Marco sent Esteban ahead as ambassador and scout, with the instructions: "If you discover an unimportant thing you should send me a white cross as large as the palm of a hand. If you see an important thing, a cross as large as one or two hands. If you sight a country better than New Spain you should send me a great cross." The friar also made it clear that if Esteban made a great discovery, he should stop and wait for the rest of the party.

Esteban did not follow the friar's instructions but pushed on ahead and made it to the gates of the first city of Cibola. Once he was there, however, his usual gifts for dealing with the Indians failed him, and he was put to death. But the adventures of Esteban inspired the later expedition of Coronado into New Mexico, and Esteban remains in American history as the great pathfinder of the Southwest.

Blacks were also companions of the French explorers such as Marquette and Joliet, and in the eighteenth century blacks explored the New World by moving down the St. Lawrence Valley or following the Mississippi River downstream to the mouth of the Arkansas. They were farmers, trappers, traders, carpenters, blacksmiths, and miners. One such black trader was Jean Baptiste Pointe Du Sable.

Brother Du Sable was born in Saint-Marc, Haiti, probably in 1745, the son of a free black woman. Nothing is known of his father. As a youth Jean Baptiste was sent to be educated in France. He returned to the islands at the age of twenty and became a trader, and he soon moved to New Orleans looking for business. From New Orleans fur trapper and trader Du Sable frequently made the thousand-mile trip up and down the Mississippi and Illinois rivers to a place on the shores of Lake Michigan named by the Indians *Eschi-ka-gou,* "place of bad smells."

Finally he settled down with his Indian wife near what is now Peoria, Illinois. In 1772, Du Sable built a trading post at Eschikagou because it was a place of many trail crossings. Two years later he moved his wife and newborn son to Eschikagou, along with a number of Indians. Thus the birth of the second city of the United States, Chicago, Illinois. Today a tiny plaque at the corner of Pine and Kinzie streets credits Du Sable as the first settler of Chicago, though the historical facts are somewhat in error:

Site of the first house in Chicago, erected about 1779 by Jean Baptiste Pointe Du Sable, a Negro from Santo Domingo.

In 1619, a year before the landing of the *Mayflower* at Plymouth Rock, a Dutch man-of-war sailed into the harbor at Jamestown, Virginia, and dropped anchor. She was a mystery ship, manned by pirates and thieves, her captain a man named Jope and her navigator an

Englishman named Marmaduke. From somewhere in the high seas she had looted a Spanish vessel of a cargo of Africans bound for the West Indies. The Africans bore such Spanish names as Antony, Isabella, and Pedro.

John Rolfe noted that the captain "ptended" he was in great need of food, and he offered to exchange his human cargo for "victualle." The human life and food exchange was made, and Antony, Isabella, Pedro, and seventeen other Africans stepped ashore in August 1619, thus beginning the black slave trade in America. Of course, the black slave trade was an established practice in other parts of the world, having begun in 1444, and it continued for over four hundred years.

Lerone Bennett, Jr., in *Before the Mayflower*, dramatically recites that the slave trade was more than dates and statistics:

The slave trade was people living, lying, stealing, murdering and dying. The slave trade was a black man who stepped out of his hut for a breath of fresh air and ended up ten months later, in Georgia with bruises on his back and a brand on his chest.

The slave trade was a black mother suffocating her newborn baby because she didn't want him to grow up a slave.

The slave trade was a kind captain forcing his suicide-minded passengers to eat by breaking their teeth, though, as he said, he was "naturally compassionate."

The slave trade was a bishop sitting on an ivory chair on a wharf in the Congo and extending his fat hand in wholesale baptism of slaves who were rowed beneath him, going in chains to the slave ships.

The slave trade was a greedy king raiding his own villages to get slaves to buy brandy.

The slave trade was a pious captain holding prayer services twice a day on his slave ship and writing later the famous hymn, "How Sweet the Name of Jesus Sounds."

The slave trade was deserted villages, bleached bones on slave trails and people with no last names.

The slave trade was Caesar negro, Angelo negro and Negro Mary.

The slaves who first arrived in Jamestown seem to have been placed in the category of indentured servants, as were so many whites who came to America. Slaves had no legal status at all. They could not give testimony in a court of law, nor could they sue or be sued. Yet in 1624, John Phillip, one of the twenty servants purchased from the Dutch warship, appears in the court record as having given testimony. Historian J. A. Rogers tells of white European slavery, "mostly British, who died like flies on the slave-ships across" to the New World. On one voyage, says Rogers, 1,100 died out of 1,500; and on another, 350 out of 400. Rogers continues:

In Virginia, white servitude was for a limited period, but was sometimes extended to life. In the West Indies, particularly in the case of the Irish, it was for life. White people were sold in the United States up to 1826, fifty years after the signing of the Declaration of Independence. Andrew Johnson, President of the United States, was a runaway, and was advertised for in the newspapers.

White folks' contracts were usually cheaper than those for black slaves. Because the former were less valuable, they were given particularly harsh treatment on the voyages to the New World. Ships carrying white indentured servants sailed with hatches closed. When they reached the New World, the hatches were opened, the living were sent ashore, and the dead bodies were tossed overboard. Between 1750 and 1755 more than two thousand bodies were tossed into New York Harbor alone. So the "huddled masses yearning to breathe free" of Emma Lazarus' poem found their way into New York Harbor long before the Statue of Liberty was planted there. White children were kidnaped in the British Isles at the rate of several thousand yearly and sold into servitude in America and the West Indies during the seventeenth and eighteenth centuries. Such a practice would have been frowned upon by Cicero. In his letter to Atticus, Cicero warned: "Do not obtain your slaves from Britain, because they are so stupid and so utterly incapable of being taught that they are not fit to form part of the household of Athens."

Whites and blacks working in the fields in servitude together seemed to be less plagued by prejudicial patterns than labor unions in America are today. Kenneth M. Stampp, in his book *The Peculiar Institution,* writes:

Moreover, the Negro and white servants of the seventeenth century seemed to be remarkably unconcerned about their visible physical differences. They toiled together in the fields, fraternized during leisure hours, and, in and out of wedlock, collaborated in siring numerous progeny. Though the first southern white settlers were quite familiar with rigid class lines, they were as unfamiliar with a caste system as they were with chattel slavery.

But it did not take long for black chattel slavery to develop a colonial familiarity. Though out of the fields, in the towns and legislatures, discrimination against blacks existed before chattel slavery was formalized (as we have seen in Chapter I), economic pressures soon made slavery a formal institution. A series of official acts between 1640 and 1667 in Virginia transformed the status of blacks in the colony from indentured servants to chattel slaves, so that their children down to the last generation were to be considered slaves. In other colonies legislation was more speedy. Slavery was recognized as legal in the Carolinas in 1663, Maryland in 1664, New York in 1664, Pennsylvania and Delaware in 1682. Though the rhetoric of the New England colonies was more evasive—black slaves kidnaped and brought over on cargo ships were sometimes officially called "servants"—there was no doubt in any black person's mind, body, and hopeless future that he was indeed a slave for life.

White-black-slave-servant relationships led to complicated legal matters. Questions had to be resolved with regard to intermarriage and any children born of interracial relationships. In 1662 the Virginia legislature enacted:

> Wheras some doubts have arisen whether
> children got by any Englishman upon a
> Negro woman shall be slave or free . . .
> all children born in this colony shall
> be bond or free only according to the
> condition of the mother.

Later the Virginia legislature passed a law stating that a white woman servant who married a black would be required to serve another five years. Maryland law in 1664 required that a "freeborn white woman" who married a slave became the servant of her husband's master as long as her husband was alive, thus giving deep meaning to the marriage vow "for better, for worse." The children of such marriages became slaves as soon as they were born. Thus the law in effect made slaves of white women involved in such marriages and was later repealed when unscrupulous masters caught on to the idea of forcing white women servants to marry black men.

Lerone Bennett, Jr., reminds us of integration on the auction block saying, "Some slave merchants sold Negroes and whites, liquor, clothing and other goods. One merchant, for example, advertised: 'Several Irish Maid Servants time/most of them for Five Years one/Irish Man Servant—one who is a good/Barber and Wiggmaker/also Four or Five Likely Negro Boys.' " And, says Bennett, "the price of men, like the price of butter, fluctuated. George Washington, for example, bought a man slave for $260 in 1754. But when he went to the market ten years later, he had to pay $285." And George Fitzhugh was such a complete apologist for slavery that he fought for the opinion "that not only Negroes but all proletarian whites emigrated from Germany and Ireland should be sold as slaves for reasons of humanity."

Indentured servitude, white and black, explodes two popular myths of American history: (1) that slavery was on its way out until the invention of the cotton gin came along to resurrect it, and (2) that slaves were a necessity in providing a southern labor force. Of the latter myth, Kenneth Stampp wrote:

According to tradition, Negroes had to be brought to the South for labor that Europeans themselves could not perform. "The white man will never raise—*can* never raise a cotton or a sugar crop in the United States. In our swamps and under our suns the negro thrives, but the white man dies." Without the productive power of the African whom an "all-wise Creator" had perfectly adapted to the labor needs of the South, its lands would have remained "a howling wilderness."

Such is the myth. The fact is that, ever since the founding of Jamestown, white men have performed much of the South's heavy agricultural labor. For a century and a half white farmers have tended their own cotton fields in every part of the Deep South. In the 1850's Frederick Law Olmsted saw many white women in Mississippi and Alabama "at work in the hottest sunshine . . . in the regular cultivation of cotton." In 1855, even a South Carolinian vigorously disputed "the opinion frequently put forth, that white labor is unsuited to the agriculture of this State." All that such laborers required was to be properly acclimatized. "The white man—born, raised and habituated to exposure and labor in the field in our climate—will be found equal to the task in any part of this State free from the influence of the excessive malaria of stagnant waters." Then this Carolinian observed an important fact: in the swamplands Negroes did not thrive any better than white men. But Negro slaves, unlike free whites, could be forced to toil in the rice swamps regardless of the effect upon their health. That was the difference.

Melvin Drimmer, in his essay "Was Slavery Dying Before the Cotton Gin?" makes it clear that immediately after the Revolution the South made remarkable economic and agricultural strides, and the number of slaves and the prices they brought rose accordingly. Even before the cotton gin got itself invented, the South was producing 60 per cent of America's corn, 63 per cent of America's wheat, and 38 per cent of its flour. Rice production had risen 14 per cent, and tobacco exports 36 per cent. Drimmer dismisses the cotton gin myth with this summary:

The South had too much tied up in slavery to let it quietly go to pieces. The slaveowners, neither in word nor deed, indicated that they were through with their peculiar institution. Evidence would point strongly to the contrary. The agricultural recovery of the region after the Revolution showed the slaveowners to be imaginative and resourceful, possessing a flexible means of labor which could be adapted to new circumstances. The rise of cotton and the invention of the cotton gin should be seen as a product of an economy and system that was viable and creative. *The cotton gin brought slavery from one plateau to one yet higher, not from the desert to the mountain.*

The cotton gin has been used to justify the retention and expansion of slavery. Rather than confronting themselves with the responsibility for the continuation of slavery, Americans in the nineteenth century shifted the burden of guilt onto the cotton gin. It was in keeping with the character of a mechanistic age that they blamed their own failings upon a machine.

Some fifty million black people were taken from their native land of Africa to be scattered as slaves throughout South America, the islands of the West Indies, and the United States. Many, if not most, died on the cruel journey to their place of enslavement. In 1860 there were some four and one-half million black people living in the United States, a very small percentage of those leaving the shores of Africa. Africans fell into the clutches of slavers in a variety of ways. Most commonly they were prisoners of war—thus literally warriors in chains. Some were criminals sold by African chiefs as punishment; some were individuals sold by their own families during times of famine; some were simply kidnaped by Europeans or by native kings.

The following narratives of ex-slaves, included in Julius Lester's book, *To Be a Slave,* indicate both the cunning of European slave traders and the cooperation between slavers and tribal chieftains. The first story is told by one Richard Jones:

Granny Judith said that in Africa they had very few pretty things, and that they had no red colors in cloth. In fact, they had no cloth at all. Some strangers with pale faces come one day and dropped a small piece of red flannel down on the ground. All the black folks grabbed for it. Then a larger piece was dropped a little further on, and on until the river was reached. Then a large piece was dropped in the river and on the other side. They was led on, each one trying to get a piece as it was dropped. Finally, when the ship was reached, they dropped large pieces on the plank and up into the ship till they got as many blacks on board as they wanted. Then the gate was chained up and they could not get back. That is the way Granny Judith say they got her to America.

Charles Ball, a slave during the nineteenth century, recalls a childhood story of a slave who was brought directly from Africa to America:

. . . we were alarmed one morning, just at the break of day, by the horrible uproar caused by mingled shouts of men, and blows given with heavy sticks, upon large wooden drums. The village was surrounded by enemies, who attacked us with clubs, long wooden spears, and bows and arrows. After fighting for more than an hour, those who were not fortunate enough to run away were made prisoners. It was not the object of our enemies to kill; they wished to take us alive and sell us as slaves. I was knocked down by a heavy blow of a club, and when I recovered from the stupor that followed, I found myself tied fast with the long rope I had brought from the desert. . . .

We were immediately led away from this village, through the forest, and were compelled to travel all day as fast as we could walk. . . . We traveled three weeks in the woods—sometimes without any path at all—and arrived one day at a large river with a rapid current. Here we were forced to help our conquerors to roll a great number of dead trees into the water from a vast pile that had been thrown together by high floods.

These trees, being dry and light, floated high out of the water; and when several of them were fastened together with the tough branches of young trees, [they] formed a raft, upon which we all placed ourselves, and descended the river for three days, when we came in sight of what appeared to me the most wonderful object in the world; this was a large ship at anchor in the river. When our raft came near the ship, the white people—for such they were on board—assisted to take us on the deck, and the logs were suffered to float down the river.

I had never seen white people before and they appeared to me the ugliest creatures in the world. The persons who brought us down the river received payment for us of the people in the ship, in various articles, of which I remembered that a keg of liquor, and some yards of blue and red cotton cloth were the principal.

Once on board, and on his way to America, a slave could never think of his means of transportation as "the most wonderful object in the world." The hold of a slave ship was generally about five feet high, but it was divided by a shelf, so that tiers of slaves could be accommodated. Thus slaves had about twenty-five inches of head room and could not sit up straight during the entire voyage. Every available inch of the slave hold was packed with human flesh, and often slaves could only sleep on their sides, "packed like spoons in a drawer."

Sanitary conditions for slaves often consisted of two or three buckets, so the imaginative reader can readily understand what the average slave ship was full of. The stench of slavery was both moral and physical. Slave ships could often be smelled coming from five miles away. The condition was complicated by the fact that the only ventilation allowed for the slave deck was the heavy gratings above it, and these were often closed during a storm.

Slaves were brought above deck in the morning, their irons attached to a long chain that ran the length of the ship, and were given a meal consisting of boiled rice or corn meal or stewed yams and a half pint of water. Then the ceremony of "dancing the slaves" commenced. For exercise slaves were made to jump around as best they could wearing chains, to the soulless accompaniment of a drum or a banjo, and the slaves were also supposed to sing. Perhaps this was the beginning of the natural rhythm black folks are supposed to have. Crew men with whips stood by to make sure the slaves lived up to their image. Of course, such exercise resulted in bleeding and swollen ankles from the irons rubbing against them. In the midafternoon, the slaves were again fed something like horse bean pulp, and packed away again below decks.

Quite understandably, many slaves went mad under such conditions. When such derangement occurred, a slave was flogged to make sure he was not pretending, and was eventually knocked on the head and thrown overboard. Often slaves would jump to their own deaths overboard, and crew members had to keep a watchful eye against such willful destruction of property. Whether a slave was thrown overboard or jumped overboard, his presence was always welcomed by the school of sharks which followed slave ships in anticipation.

Some slaves attempted to commit suicide by refusing to eat. Slavers developed an instrument known as the *speculum oris,* or mouth opener, which was wedged between an uncooperative slave's teeth like a pair of dividers, then screwed to open the slave's mouth so that the gruesome gruel could be poured down his throat. Sometimes slaves were thrown overboard if rations ran low. Slaves who looked as if they might not make the voyage, or who were so sickly that they would not bring a good price on the auction block, were "jettisoned" and thus became not a total loss, as insurance companies would pay the owners something for them.

When the slave ship finally docked, and the slaves were assembled at the public square, a signal was given, and prospective buyers raced each other to tag the healthiest and strongest merchandise. When the slaves saw so many white folks coming down upon them like a blizzard, some went "mad with fright," because they still felt they were to be eaten. After a slave was purchased, a three- to four-month "seasoning" period began during which discipline was learned and spirits were broken. Probably most slaves who did not survive died during this period of taming the warriors, though many had died during the march to the coast in Africa, and more during the trip over.

Social and political philosopher Henry David Thoreau recalled the horrors of the slave ships in 1859 when he responded to Horace Greeley's admonition against violence and to his suggestion that an end to slavery could be accomplished "by the quiet diffusion of the sentiments of humanity without outbreak." Said Thoreau:

The slave ship is on her way crowded with its dying victims; new cargoes are being added in mid ocean; a small crew of slaveholders, countenanced by a large body of passengers, is smothering four millions under the hatches, and yet the politician asserts that the only proper way by which deliverance is to be obtained is by "the quiet diffusion of the sentiments of humanity without any outbreak." As if the sentiments of humanity were ever found unaccompanied by its deed, and you could disperse them all finished to order, the pure article, as easily as water with a watering pot, and so lay the dust. What is that I hear cast overboard? The bodies of the dead that have found deliverance. This is the way we are "diffusing" humanity and its sentiments with it.

Perhaps the "Massa/Missy" idyllic version of life on the old plantation is best refuted by a more down-to-earth description given by one who lived outside the big house and spent his days in the sweltering fields. Solomon Northrup was a free black who was kidnaped and sold in 1845 to labor twelve years on a Louisiana cotton plantation. He left the following account, contained in Robert Goldston's *The Negro Revolution*:

During all these hoeings the overseer or driver follows the slaves on horseback with a whip. . . . The fastest hoer takes the lead row. He is usually about a rod in advance of his companions. If one of them passes him, he is whipped. If one falls behind or is a moment idle, he is whipped. In fact, the lash is flying from morning until night, the whole day long. The hoeing season thus continues from April until July, a field having no sooner been finished once, than it is commenced again.

In the latter part of August begins the cotton picking season. . . . An ordinary day's work is two hundred pounds. A slave who is accustomed to picking, is punished, if he or she brings in less quantity than that.

The hands are required to be in the cotton field as soon as it is light in the morning, and, with the exception of ten or fifteen minutes, which is given them at noon to swallow their allowance of cold bacon, they are not permitted to be a moment idle until it is too dark to see and when the moon is full they often times labor till the middle of the night. They do not dare to stop, even at dinner time.

When the day's work in the field is completed, and the cotton is weighed, and whippings are administered to those who did not make their quota, Northrup continues:

the labor of the day is not yet ended, by any means. Each one must then attend to his respective chores. One feeds the mules, another the swine—another cuts wood, and so forth. . . . Finally, at a late hour, they reach the quarters, sleepy and overcome with the long day's toil. Then a fire must be kindled in the cabin, the corn ground in a small hand-mill, and supper, and dinner for the next day in the field, prepared. All that is allowed them is corn and bacon. . . . Each one receives as his weekly allowance, three and a half pounds of bacon, and corn enough to make a peck of meal. That is all.

And Northrup describes that cheerful row of slave cabins behind the big house where "Missy" sees so many smiles and hears those songs:

The softest couches in the world are not to be found in the log mansion of the slave. The one whereon I reclined year after year, was a plank twelve inches wide and ten feet long. My pillow was a stick of wood. The bedding was a coarse blanket, and not a rag or shred beside. . . .

The cabin is constructed of logs, without floor or window. The latter is altogether unnecessary, the crevices between the logs admitting sufficient light. In stormy weather, the rain drives through them, rendering it comfortless and extremely disagreeable. . . .

An hour before daylight the horn is blown. Then the slaves arouse, prepare their breakfast, fill a gourd with water . . . and hurry to the field again. It is an offense invariably followed by a flogging, to be found at the quarters after daybreak. Then the fears and labors of another day begin; and until its close there is no such thing as rest.

In his *Narrative,* Frederick Douglass describes the "provisions" that the myth of black content says gave slaves a "carefree" existence:

The men and women slaves received, as their monthly allowance of food, eight pounds of pork, or its equivalent in fish, and one bushel of corn meal. Their yearly clothing consisted of two coarse linen shirts, one pair of linen trousers, like the shirts, one jacket, one pair of trousers for winter, made of coarse negro cloth, one pair of stockings, and one pair of shoes; the whole of which could not have cost more than seven dollars. . . . The children unable to work in the field had neither shoes, stockings, jackets, nor trousers, given to them; their clothing consisted of two coarse linen shirts per year. When these failed them, they went naked until the next allowance-day. Children from seven to ten years old, of both sexes, almost naked, might be seen at all seasons of the year.

It is interesting to note that slavery in America is often referred to as the South's "peculiar institution." Our word "peculiar" is derived from the Latin word *peculium,* or the allowance which Roman masters often gave to their slaves. Perhaps meager allowances constitute the outstanding mark of America's inhumanity in the history of world slavery. Frederick Douglass recites how allowances were used to further oppress, rather than to relieve, slaves:

The holidays are part and parcel of the gross fraud, wrong, and inhumanity of slavery. They are professedly a custom established by the benevolence of the slaveholders; but I undertake to say, it is the result of selfishness, and one of the grossest frauds committed upon the down-trodden slave. They do not give the slaves this time because they would not like to have their work during its continuance, but because they know it would be unsafe to deprive them of it. This will be seen by the fact, that the slaveholders like to have their slaves spend those days just in such manner as to make them as glad of their ending as of their beginning. Their object seems to be, to disgust their slaves with freedom, by plunging them into the lowest depths of dissipation. For instance, the slaveholders not only like to see the slave drink of his own accord, but will adopt various plans to make him drunk. One plan is, to make bets on their slaves, as to who can drink the most whisky without getting drunk; and in this way they succeed in getting whole multitudes to drink to excess. Thus, when the slave asks for virtuous freedom, the cunning slaveholder, knowing his ignorance, cheats him with a dose of vicious dissipation, artfully labelled with the name of liberty. The most of us used to drink it down, and the result was just what might be supposed: many of us were led to think that there was little to choose between liberty and slavery. We felt, and very properly too, that we had almost as well be slaves to man as to rum. So, when the holidays ended, we staggered up from the filth of our wallowing, took a long breath, and marched to the field,—feeling, upon the whole, rather glad to go, from what our master had deceived us into a belief was freedom, back to the arms of slavery.

I have said that this mode of treatment is a part of the whole system of fraud and inhumanity of slavery. It is so. The mode here adopted to disgust the slave with freedom, by allowing him to see only the abuse of it, is carried out in other things. For instance, a slave loves molasses; he steals some. His master, in many cases, goes off to town, and buys a large quantity; he returns, takes his whip, and commands the slave to eat the molasses, until the poor fellow is made sick at the very mention of it. The same mode is sometimes adopted to make the slaves refrain from asking for more food than their regular allowance. A slave runs through his allowance, and applies for more. His master is enraged at him, but, not willing to send him off without food, gives him more than is necessary, and compels him to eat it within a given time. Then, if he complains that he cannot eat it, he is said to be satisfied neither full nor fasting, and is whipped for being hard to please! I have an abundance of such illustrations of the same principle, drawn from my own observation, but think the cases I have cited sufficient. The practice is a very common one.

Though whippings, chains, and irons were used to keep slaves under control, the lash became a cunning instrument in the hands of some soul brothers who found themselves in the role of black overseers. Ex-slave West Turner describes how such soul brothers would trick the master:

Anytime ol' massa got a slave that been cuttin' up or something, he tell Gabe to give that slave a lashin'. Some-time he come down to the barn to watch it, but most time he just set on the porch and listen to the blows. Ol' Gabe didn't like that whipping business, but couldn't help him-self. When massa was there, he would lay it on, because he had to. But when ol' massa wasn't, he never would beat them slaves. Would tie the slave up to one post and lash another one. Of course, the slave would scream and yell to satisfy massa, but he wasn't getting no lashing. After while Gabe would come out of the barn and ask massa if that was enough. "Sho', that's plenty," say massa. Once ol' Gabe was beating the post so hard and the slave was yelling so that massa call out to Gabe, "Quit beating that nigger, Gabe. What you trying to do? Kill him?" Slave come running out screaming, with berry wine rubbed all over his back and massa told Gabe if he didn't stop beat-ing his slaves so hard, he gonna git a lashin' himself.

But when the master did his own flogging, giving vent to all the brutality and viciousness slave disobedi-ence aroused within him, the result was an inhumane spectacle defying description. Again it is Frederick Douglass who in the printed word comes closest to capturing the horror of such lashing. When Douglass was only a little boy, he witnessed the beating of his Aunt Hester. Her master had told Douglass' aunt not to go out in the evenings, and had further warned her never to be caught in the company of a young man named Ned Roberts, who belonged to a Colonel Lloyd. Frederick Douglass describes this horrible childhood memory:

Aunt Hester had not only disobeyed his orders in going out, but had been found in company with Lloyd's Ned; which circumstance, I found, from what he said while whipping her, was the chief offence. Had he been a man of pure morals himself, he might have been thought interested in protecting the innocence of my aunt; but those who knew him will not suspect him of any such virtue. Before he commenced whipping Aunt Hester, he took her into the kitchen, and stripped her from neck to waist, leaving her neck, shoulders, and back, entirely naked. He then told her to cross her hands, calling her at the same time a d——d b——h. After crossing her hands, he tied them with a strong rope, and led her to a stool under a large hook in the joist, put in for the purpose. He made her get upon the stool, and tied her hands to the hook. She now stood fair for his infernal purpose. Her arms were stretched up at their full length, so that she stood upon the ends of her toes. He then said to her, "Now, you d——d b——h, I'll learn you how to disobey my orders!" and after rolling up his sleeves, he commenced to lay on the heavy cowskin, and soon the warm, red blood (amid heart-rending shrieks from her, and horrid oaths from him) came dripping to the floor. I was so terrified and horror stricken at the sight, that I hid myself in a closet, and dared not venture out till long after the bloody transaction was over. I expected it would be my turn next. It was all new to me. I had never seen any thing like it before. I had always lived with my grandmother on the outskirts of the plantation, where she was put to raise the children of the younger women. I had therefore been, until now, out of the way of the bloody scenes that often occurred on the plantation.

Thus, life on the old plantation was hardly conducive to the mass production of contented black folks, in spite of what the myth insists; and the brutal realities of slavery account for the fact that there were some four hundred slave uprisings during the hundred-year period between 1750 and 1850. Herbert Aptheker listed more than 250 recorded revolts or conspiracies within the continental United States, but there were also small unorganized rebellions, which involved a handful of slaves, the destruction of individual plantations, and the murder of solitary families. Sometimes plans of such revolts on a plantation were thwarted by a tipoff from a loyal "house" slave. For example, on June 7, 1802, a Mr. Mathews of Norfolk, Virginia, received the following note:

White pepil be-ware of your lives, their is a plan now forming and intent to put in execution this harvest time —they are to commence and use their Sithes as weapons until they can get possession of other weapons . . . the scream is to kill all before them, men, women and children. . . . I am a favorite Servant of my Master and Mistis, and love them dearly.

During the summer of 1800 a twenty-four-year-old black slave named Gabriel, a coachman who was the property of Thomas Henry Prosser of Henrico County, Virginia, began sending word throughout the plantations that the time had come for slaves to strike. The uprising was planned for harvest time, when the army of slaves could live most conveniently from the fruits of the countryside. Gabriel was a tall and powerful man, six feet two inches, and he appointed himself general of the rebellion. On August 30 all the slaves in Henrico County were to rise up simultaneously, murder their masters and any other white folks who got in their way, and march on Richmond. Gabriel reasoned that if he seized Richmond, the slaves in neighboring counties would be inspired to join the movement. Seizing Richmond would also give Gabriel command of the state treasury and arsenal.

White folks were to be given a chance to surrender, but if they refused, all would be put to death except Methodists, Quakers, and Frenchmen. Even if the white folks did surrender, the slaves would "at least cut off one of their arms."

Throughout the summer, secret meetings were held in various hideaways, and Gabriel's agents spread the word from plantation to plantation. Black discontent was so rampant and Gabriel's agents so effective that by August more than ten thousand slaves had agreed to join the uprising, one thousand of them in Richmond itself. Gabriel's arsenal consisted of twelve shillings, which he gave to his agents; twelve dozen handmade swords, the blades having been forged by a slave named Solomon and the handles whittled by Gabriel; about one peck of bullets, hand-cast by Gabriel; and ten pounds of gunpowder. Until their masters' weapons could be seized, the slaves would fight with axes, shovels, scythes, or anything else they could get their hands on.

Gabriel had many things going for him. He had numbers. He had the element of surprise; in fact not a word of the uprising reached the ears of whites until the day itself. He had the passion of a just cause on his side. And he had a carefully worked-out battle plan. Gabriel had planned a three-pronged attack on Richmond, deploying 1,100 men. One column would be directed toward the arsenal to get guns. Another would capture the powder house. The third column would split in two near the outskirts of Richmond, swing in opposite directions, and attack from different sides at the same time in a pincers action. The latter division was under orders to inflict as many casualties as possible and to take possession of the treasury, the flour mills, and the bridge across the James River, thus controlling the access routes to the city. In case of defeat Gabriel had even organized a phased withdrawal into the mountains, where those who survived would divide the spoils of conquest and enjoy their freedom. The motto of the slave action was to be Patrick Henry's "Give me liberty or give me death."

There were two factors Gabriel could not control, and they did him in—the weather and slave betrayal. On the night of the march the rain fell in deluges, causing floods and making it all but impossible for the slaves to gather. The effort had to be abandoned for that night, but white folks would have been none the wiser. (Later white folks said God had sent the floods for their protection.) But even as Gabriel was dismissing his army, two house slaves of a Mr. Moseby Sheppard, Tom and Pharaoh, were betraying the secret. Sheppard immediately notified Governor James Monroe, who called out the troops and alerted every militia commander in the whole state.

Sunday morning, September 1, Richmond was an armed camp under martial law. White folks were filling the churches to thank God for taking sides. Panic swept the state, and hundreds of suspected slaves were rounded up, and many were put to death as a precautionary measure. For the most part the insurrectionists went to their deaths in silence, displaying a dignity, a determination, and a courage which was upsetting to white folks who expected slaves to cringe and beg for mercy.

Gabriel escaped but was found in the hold of the schooner *Mary* when it docked at Norfolk after a trip from Richmond. Gabriel was questioned by Governor Monroe himself, but he remained silent and refused to implicate any of his comrades. On October 7, 1800, Gabriel was hanged, displaying what one newspaper called "utmost composure" and "the true spirit of heroism." But there is no doubt that the "composure" of Virginia slaveholders was quite shattered by the awful fate that only nature and betrayal had spared them.

In the same year of Gabriel's revolt a slave named Denmark Vesey won $600 in a cash lottery and bargained it all to his master for his freedom. He then became a carpenter in Charleston, South Carolina. While he was a slave, Vesey had traveled with his master. He had actually seen the bargaining process for the purchase of slaves in the land of his ancestors, learned at first hand of the terrible conditions aboard slave ships, watched the branding and selling processes at the auction block. Vesey grew to hate the system and all who benefited from it.

Denmark Vesey became an inside agitator in Charleston, inspiring slave resistance and organizing for action. He was literate and had read of Toussaint L'Ouverture and his successful slave uprising which led to independence in Haiti. He was also a student of the Bible. Vesey reminded slaves how God had freed the people of Israel from their bondage in Egypt, but he insisted the slaves must take the initiative. The action Vesey was inspiring would differ from that of Gabriel in that no whites at all were to be spared. He remembered God's instructions to Joshua during the siege of Jericho, and Vesey was fond of quoting Joshua 6:21, "And they utterly destroyed all that was in the city, both man and woman, young and old, and ox, and sheep, and ass, with the edge of the sword."

By December 1821, Vesey had enlisted to his cause two African practitioners of magic—Gullah Jack and Blind Philip—who were to help maintain discipline among the slaves Vesey was organizing. A man named Peter Poyas became second in command to Vesey. A date was set for an assault on Charleston, the second Sunday in July 1822. It was a perfect time. Large numbers of blacks were accustomed to swarm into Charleston on a Sunday. And in July many white folks were away on vacation.

Vesey and his comrades had made or collected several hundred weapons, such as bayonets, pike heads, and daggers. The battle plan included men patrolling the streets of Charleston on horseback, while the vital points of the city—naval stores, powder magazines, arsenals, and guardhouses—were being struck from five different approaches. Many thousands of slaves were in on the plans, and Vesey had recruited them from as great a distance as eighty miles.

Vesey tried to take all necessary precautions. Peter Poyas instructed his recruiters not to involve any household servants, as it was felt any man who would accept his master's old coat as a gift would betray his brothers. But an unauthorized recruiter named William Paul did enlist a house servant; and, sure enough, in a short time rumors of the plot were spreading through the white community. Vesey, as a free black, had a good reputation in Charleston which he had built up over a twenty-year period. White folks thought he was a co-operative citizen. So Vesey was able to approach the authorities in an effort to convince them that the rumor was a hoax. He even got some of his arrested compatriots released in his custody! But Vesey was still not sure how much the white folks really knew, so he moved the date up to the second Sunday in June.

The mayor enlisted the services of three black spies, who infiltrated the ranks; and on May 30, 1822, Vesey was identified as the ringleader. The informer in the case was a "favorite and confidential slave" named Peter, who was the property of Colonel J. C. Prioleau.

Peter was given as a reward a $50-a-year pension, which was raised to $200 a year in 1857.

Vesey was arrested with 138 of his companions, and once again white folks were amazed that the leadership "never divulged any of their secrets in court." The blacks who did talk were "those who knew but little." Four whites who were convicted of sympathizing with the black rebels were fined and jailed. Forty-six blacks, including Vesey, were hanged, and various other punishments were meted out to the others, including the banishment of thirty-five.

Again the year 1800, the year of Gabriel's revolt and Vesey's purchase of freedom, has special meaning for the myth of black content. It was the year Nat Turner was born. Nat Turner was born in Southampton County, Virginia, on October 2, 1800. Bryan Fulks, in *Black Struggle,* writes: "Although Nat Turner was born *in* slavery, he was not born *to* slavery. An intelligent and sensitive man, he could never accept slavery for himself or for others."

Like Gabriel and Vesey, Nat Turner found the words of the Bible a particular inspiration to opposing cruel oppression. Nat taught himself to read and became an avid Bible reader. Though his parents were illiterate, they had instilled in Nat the belief that he was singled out for a special destiny, that he had the gift of prophecy, and that he would emerge as a gifted preacher.

Brother Nat was somewhat of a mystic, whose religious devotion gave him a profound belief in the supernatural, and he heard voices of inspiration and saw visions. He was a serious man and a teetotaler. He was a gifted orator, and fellow slaves stood in awe of him, some feeling he was somewhat of a messiah sent to deliver them from oppression.

One day in 1828, while working in the field, Nat felt sure that the time was near when the promise of Christ would be fulfilled: "But many that are first shall be last; and the last shall be first." Rather than taking place at a banquet table in heaven, Nat felt the fulfillment would occur here on earth, in the midst of the institution of slavery.

But Brother Nat waited patiently for a further sign from heaven. On February 12, 1831, the sign came. It was a total eclipse of the sun. Others saw it as a sign of a different sort. A white minister in New York City interpreted the sign to mean that a certain part of the city would sink. Some religious white folks heeded his warning and moved out.

The message Nat received from the sign was to "arise and prepare" himself to slay his enemies "with their own weapons." He disappeared into the swamps with four of his companions to brood over the meaning of what they must do. He emerged with the conviction that God had ordained the deliverance of the black race from slavery. All whites were to be slain; weapons were to be taken from the oppressor; and a Christian army was to effect the cause of black liberation.

The first blow was to be struck the night of August 21, 1831. Nat arrived at the agreed meeting place and found a stranger among his known and trusted compatriots. His name was Will, and he passed the membership test by vowing that he loved liberty rather than life. Under cover of night Nat and a party of six or eight slaves, armed only with a broadax and a hatchet, marched up to the big house of Turner's master, Joseph Travis, himself somewhat of a religious fanatic and a preacher. They killed both master and family.

The little band of liberators marched on to the next plantation, expecting to pick up crusaders along the way. The band soon numbered seventy, and they marched through the countryside proclaiming Judgment Day and in twenty-four hours had killed sixty whites. Not a white was spared, with the singular exception of a family of poor whites who had never owned a slave. The liberators gathered guns, swords, and bayonets as they moved from plantation to plantation. The newcomer Will, a large, powerful man with a scar of slavery extending from his eye to his chin, was so skillful with the broadax that Nat gave him the name "Will the Executioner."

Turner was heading for the seat of Southampton County, Jerusalem (now Courtland). Three miles from his destination, Nat allowed his companions to talk him into hitting another plantation. The little side trip caused the liberators to meet up with state and federal troops, who had been summoned at word of the uprising. The band was overwhelmed by the soldiers, and Turner escaped into the Great Dismal Swamp, where he holed up for two months before being sniffed out by bloodhounds.

Fear and panic spread throughout the area, and white folks began torturing and killing slaves at the slightest suspicion of involvement in the uprising. Some one hundred blacks were killed, only nineteen of whom were tried. Southern nerves were on edge.

As for Nat Turner, he was taken to Jerusalem and tried and convicted and hanged on November 11, 1831. But finding an executioner was difficult, since the white sheriff and his black neighbors feared having the blood of Nat Turner on their hands, so convincing was Brother Nat's gift of prophecy. He predicted that the heavens would show divine disapproval on the day of his execution, and the thunder and lightning of the storm that actually occurred at his execution must have caused absolute terror.

Not all whites who died during the years of resistance to slavery were killed by angry blacks. A white man by the name of John Brown was so horrified by the South's peculiar institution that he determined to raid the South and free the slaves. He had raised enough money in the New England states and in New York to establish a stronghold in western Virginia to assist fugitive slaves. The private war he waged against slaveholders in Kansas had earned him the title of "God's Angry Man." Through his invasion of the South, John Brown hoped to initiate a dramatic action that would strike such a chord of rebellion among the slaves that they would rise and liberate themselves.

On the night of October 16, 1859, John Brown led a group of twenty-one men, including his own sons and five blacks, against the government arsenal at Harpers Ferry. Brown seized the arsenal, killed the town mayor, and took prisoner some of the leading townspeople. Daybreak brought the Maryland and Virginia militia swarming against Brown. Governor Wise called out the entire militia and appealed to the federal government for help. John Brown retreated into a locomotive roundhouse, knocked holes through the brick wall, and proceeded to defend himself. One of Brown's prisoners, Lewis Washington, left this description of the scene: "Brown was the coolest and firmest man I ever saw in defying danger and death. With one son dead by his side, and another shot through, he felt the pulse of his dying son with one hand and held his rifle with the other, and commanded his men with the utmost composure, encouraging them to be firm and to sell their lives as dearly as they could."

The next day Colonel Robert E. Lee arrived with a company of United States Marines. Only four of Brown's men remained alive and unwounded. Marines forced an entrance and captured John Brown and his handful of survivors. John Brown was tried in Virginia on charges of insurrection, murder, and treason; was convicted on October 31, 1859; and hanged on December 2. He became the instant martyr of Northerners opposed to slavery; the shining example of a white man who valued the cause of black liberation more than the lives of his own sons. John Brown's last words before the court were quoted and requoted:

Had I so interfered in behalf of any of the rich, the powerful, the intelligent, the so-called great, or in behalf of any of their friends, either father, mother, brother, sister, wife, or children, or any of that class, and suffered and sacrificed what I have in this interference, it would have been all right, and every man in this court would have deemed it an act worthy of reward rather than punishment. This Court acknowledges, too, as I suppose, the validity of the law of God. I see a book kissed, which I suppose to be the Bible, or at least the New Testament, which teaches me that all things whatsoever I would that men should do to me, I should do even so to them. It teaches me further to remember them that are in bonds, as bound with them. I endeavored to act up to that instruction. I say I am yet too young to understand that God is any respecter of persons. I believe that to have interfered as I have done, as I have always freely admitted I have done in behalf of His despised poor, is no wrong, but right. Now, if it is deemed necessary that I should forfeit my life for the furtherance of the ends of justice, and mingle my blood further with the blood of my children and with the blood of millions in this slave country whose rights are disregarded by wicked, cruel, and unjust enactments, I say let it be done.

Little remembered were the words of John A. Copeland, who was a free black who had taken part in Brown's raid and was hanged on December 16, 1859. The night before his death Copeland wrote to his family saying:

It was a sense of the wrongs which we have suffered that prompted the noble but unfortunate Captain John Brown and his associates to give freedom to a small number, at least, of those who are now held by cruel and unjust laws. . . . And now, dear brother, could I die in a more noble cause? . . . I imagine that I hear you, and all of you, mother, father, sisters and brothers, say—"No, there is not a cause for which we, with less sorrow, could see you die."

One of the persons John Brown had asked to join him in the Harpers Ferry raid was the brilliant black orator and writer Frederick Douglass. Douglass, now having bought his freedom, had started his abolitionist newspaper in Rochester, New York, *The North Star*. Douglass hated slavery as much as any man and was certainly an activist, but he considered his actions carefully. Douglass implored John Brown to reconsider his Harpers Ferry plans, saying, "To me such a measure would be fatal to running off slaves, and fatal to all engaged in doing so. It would be an attack upon the federal government, and would array the whole country against us."

But on July 5, 1852, delivering a "Fourth of July Address" in Rochester, Frederick Douglass had let the whole world know how he felt about slavery:

At a time like this, scorching irony, not convincing argument, is needed. Oh! had I the ability, and could I reach the nation's ear, I would pour out a fiery stream of biting ridicule, blasting reproach, withering sarcasm, and stern rebuke. For it is not light that is needed, but fire; it is not the gentle shower, but thunder. We need the storm, the whirlwind, and the earthquake. The feeling of the nation must be quickened; the conscience of the nation must be roused; the propriety of the nation must be startled; the hypocrisy of the nation must be exposed; and its crimes against God and man must be denounced.

What to the American slave is your Fourth of July? I answer, a day that reveals to him more than all other days of the year, the gross injustice and cruelty to which he is the constant victim. To him your celebration is a sham; your boasted liberty an unholy license; your national greatness, swelling vanity; your sounds of rejoicing are empty and heartless; your denunciation of tyrants, brass-fronted impudence; your shouts of liberty and equality, hollow mockery; your prayers and hymns, your sermons and thanksgivings, with all your religious parade and solemnity, are to him mere bombast, fraud, deception, impiety, and hypocrisy—a thin veil to cover up crimes which would disgrace a nation of savages. There is not a nation of the earth guilty of practices more shocking and bloody than are the people of these United States at this very hour.

Go where you may, search where you will, roam through all the monarchies and despotisms of the Old World, travel through South America, search out every abuse and when you have found the last, lay your facts by the side of the everyday practices of this nation, and you will say with me that, for revolting barbarity and shameless hypocrisy, America reigns without a rival.

Just before he died suddenly in Washington, D.C., February 20, 1895, very close to his seventy-eighth birthday, Frederick Douglass left a simple program for race relations in America, which even if implemented today would go a long way toward making a reality of the myth of black—and white—content:

Let the white people of the North and South conquer their prejudices.

Let the Northern press and pulpit proclaim the gospel of truth and justice against the war now being made upon the Negro.

Let the South abandon the system of mortgage labor and cease to make the Negro a pauper, by paying him a dishonest scrip for his honest labor.

Let him give up the idea that they can be free while making the Negro a slave.

Let the organic law of the land be honestly sustained and obeyed. Let the political parties cease to palter in a double sense and live up to the noble declarations we find in their platforms.

The myth of black content continues to struggle to find expression today when white America reminds black America of the progress black folks have made. Usually white America is talking about jobs, housing, education, and the like. I don't like to talk about black progress, because so few people really understand where real progress has been made. The biggest breakthrough for black folks in the history of America occurred a couple of years ago in the state of Texas, and nobody even noticed it. We got our first colored hurricane— *Beulah*. When you can integrate that big breeze, that's progress.

I am the father of eight children, and every time I see my black wife pregnant, I realize the progress black folks have made. I realize that only a little more than one hundred years ago in America a black slave couple went through the same experience. Close your eyes, especially those of you who have children, and imagine yourself a slave. Your wife comes to you and tells you she is pregnant. Visualize the slave couple falling to their knees in prayer, begging God Almighty that their child be born deformed so that he might be free from being sold on the slave block.

The slave couple would pitifully petition the Lord God to grant that their baby be born without an arm or a leg, so that he could escape the labor of the fields. Sometimes the prayer was answered. And the black woman would look at the black man, with tears of joy streaming down her face, and exclaim, "Our prayer has been answered." Can you see both of them falling to their knees in a prayer of thanks—thanking their God for blessing them with a deformed child?

Black folks have suffered and survived more than four hundred years of such indignities and inhumanities and yet are able to stand proud and tall today. That is why we can look America straight in the eye and say, "Yes, my white brothers and sisters, BLACK IS BEAUTI-FUL."

> "Every American child should learn at school
> the history of the conquest of the West. The
> names of Kit Carson, of General Custer and
> of Colonel Cody should be as household words
> to them. These men as truly helped to form
> an empire as did the Spanish conquistadores.
> Nor should Sitting Bull, the Short Wolf, Crazy
> Horse, and Rain-in-the-Face be forgotten. They
> too were Americans, and showed the same
> heroic qualities as did their conquerors."
>
> ROBERT GRAHAM
> LETTER TO THEODORE ROOSEVELT, 1917

V

THE MYTH OF THE COURAGEOUS WHITE SETTLER AND THE FREE FRONTIER

or The Cowboy and the Campus

On September 26, 1872, three men rode up on their horses to the gate of the Kansas City fair. As a crowd of ten thousand were enjoying themselves inside, the bandits shot at the ticket seller, hit a little girl in the leg, and rode off into the woods with a little less than a thousand dollars. John N. Edwards, writing in the Kansas City *Times,* described the robbery as "so diabolically daring and so utterly in contempt of fear that we are bound to admire it and revere its perpetrators."

Two days later the *Times* was comparing the outlaws with the knights of King Arthur's Round Table:

It was as though three bandits had come to us from storied Odenwald, with the halo of medieval chivalry upon their garments and shown us how the things were done that poets sing of. Nowhere else in the United States or in the civilized world, probably, could this thing have been done.

Two of the three bandits were undoubtedly the James brothers: Frank and Jesse. They have been immortalized in the annals of American folklore, illustrating America's habit of freaking out over bold acts of outrageous lawlessness. The latest expression of the freakout is the current infatuation with the two bank-robbing, cop-killing degenerates, Bonnie and Clyde. Hollywood immortalized Bonnie and Clyde on film, and now America is even trying to dress like them.

Bonnie and Clyde's influence on fashion is not surprising, because the history of the American frontier illustrates that it has always been fashionable in America to take what you can get, any way you can get it.

THE MYTH

The traditional myth of the courageous white settler and the free frontier describes the taking process somewhat differently. Describing pioneers on the Oregon Trail, David S. Muzzey wrote: "Despite hunger, thirst, flash floods, and Indian ambush, the call of adventure, fertile soil, and wider horizons urged men westward." And Stephen Vincent Benét poetically extolled frontier virtue: "The cowards never started and the weak died on the road, and all across the continent the endless campfires glowed."

So, following Horace Greeley's advice, "Go west, young man, and grow up with the country," courageous settlers moved out to challenge and conquer the barren wild frontier. They moved out in covered wagons, stuck together in face of danger, and developed a beautiful sense of community spirit and sharing. Men in an area would band together and help each other build their barns and houses, while the women prepared large quantities of food to feed their hard-working, hungry menfolk.

The frontiersmen represent the true nitty-gritty of American democracy. They are the common folk, the industrious, resourceful, God-fearing individuals whose pioneer spirit made a nation out of an eastern seaboard. Preachers on horseback accompanied the pioneers, built churches in the new settlements, and kept alive the spirit of righteousness. An untamed frontier was fertile ground for the activities of ruthless bad guys, but the Wild West produced heroic lawmen who rose to the occasion and established a climate of law and order.

The triumph of the frontier spirit of true democracy over the dominance of the eastern aristocracy, wealth, and privilege is symbolized in the victory of President Andrew Jackson in 1828. Needless to say, the members of high society were not happy with the election returns. Such dignified elected officials as Daniel Webster deplored the rule of the common masses, calling the Jackson administration the "reign of King Mob." When the common folks traveled to the White House from hundreds of miles to attend the inaugural party, standing on the damask-covered chairs wearing their muddy boots and spilling orange punch on the expensive carpets, outgoing President John Quincy Adams slipped out the back door and refused to attend Jackson's inauguration. Adams was even more upset when his old school, Harvard, conferred the degree of Doctor of Laws upon President Jackson. "Myself an affectionate child of our Alma Mater," Adams wrote, "I would not be present to witness her disgrace in conferring her highest literary honors upon a barbarian who could not write a sentence of grammar and hardly could spell his own name."

The notion that education was the special privilege of persons of wealth and property was dispelled by the common folks, and free public education took root on the expanding frontier. Rich folks objected to paying taxes to support schools to which they would never dream of sending their kids, but poor common folks replied with votes; and education became one more right.

Henry Steele Commager and Samuel Eliot Morison sum up the traditional myth as follows: "Their [the pioneers'] wild, free life gave America much of its old-time gusto and savor; and if they left a taint of lawlessness and violence, they also carried forward the robust tradition of individual prowess that has given the European mind its present 'image' of America."

And each night of the week every television station in America perpetrates the myth of the American frontier.

COLOR THEM BLACK

Until very recently the American television screen gave the impression that all cowboys, pioneers, and settlers in the Wild West were white folks. Last season black folks got their own TV western featuring a black cowboy, though it might be better these days not to call him "boy." The name of the show was *The Outcasts*, so you could tell by the name that it feaured black folks. I understand that there will soon be another black cowboy on television, so that the current black cowboy will have somebody to kill. Sometimes the black cowboy gets to kill a white cowboy. But it poses such a problem for the scriptwriters. They have to work so hard "dirtying up" a white cowboy, so that the viewing audience won't resent the black cowboy's killing him.

Some time back I did see the black cowboy kill a white bad guy. The white cat had just finished raping a blind, paraplegic, Salvation Army worker. But that's not the reason the black cowboy killed him. It turned out the white cat had stolen two thousand polio-fund canisters containing contributions and had marched off with all the dimes.

Of course, there is ample material from the pages of American history for the true story of black cowboys. Philip Durham and Everett L. Jones tell the story in their book *The Adventures of the Negro Cowboys.* More than five thousand black cowboys rode the trails north from Texas during the years following the Civil War. They were an exciting, humorous, and daring lot, and their adventures would make the staid life on the Ponderosa quite dull by comparison.

Most of the first black cowboys were slaves who came West with their masters from the plantations of the Old South. Just when these slaves had learned to adjust to the long hours and hard labor of the cotton fields, they were forced to master a new trade—breaking horses and handling longhorns.

All-black cattle crews were common in Texas, and some free blacks owned ranches even before the Civil War. Aaron Ashworth was a black ranch owner who had 2,500 head of cattle and employed a white schoolmaster to teach his children. Now there is material for a series to rival *Bonanza,* with actors Ossie Davis as the ranch owner and Hugh O'Brien teaching sons Clarence Williams and Rosie Grier.

And in the favorite location of TV westerns, Dodge City, there was a much more colorful figure than Matt Dillon, Bat Masterson, or Wyatt Earp. His name was

Ben Hodges, born of a black father and a Mexican mother. Ben Hodges was undoubtedly the first ghetto hustler, and he put to shame the schemes of Kingfish on the old *Amos 'n' Andy* series.

When Ben Hodges rode into town and heard a rumor that much of the range land surrounding Dodge was part of an old Spanish land grant, he immediately began circulating word of his ancient Spanish ancestry and laid claim to ownership of the land. Sporting the Old West equivalent of an Eldorado, Hodges rode around Dodge on an extravagant saddle, wearing the most expensive spurs and carrying the best gun made. Even when his hustle was exposed, Ben Hodges was able to call up the resources of a ghetto ingenuity. A whole herd of cattle turned up missing one day, and all the circumstantial evidence pointed directly to Hodges. Since he was broke, friendless, and without a lawyer, Ben Hodges decided to defend himself.

For two hours Ben Hodges held the jurors spellbound with interest, amusement, and bewilderment. At one point in his summary Hodges cried out, "What! Me? The descendant of old grandees of Spain, the owner of a land grant embracing millions of acres, the owner of gold mines and villages and towns situated on that grant of which I am sole owner, to steal a miserable, miserly lot of old cows? Why, the idea is absurd. No, gentlemen, I think too much of the race of men from which I sprang, to disgrace their memory."

Later on in the summation Hodges portrayed himself as a poor but honest cowboy, harassed and falsely accused by personal enemies. The whole display was too much for the jury to handle, and Hodges was acquitted.

A few days later the missing cows came home, leaving tracks that told the whole story. Hodges had indeed stolen them and hidden them, unguarded, in a canyon. Weather forced the cows to start moving. But the condemning evidence showed up too late, and the accused remained a free man.

The legendary Billy the Kid rode with blacks and found himself engulfed in blackness much of the time. When Billy and his gang were trapped in a burning building, blacks were right in there with him. And outside, black troops surrounded the house.

An unidentified black cook holds the singular distinction of being the first prisoner in the new jail in Abilene, Kansas—and the first man to break out of it. Soon after the Civil War, Abilene became the first big cowtown, a market place and railroad-shipping point for cattle. Thousands of cattle moved toward Abilene every summer, grazing on the surrounding plains and filling up the pens. Cowboys came into town on their night off, took hot baths, filled up the barber shops and got clipped, shaved, and sprinkled with bay rum. Then they filled the saloons, drank, gambled, and got into fights. A new jail was constructed to hold the trouble-making rowdies.

One such night the black cook rode into town, bought a hot meal he didn't have to cook, and began boozing heavily. When his whisky got to talking to him, he went outside and started shooting, not doing much damage but making a lot of noise.

The town marshal came running, disarmed the drunken cook, and slapped him into jail. But the cook's crew soon got hungry. When they heard their next meal was locked up in Abilene, the crew rode into town, drove the marshal into hiding, shot the lock off the cell door, and freed the cook. On their way out of town they rode past the office of the town trustees and shot it full of holes. Then they rode back to camp for some soul cooking.

Black folks have always had to use their wits to survive, but a black cowboy named Tony Williams must hold some sort of record for ingenuity. Brother Tony was leading a herd of cattle through the treacherous waters of the swollen Red River in 1873. When Tony and the herd were well out into the river, a big wave knocked him off his mule. He sank out of sight, and his mount kept leading the herd on across.

"We thought he had drowned," one of Tony's friends said later. "But in a little while we discovered him holding on to the tail of a big beef steer. When the steer went up the bank Tony was still holding on and went with him."

A picture of Billy the Kid shows a shabby, popeyed, bucktoothed white boy staring into the camera lens. Yet Billy became the legendary bad man of the Wild West, the hero of books, stories, ballads, and ballets. There was another youngster on the scene about ten years after Billy's death, just as tough and twice as vicious as the Kid, whose photographs would need no retouching. He was a handsome, daring woman-charmer, the son of part black, part white, part Indian parents, and his name was Cherokee Bill.

Bill got his start at the age of fourteen when he shot and killed his brother-in-law. He then became a professional killer shooting railroad agents, Indian police, express agents, and storekeepers. He rode with a gang which specialized in armed robbery—stores, trains, and express offices. One writer said Cherokee Bill made legendary bad men like John Wesley Hardin and Sam Bass look like "small potatoes" at a time when "there was no Sunday west of St. Louis and no God west of Fort Smith."

Bill was so bad that at least one town passed a law saying nobody could bother him while he was in the city limits. But his woman-chasing activities led to his downfall at the ripe old age of twenty. Bill was visiting his favorite lady, Maggie Glass. As he was getting down to business with his lady, he also let down his guard. Maggie's cousin, Ike Rogers, banged Bill on the head with a poker.

Bill was chained and handcuffed and turned over to deputy United States marshals and carted off to Fort Smith, Arkansas. He was tried before the notorious federal judge Isaac C. Parker, known for his speedy trials and his frequent passing out of the death sentence. Judge Parker sentenced Bill to hang and said he was sorry there was no harsher penalty. I guess the judge wished he could have sentenced Cherokee Bill to thirty days in the electric chair—with wet drawers on.

"Your record," said Judge Parker to Cherokee Bill, "is more atrocious than that of all the criminals who have hitherto stood before this bar. To effect your capture brave men risked their lives and it was only by the keenest strategy that it was effected. Even after you had been placed within the prison walls your ferocity prevented docility, and your only thought was to break away that you might return to the scenes of bloodshed from which an outraged law had estranged you. In order to make your escape you would have trampled under foot the will of the people, and releasing hundreds of your ilk, fled to your mountain and forest haunts, there to gather around you a larger and more bloodthirsty band; there to defy all power under heaven while you indulged your passion for crime; there to burn and pillage and destroy the lives of whoever stood for a moment in the way of your campaign of destruction."

Unlike Judge Parker, Cherokee Bill was not one to talk a lot. As he faced his executioner before the large crowd gathered to watch him hang, Bill was asked if he had anything to say. Bill replied simply, "No. I came here to die—not to make a speech." Then, tying the noose around his own neck, Cherokee Bill departed from this life.

Bose Ikard was born a slave in Mississippi before the Civil War. His master's family, the Ikards, brought Bose to Texas when he was five years old. Raised on the frontier near Weatherford, Texas, Bose learned to ride, rope, and fight. He became a skilled and valuable cowhand.

Bose Ikard rode for two Texas cattlemen. He first rode for Oliver Loving. When Loving died after a fight with the Comanches, Ikard began to ride for Colonel Charles Goodnight. The Goodnight-Loving Trail went through central Texas, then north through New Mexico, Colorado, and Wyoming. The trail was particularly hazardous in that just before reaching the Pecos River, it went through about eighty miles of waterless desert. Bose Ikard was the backbone of those hard cattle drives.

Colonel Goodnight said that Bose

surpassed any man I had in endurance and stamina. There was a dignity, a cleanliness, and a reliability about him that was wonderful. He paid no attention to women. His behavior was very good in a fight, and he was probably the most devoted man to me that I ever had. I have trusted him farther than any living man. He was my detective, banker, and everything else in Colorado, New Mexico and the other wild country I was in. The nearest and only bank was at Denver, and when we carried money I gave it to Bose, for a thief would never think of robbing him—never think of looking in a Negro's bed for money.

We went through some terrible trials during those four years on the trail. While I had a good constitution and endurance, after being in the saddle for several days and nights at a time, on various occasions, and finding that I could stand it no longer, I would ask Bose if he would

South Dakota, in Deadwood, shot in the back while gambling in a saloon. Wild Bill was holding a poker hand of aces and eights. Since that time a poker hand of two aces and two eights has been known as a "dead man's hand."

George H. Hendricks in *The Bad Men of the West* lists Bill Hickok among the bad guys, along with Judge Roy Bean, who dispensed the "Law West of the Pecos." A man was once hauled before Judge Bean for murdering a Chinese laborer along the Southern Pacific railroad tracks being built beyond the Pecos. Judge Bean freed the accused man, saying that nowhere in his law books could he find a ruling against killing a Chinese. Said Judge Bean: "There's no law in my book against killin' a Chinaman, but I'll have to fine the corpse for carryin' a concealed weapon." Roy Bean was the poet laureate of frontier justice, as some of his sentences from the bench will indicate: "Tomorrow is goin' to be a beautiful day in Texas. The sun will rise, the cactus will bloom, the sage will smell like sweet perfume—but not for you, José, 'cause you're hangin' at daybreak."

Many notorious gun fighters ended up as "peace officers." Ben Thompson shot up Kansas and almost had a run-in with Bill Hickok, and finally wound up as city marshal of Austin, Texas. Deputy Sheriff Bill Longley was one of the most notorious killers in the business. Doc Holliday served as a lawman with Wyatt Earp in Kansas and Arizona. It is still an open question whether Earp belongs with the good guys or the bad guys in spite of his being immortalized on the American television screen.

Sometimes their "peace officers" let them down, so the good folks of the frontier had to take matters into their own hands. The spirit of frontier democracy was embodied in the "instant justice" of posses, mobs, and vigilante groups. The following warning was tacked up in Las Vegas, New Mexico, in 1880:

To murderers, confidence men, thieves:
The citizens of Las Vegas are tired of robbery, murder and other crimes that have made this town a byword in every civilized community. They have resolved to put a stop to crime, even if in obtaining that end they have to forget the law, and resort to a speedier justice than it will afford. All such characters are, therefore, notified that they must either leave this town or conform them-selves to the requirement of law, or they will be sum-marily dealt with. The flow of blood MUST and SHALL be stopped in this community, and good citizens of both the old and new towns have determined to stop it if they have to HANG by the strong arm of FORCE every violator of law in this country.

VIGILANTES

So in 1877, Texas alone had five thousand men on its wanted list. Theodore Roosevelt, commenting upon the frontier, emphasized "the fact of such scoundrels being able to ply their trade with impunity for any length of time can only be understood if the absolute wildness of our land is taken into account." That wildness was de-scribed by Roosevelt in 1888 when he said "notorious bullies and murderers have been taken out and hung, while the bands of horse thieves have been regularly hunted down and destroyed in pitched fights by parties of armed cowboys."

An English visitor to Denver, Colorado, observed that murder was a "comparatively slight offense."

Until two or three years ago, assassination—incidental not deliberate assassination—was a crime of every day. . . . Unless a ruffian is known to have killed half-a-dozen peo-ple, and to have got, as it were, murder on the brain, he is almost safe from trouble in these western plains. A notorious murderer lived near Central City; it was known that he had shot six or seven men; but no one thought of interfering with him on account of his crimes.

The commonplace nature of killing on the old frontier encouraged the most unbridled notions of law and order among the private citizenry. Texas led all other states, with fifty-two vigilante groups. Montana held the "instant justice" execution record with a human roundup, led by Granville Stuart, which claimed thirty-five lives.

Montana sheriff Henry Plummer was the victim of vigilante execution along with two confederates. The account of that execution gives the historic roots for the increasingly common demand for law and order today.

Terrible must have been its [the gallows that Plummer himself had erected the previous year] appearance as it loomed up in the bright starlight, the only object visible to the gaze of the guilty men, on that long waste of ghastly snow. A negro boy came up to the gallows with rope before the arrival of the cavalcade. All the way, Ray and Stinson filled the air with curses. Plummer, on the contrary, first begged for his life, and, finding that unavailing, resorted to argument. . . .

"It is useless," said one of the Vigilantes, "for you to beg for your life; that affair is settled, and cannot be altered. You are to be hanged. You cannot feel harder about it than I do; but I cannot help it if I would."

Plummer asked for time to pray. "Certainly," replied the Vigilante, "but say your prayers up there," at the same time pointing to the crossbeam of the gallows-frame.

The spirit of frontier democracy exemplified in the vigilante tradition meant that the majority took matters into their own hands and decide a man's guilt or innocence without going through the motions of a jury trial or a legal defense. The majority insisted upon conformity with community standards and sentiments while it bypassed the established official means of dispensing justice. The fact that courtrooms were either absent or overcrowded on the old frontier contributed to lynch-mob rule. But even today, when this is no longer the case, a simplistic law-and-order tradition still dominates the American mentality.

During the 1968 national elections I was an independent write-in candidate for President of the United States. Personally I felt I was the *only* candidate running for President. The three major candidates seemed to be running for sheriff. They all placed heavy emphasis in their campaign rhetoric on the need for law and order. But they did not place equal emphasis upon the conditions of social injustice that breed lawlessness and create disorder. When law and order is demanded in the absence of social justice, the term "law and order" becomes America's new way of saying "nigger."

Professor Frantz articulates the link between frontier tradition and sentiment and contemporary America's violent mentality:

The prevalence of arms over the fireplace of every frontier cabin or stacked by the sod-house door endures in the defense which groups like the National Rifle Association membership carry on today against attempts to register arms and control the sale of guns and ammunition. A man had to have a gun, not solely for game to feed his family but because he had to be ready to defend. This heritage continues. As of this writing, it still prevails in most parts of the Nation. Almost no other country permits such widespread individual ownership, but the United States through its frontier experience has historical justification. In pioneer days a frontier boy came of age when his father presented him wtih his own gun as surely as a town boy came of age by putting on long pants or his sister became a woman by putting up her hair. In many areas of the United States in A.D. 1969 a boy still becomes a man, usually on his birthday or at Christmas, when his father gives him a gun. A generally accepted age is twelve, although it may come even a half-dozen years sooner. The gun may be nothing more than a target weapon, but the boy is shown how to use it and how to take care of it, and he is a gun owner and user, probably for the next 60 years of his expected life on this earth. Whether he shoots sparrows out of the eaves of the house, quail and deer in season, or his fellowman with or without provocation remains for his personal history to unfold. The fact is that in his gun ownership he is following a tradition that goes back to John Smith and Jamestown and has persisted ever since.

The frontier tradition abuses the intention of the United States Constitution. The framers of the Constitution gave every American citizen the right to carry a gun to protect his life and property. Article II of the Bill of Rights states: "A well-regulated Militia, being necessary to the security of a free State, the right of the people to keep and bear Arms, shall not be infringed." I have profound respect for the Constitution, and I think Article II of the Bill of Rights preserves an important right of every citizen.

But we must remember that there were no automatic weapons and no hand guns when the first ten amendments to the Constitution were written. Constitutional mandate was limited to shotguns and rifles. It is very difficult to slip a shotgun or a rifle into your pocket and travel across town. Any time a man comes out of his home bearing a shotgun or a rifle, there is a good chance it will be noticed.

Even though I am nonviolent, I uphold the essential wisdom of the Constitution—namely, the right of a citizen to protect himself. The spirit of the Constitution guarantees the right of self-defense. But I cannot support the spirit of the frontier tradition. I happen to feel that a man can protect both himself and his family, or property, quite well with a shotgun or a rifle, and I would urge gun legislation to interpret constitutional mandate to apply only to shotguns or rifles and to rule out small automatic weapons. The intent of the Constitution is to preserve a safe America. This country is much safer in dealing with a man whose weapon can be seen than in dealing with a man who has a pistol hidden in his pocket. But America's frontier mentality shows more respect for the Colt .45 than for the United States Constitution.

America's mental link with her frontier tradition is symbolized in both television westerns and the childhood game of cowboys and Indians. The cowboy of the Wild West frontier—always a white Anglo-Saxon—symbolizes the rugged individual, the courageous, "good guy," "do-it-yourself" American who defends his property and honor against all would-be "bad guys." And those "bad guys," according to the myth, are most frequently Indians, wild, savage, ruthless, who stalk the courageous cowboy, posing a threat to his life and property and not infrequently massacring his entire family.

The Cartwrights of the television show *Bonanza* are an all-American family, having amassed a personal fortune and carved a veritable empire—the Ponderosa—on the old frontier. On the surface the Cartwrights appear to be honorable men, upholding the virtues of honesty, justice, and fair play, until one remembers that all of the Ponderosa was once Indian land and Ben Cartwright and his boys are at best unwelcome stewards of stolen Indian territory.

And in a country that tries desperately to perpetuate

the myth of nonviolence upon her young, Marshal Matt Dillon comes into every American living room once a week showing little kids it is a virtue to shoot straight. Matt Dillon should probably be heralded more than Herbert Marcuse as the father of the New Left. Marshal Dillon has had a much longer influence upon the minds of youth, and his basic message has always been that the ends of justice are most frequently won at gunpoint, that evil must be violently wiped out, and that "bad guys" deserve to die.

So children in America grow up watching television and going outside to play cowboys and Indians. And parents think it is so cute. They enjoy watching their little ones hiding behind trees, pointing their fingers or toy guns at one another, and shouting, "Bang! Bang! I got you. You're dead." Because Americans have always thought of themselves as the courageous cowboys, the rugged individualists carving out the new frontier of freedom. And as America has grown, so also have the boundaries of the new frontier. The whole world has become the Wild West, and each time America sends her troops abroad, it is Matt Dillon making the frontier safe for democracy and law and order.

Now America's favorite myth is in danger. The children who grew up playing cowboys and Indians have discovered that the "good guy—bad guy" roles were reversed. The Indians were those who were denied justice. The cowboys were the invaders. Matt Dillon's personal virtues are inconsequential when matched against the genocide involved in settling the new frontier.

But young folks in America have retained one important lesson of Matt Dillon's—that evil must be resisted, and that those who represent justice have every right to fight in the streets. Is it any wonder that some of those same young folks have followed Matt Dillon all the way and reached the decision that guns are an appropriate means for resisting evil and creating an atmosphere of justice?

Perhaps the cowboys and the common folks of the free frontier made their biggest mistake when they established schools, colleges, and universities. Those educational institutions have produced a generation of youth who refuse to play cowboy any more. The old cowboys—President Nixon, Vice President Agnew, Attorney General Mitchell, and the National Guard—see themselves as defending their property, their territory—America, if you will—against increasingly savage student attackers.

They ride onto the campuses of Kent State University and Jackson State College, and a shoot-out takes place. When the posse leaves the campus, it leaves the dead behind. And the posse rides on into Cambodia. But the world knows Matt Dillon has traveled far beyond his legitimate boundaries of jurisdiction. The whole world sees that America's rugged individualist is really a bully.

So the campus has become the new frontier. The old cowboys are losing their control. Colleges and universities today are controlled not by presidents and faculty but by boards of directors. The average board of directors in an educational institution comprises not education or human-relations experts but rather people whose only qualification is that they have made some money. Nobody even asks them how they made it. But a quick survey of the lists of boards of directors will reveal the same names of the same wealthy families who are causing problems all over the world. They have projected the spirit of the old frontier on a worldwide scale—the spirit of taking what is there to be taken.

But they are being closely watched by the free young spirits of the new frontier. Those youths are posting their own warning to the "thieves, confidence men and murderers." There is one major difference between the old and the new frontiers. The watchful vigilantes of the new frontier are not seeking to bypass justice; rather, they are demanding its implementation.

> "You degrade us and then ask why we are
> degraded. You shut our mouths and then ask
> why we don't speak. You close your colleges
> and seminaries against us, and then ask why
> we don't know more."

FREDERICK DOUGLASS, 1847

VI

THE MYTH OF THE MASON-DIXON LINE

or Searching for Boundaries

The reality of the Mason-Dixon line is that it lies along latitude 39° 43′ 26.3″ N between the southwestern corner of Pennsylvania and the arc of a circle of twelve miles' radius drawn from Newcastle (Delaware) as a center; and along that arc to the Delaware River. The line was drawn by two English astronomers, Charles Mason and Jeremiah Dixon, in 1763–1767, to settle a longstanding border dispute between the colonies of Pennsylvania and Maryland.

The myth is that the Mason-Dixon line served to designate the boundary between the farming (or commercial) states and the plantation states—the free and the slave states respectively before the Civil War—and continues to be the boundary of sentiment between the North and the South today. The late Malcolm X was closer to a correct border distinction regarding racial attitudes in America when he suggested the term "South" means "south of the Canadian border."

Whereas the Mason-Dixon line is a physical boundary, distinctions regarding northern and southern racial attitudes are verbal. When southern white folks display a contempt for the rights of black folks, poor folks, and all oppressed people, northern white folks call them "bigots." When those same attitudes are displayed in the North, the persons who display them are called "conservatives." When George Wallace ran for the presidency in 1968, liberal northern white folks said he was a bigot. But when Mario Procaccino ran as the Democratic candidate for mayor of New York City in 1969, saying essentially the same things George Wallace had said, folks said Brother Mario was a conservative.

If I go to the South and deliver a lecture, and afterward I am beaten up by a group of people who do not agree with my views, northern newspapers will report, "Dick Gregory Attacked By Racist Mob." If I deliver a lecture in New York City and the same thing happens, the newspapers will say, "Dick Gregory Stirs White Backlash."

During the early and mid-1960's liberal folks from the North, white and black, frequently crossed the Mason-Dixon line to participate in civil rights demonstrations. They seemed to be under the impression that racial problems in America existed only below that line. But Memorial Day 1970 illustrated how thin the Mason-Dixon line really is today. Antiwar demonstrators planned a series of protest marches in New York City. A few weeks earlier peace demonstrators had been attacked and beaten by construction workers in the Wall

Street area of New York, and the accusation was leveled against the police department that many officers stood by and watched the beatings. The New York Civil Liberties Union and three other legal organizations representing the antiwar demonstrators requested a court order requiring police to protect Memorial Day demonstrators. The order was virtually identical to orders issued to Southern sheriffs in Alabama after they had allowed civil rights workers to be beaten in 1965.

But there has always been a closer alignment than traditional American history admits between the racial attitudes of the North and the South. Before the Civil War the Ohio River extended the boundary of the Mason-Dixon line to designate the border between slave and free states. Yet there was considerable antiblack sentiment north of the Ohio River.

On June 6, 1862, the Honorable S. S. Cox, Congressman from Ohio, spoke in dismay of the actions of the Thirty-seventh Congress and its pro-black legislation:

My belief is, that the people will write the epitaph of this Congress, nearly as Gladstone wrote that of the Coalition ministry during the Crimean War:

Here lies the ashes of the XXXVII Congress!
It found the United States in a war of
gigantic proportions, involving
its very existence.
It was content to wield the sceptre of Power
and accept the emoluments of office:
and used them to overthrow
the political and social system of the country, which
it was sworn to protect.
It saw the fate of thirty-four white commonwealths
in peril; but it babbled of the
NEGRO!
It saw patriotic generals and soldiers in the
field under the old flag:

It slandered the one, and in the absence of the other,
  it destroyed his means of labor.
It talked of Liberty to the black, and
  plied burdens of taxation on white people
    for schemes utopian.
The people launched at it the thunderbolt
  of their wrath;
and its members sought to avoid punishment,
  by creeping into dishonored
    political graves!
    Requiescat!

The Providence *Post* was a little more systematic that same year in summing up the actions of the Thirty-seventh Congress, First Regular Session:

(Not copied from the Record, but put down according to our recollection, and warranted correct in the main:)

1. An act in relation to niggers.
2. An act to emancipate niggers.
3. An act to prohibit what-ye-call-it, in the Territories.
4. An act to abolish what-ye-call-it in the District of Columbia.
5. An act concerning niggers.
6. An act to confiscate niggers.
7. An act to emancipate the wives and babies of contrabands.
8. An act to emancipate niggers who fight for the Confederacy.
9. An act to make 'em fight for the Union.
10. An act to make freed niggers love to work.
11. An act to educate said freed niggers.
12. An act to make paper worth more than gold.
13. An act to make a little more paper worth more than a good deal more gold.
14. An act to free somebody's niggers.
15. An act in relation to niggers.
16. An act to prohibit importations by increasing duties.

17. An act to make white folks squeal, otherwise known as the Tax Bill.
18. An act authorizing the President to draft white folks.
19. An act authorizing the President to arm niggers.
20. An act to give us a little more paper.
21. An act concerning niggers.
22. An act to make omnibus tickets a legal tender.
23. An act to compensate Congressmen for using their influence in obtaining contracts.
24. An act authorizing the issue of more omnibus tickets.
25. An act declaring white men almost as good as niggers, if they behave themselves. (Laid on the table.)
26. An act to repeal that clause of the Constitution relating to the admission of new States.
27. An act to repeal the rest of the Constitution.
28. Resolutions pledging the Government to pay for emancipated niggers.
29. An act authorizing the President to pay for said niggers. (Went under.)
30. Act to confiscate things.
31. Resolution explaining that some other things are not meant.
32. An act in relation to niggers.
33. An act to make niggers white.
34. An act to make 'em a little whiter.
35. An act to make them a good deal whiter.
36. An act in relation to colored people.
37. An act in relation to contrabands.
38. An act concerning niggers.
39. Resolutions of adjournment.

The Lancaster (Pa.) *Intelligencer* also had something to say about one of the acts of the Thirty-seventh Congress. In reporting a celebration of the emancipation of black folks in Washington, D.C., the *Intelligencer* exhorted:

What do you think of it, white men? Is this the feast to which the laboring class of the North is invited? These woolly heads intend to amalgamate with the whites and establish a society "far superior to any ever produced by any nation in the world." And to accomplish this they do not intend to leave the country, either, nor do they care whether their freedom is obtained "through the preservation or *dissolution* of the Union." Is this treason or is it not?

Word of a better way of life north of the Mason-Dixon line infiltrated Southern plantations, and many slaves were encouraged to run away to the North, risking the terrible consequences of being caught. An organized system for helping slaves to run away, known as the "Underground Railroad," began in the 1820's, and between 1830 and 1860 it was responsible for helping no less than 75,000 slaves to find "freedom" in the North. One of the most ingenious runaway slaves was a man named Henry Brown. He had a special box made, two feet wide and three feet long, containing cleverly designed receptacles for food and water. Labeling the box "THIS SIDE UP," Brother Brown climbed in, had it sealed and shipped by the Adams Express Company. The trip from Richmond to Philadelphia lasted twenty-six hours. Four men were on hand to receive the crate. When they pried open the lid, one of the men, William Still, reports "the marvelous resurrection of Henry Brown ensued. Rising up in his box, he reached out his hand, saying, 'How do you do, gentlemen?' "

But runaway slaves discovered that life for black folks in America bears a universal stamp whether they find themselves north or south of the Mason-Dixon line. Sometimes slaves who successfully made it to the North were discovered, arrested, kidnaped, or otherwise returned to their masters, where unspeakable horrors

awaited their arrival "home." An Ohio newspaper, the
Ravenna *Democrat,* reported the eyewitness account of
a Mrs. A. Wilcox:

She relates instances that came under her observation, of
the destitution and desperation of the Southern chivalry,
and instances of the terrible punishment they apply to
contrabands. The man with whom she boarded had seven
slaves, who escaped to the Federal lines, and were by our
soldiers returned or driven back. They were taken to the
whipping-yard, placed prostrate upon the ground, and
stocks placed upon their necks, and their feet were fastened tight. The lash was then applied to their naked
backs, *gashing them at every blow.* They were then sent
to Gen. Pillow, and set to work on the entrenchments.

The brother of this man uses a different method of
punishment. Instead of the whip, he keeps for the especial
purpose, a cage of tom-cats, and when he wishes to punish
a slave, he raises up the fence and puts his neck between
the rails, back up, then takes a cat by the tail and drags
it the whole length of the back of his unfortunate and
helpless victim—and this is proud, happy America! Heaven
save the mark!

John H. Aughey, a Northerner residing in Kosciusko,
Mississippi, wrote a Christmas letter in 1861 to his
friend in Jefferson County, Ohio, in which he spoke of
the runaway slave situation:

Every night the woods resound with the deep-mouthed
baying of the bloodhounds. The slaves are said by some
to love their masters; but it requires the terror of bloodhounds and the Fugitive Slave Law to keep them in bondage. You in the North are compelled to act the part of
the bloodhounds here, and catch the fugitives for the
planters of the South. Free Negroes are sold into bondage
for the most trivial offenses. Slaveholders declare that the
presence of free persons of colour exerts a pernicious influence upon the slaves, rendering them discontented with

their condition and inspiring a desire for freedom. They, therefore, are desirous of getting rid of the free Negroes, either by banishing them from the State, or by enslaving, or re-enslaving them.

Aughey also wrote of the daily punishment facing each slave:

Every night the Negroes are brought to the judgment-seat. The overseer presides. If they have not laboured to suit him, or if their tasks are unfulfilled, they are chained to a post and severely whipped. The victims are invariably stripped; to what extent is the option of the overseer. In Louisiana, women preparatory to whippings are often stripped to the state of perfect nudity. Old Mr. C——, of Waterford, Mississippi punished his Negroes by slitting the soles of their feet with his Bowie knife! . . . Such cruel scourgings are of daily occurrence. Col. H——, a member of my church, told me yesterday that he ordered a boy who he supposed was feigning sickness to the whipping post, but that he had not advanced ten steps toward it when he fell dead!

One further note of interest. Aughey's letter gives documentation concerning the cross-breeding process of the "peculiar institution":

The next peculiar abomination which I observed was the licentiousness engendered by it. Mr. D. T. ——, of Madison County, Kentucky, had a white family of children, and a black, or rather mulatto family. As his white daughters married, he gave each a mulatto half-sister, as a waiting girl, or body servant. Mr. K——, of Winchester, Kentucky, has a mulatto daughter, and was also the father of her child, thus re-enacting Lot's sin. Dr. C——, of Tishomingo County, Mississippi, has a Negro concubine, and a white servant to wait on her. Mr. B——, of Marshall County, Mississippi, lived with his white wife till he had grandchildren, some of whom came to school to me, when he repudiated his white wife, and attached himself to a very homely old African, who superintends his household, and rules his other slaves with vigor. Mr. S——, of Tishomingo County, Mississippi, has a Negro concubine, and a large family of mulatto children. He once brought this woman to church in Rienzi, to the great indignation of the white ladies, who removed themselves to a respectful distance.

Slaves who were not apprehended also found that life above the Mason-Dixon line held little promise for them. The *New York Times* told the following little tale:

Yesterday afternoon a very black individual, belonging to that class of beings commonly designated "contrabands," made his appearance at an office in Wall Street, and told a very woeful tale about his troubles. He confessed that he was from Wilmington, N.C., which place he had been influenced to leave, and subsequently was induced, by plausible stories, to visit the North, as a paradise of Freedom, where work was to be had in abundance, and fabulous sums would be given for labor. He made his way to this city in a Government vessel or otherwise; but instead of finding plenty and freedom, he was encountered with cool indifference wherever he applied for assistance. He professed to be a cooper by trade, and said he could find no employment here and was weary seeking for aid and comfort. The "bosses" told him they dare not give him work, because all their white hands would instantly leave them in disgust. Coming to the conclusion that Northern freedom and equality were all gammon, he only asked for a little assistance to get back to Wilmington once more, where he expected at least to get enough to eat and drink.

So blackness was the real "peculiarity" on both sides of the Mason-Dixon line, and slavery need not be institutionalized to still be very real in the lives of black folks. One young man who made history in the annals of black achievement, after the Civil War was over, found out painfully how much his blackness was despised in the North. The New York *Truth Seeker* reported April 17, 1880: "James Webster Smith, the first colored cadet in the history of West Point, was recently taken from his bed, gagged, bound, and severely beaten, and then his ears were slit. He says he cannot identify his assailants. The other cadets claim he did it himself."

Free blacks were still black, and they were lynched and burned on both sides of the Mason-Dixon line, in New York *and* Mississippi, in Illinois *and* Alabama, in short, wherever their blackness enraged the emotions of white folks.

One northern burning example will suffice. The *Montgomery Advertiser,* August 15, 1911, carried the following account of an incident in Coatesville, Pennsylvania:

Zachariah Walker, a negro desperado, was carried on a cot from the hospital here last night and burned to a crisp by a frenzied mob of men and boys on a fire which they ignited about a half mile from town.

Walker had been cornered in a cherry tree yesterday by a sheriff's posse which suspected him of the murder of Edgar Rice, a special policeman at the Worth Iron Mills.

When he was cornered, Walker shot himself in the mouth, falling from the tree. The posse then brought him to the hospital.

News of the murder of Rice, who was very popular among the people here, spread rapidly. There had been no other crimes committed in this neighborhood that had been blamed on negroes and talk of lynching fell on willing ears. The main street of Coatesville is usually filled with people from the surrounding towns Sunday nights and a crowd soon gathered at the hospital. As the crowd increased the talk of lynching spread and finally a masked man mounted the steps of the hospital and shouted:

"Men of Coatesville, will you let a drunken negro do up such a white man as Rice?"

The orderly crowd was instantly transformed into a riotous mob. The attack on the hospital was then made. There were only the superintendent, four nurses and a policeman in the institution at the time and a defense of the negro was impossible. The crowd swarmed into the place through smashed doors and windows and before most of the mob knew it, the wounded and frightened negro was being taken out of the building screaming piteously. Still lying on the cot, he was carried through the streets and out of the city to the Newland farm. He had been tied to the bed with ropes and as the crowd tore fence rails and gathered wood and other inflammables, Walker writhed on his cot and tugged at his bonds, but could not free himself.

All the leaders of the crowd wore masks made of handkerchiefs tied around their faces up to the eyes. They carried on their work quickly and after piling up the rubbish placed the cot, with its shuddering victim on it, over the pile. A dozen matches, it seemed, were simultaneously applied to the pyre and in an instant the negro was enveloped in the flames. The fire burned the ropes that held him and he made a dash for liberty. Walker reached a fence and was about to climb it when stalwart hands seized him and dragged him back to his funeral pyre.

As he was thrust back into the flames, he shrieked, "Don't give me a crooked deal because I ain't white."

Only vile oaths greeted his plea.

Good white folks, of course, wanted to see a better way of life for blacks and urged education as a necessary prerequisite to full liberation. Black parents dreamed of educational benefits for their children, perhaps even of sending their son to Harvard! A fortunate black youth who made it to Harvard might have been enrolled in the class of Professor Albert Bushnell Hart, who spoke before the American Historical Association's convention in Detroit, December 29, 1900. The New York *World* reported the following day that Professor Hart "said that if people of certain States are determined to burn colored men at the stake, those States would better legalize the practice."

Thus began the twentieth century in America, a century in which the "burning" issue remains one of blackness rather than boundaries. New fires of rage sweep through black ghettos of the North, and, like the white folks' practice of burning "colored men" at the stake in the early part of the century, they indicate hostility and resentment. I wonder if Professor Bushnell would apply the same logic and suggest that if such fires of rage persist, states would be well advised to legalize them, too.

> "After God had finished the rattlesnake, the
> toad and the vampire, he had some awful
> substance left with which He made a SCAB.
> A SCAB is a two-legged animal with a cork-
> screw soul, a water-logged brain and a combi-
> nation backbone made of jelly and glue. Where
> others have hearts he carries a tumor of rotten
> principles. A strikebreaker is a traitor to his
> God, his country, his family and his class!"
>
> JACK LONDON, 1904

VII

THE MYTH OF FREE ENTERPRISE

or Labor Pains

After the Civil War, as enterprising blacks were discovering how little it meant to be free, "free enterprise"
was taking root in America for the benefit of the fortunate few. Free enterprise is an extension of the doctrine
of laissez faire, which holds that an economic system
functions best free of governmental interference. So
while government in America was busying itself with
picking up the pieces left by the ravages of the Civil War
and "reconstructing" the South, a few white folks were
building financial empires for themselves.

Andrew S. Berky and James P. Shenton, in their two-
volume collection *The Historians' History of the United
States*, sum up the situation:

But once the war had ended, the explosive marshalling of the industrial resources of the nation, already in the take-off stage of development at the war's beginning, set in motion an accumulation of wealth for the fortunate few without parallel in history. Whereas before the war the number of millionaires ranged in the low hundreds, by 1892 the number was somewhere between 3,045 and 4,047, and in 1900 no fewer than twenty-five of their number had found their way into the Senate. The single fortune of John D. Rockefeller, on the eve of the depression of 1892, was reputed to be $815,647,796.89, while Andrew Carnegie, in 1900 alone, garnered a profit from his steel enterprise of $40,000,000. Gentility had been superseded by opulence, and, as many critics complained, an arrogant, unbridled power. The corporations which managed whole segments of the American economy loomed up as states within a state; their captains resembled increasingly the nobles of old, answerable to none but their imprecise consciences.

Even though laissez-faire policy dictated that government not interfere with business, newly developed big business had no qualms about interfering with government. Paid lobbyists took residence in Washington to prevent any legislation by Congress harmful to business interests. The old cliché "money talks" became embodied in state legislators and state judges who were bribed and controlled by the enormous wealth of the captains of industry. Such actions substantiated the observation of Honoré de Balzac (1799–1850) that behind every fortune there is a crime. Though later anti-trust legislation by government aimed at breaking up mass consolidations of wealth and monopolistic practices in the interest of maintaining some semblance of a free enterprise system, the captains of industry left a legacy which still determines political decisions in America and keeps the concept of true democracy in the realm of myth.

Ferdinand Lundberg in his monumental work *The Rich and the Super-Rich* writes:

First, the present concentration of wealth confers self-arrogated and defaulted political policy-making power at home and abroad in a grossly disproportionate degree on a small and not especially qualified mainly hereditary group; secondly, this group allocates vast economic resources in narrow, self-serving directions, both at home and abroad, rather than socially and humanly needed public directions. . . . So, concentrated asset-wealth not only brings in large personal incomes, but confers on the owners and their deputies a disproportionately large voice in economic, political and cultural affairs. Thus the owners may make or frustrate public policy, at home and abroad.

Thus labor reforms and antitrust legislation have had little to do with breaking up vast concentrations of wealth, and Lundberg observes:

The Constitution of the United States bars the bestowal of titles of nobility. But in many ways it would clear up much that is now obscure if titles were allowed. Not only would they show, automatically, to whom deference was due as a right but they would publicly distinguish those who held continuing hereditary power from people who are merely temporarily voted in or appointed for limited terms. The chronicles of High Society—that is, the circles of wealth—recognize this need and, in order to show hereditary status and family position, they allude to males in the line of descent by number, as in the case of royal dynasties. Thus in the English branch of the Astor family there is a John Jacob Astor VII. But there are also George F. Baker III, August Belmont IV, William Byrd III, Joseph H. Choate III, Irénée and Pierre du Pont III, Marshall Field V, Potter Palmer III, John D. Rockefeller IV, Cornelius Vanderbilt V and so on.

Among the wealthy elite in America are the Du Ponts, the Mellons, the Rockefellers, the Fords, and the Pews. Their primary but not sole sources of wealth have been E. I. du Pont de Nemours and Company, the Aluminum Company of America, the Standard Oil group of companies, and the Ford Motor Company. "Each of these companies," says Lundberg, again reminding us of Balzac's observation, "has many times been formally adjudicated in violation of the laws, the first three repeatedly named in crucial successful prosecutions charging vast monopolies. Aluminum, Standard Oil and Du Pont achieved their positions precisely through monopoly, as formally determined by the courts."

Influence of corporate wealth on governmental decisions in America can be seen in a couple of examples—the persisting injustices of the tax structure, for one. Oil-depletion allowances allowed the Rockefeller-controlled Atlantic Oil Company to collect a cool $410,000,000 in 1964 without paying a penny of taxes. Another Rockefeller company, Marathon Oil, got by for four years without paying any taxes before finally coughing up 1.8 per cent of its vast earnings. And Rockefeller's Standard Oil of New Jersey, which has a greater income than most members of the United Nations, paid only 0.6 per cent of its staggering profits to Internal Revenue in 1962.

When President Lyndon Johnson and the CIA sent the Marines into the Dominican Republic in 1967, under the usual guise of the threat of communism, it really meant that American business interests were in danger. Which in turn meant that the wealth of the aforementioned families was threatened. The Mellon family's Aluminum Company of America gets about one million tons of aluminum ore a year from its mines in the Dominican Republic. The South Porto Rico Sugar

Corporation, whose board of directors intertwines with the Rockefellers' Chase Manhattan Bank, owns 300,000 acres of sugar land in the Dominican Republic. And the United Fruit Company—incidentally a Kennedy family interest—owns 2,300 acres of banana cultivation in the same place.

Wealth and oppression have always gone hand in hand in America; and during the heyday of the captains of industry, oppressive practices against the working class gave rise to some of the most radical words to pass the lips of white folks since the days of the American Revolution. Chicago, Illinois, which seems to have a peculiar attraction for radical activities and "conspiracies," was the scene in May 1886 of a workers' rebellion known as the Haymarket Riot.

The working class of Chicago and elsewhere lived in squalor, working long hours for very small wages. Berky and Shenton describe the prevailing condition:

The booming condition of industry brought with it dismal consequences for the worker. His housing conditions were characterized by "filth, over-crowding, lack of privacy and domesticity, lack of ventilation and lighting, and absence of supervision and of sanitary regulations." Streets were often cluttered with debris, not infrequently with dead animals. The factory fitted its environment well. The worker's ears were assaulted by a constant din, and, as one worker recalled, an iron factory was filled with "half-naked, soot-smeared fellows . . . their scowling faces . . . lit with fire." Outside of thousands of factories, as the evening whistle blew ending a ten-hour day, crowds "of tired, pallid, and languid looking children," worn by a long day of work, usually undernourished, poured home-ward to their warrens to sleep and prepare for another day's work.

Trouble in Chicago began in February when Cyrus McCormick locked out his 1,400 employees who were demanding that the company stop discriminating against the employees who had taken part in an earlier strike. An eight-hour work day was at issue. For two months strikebreakers, Pinkerton agents (the FBI of the time), and police had attacked locked-out men with unbridled savagery. A confrontation occurred on Monday afternoon, May 3, which spurred the workers' underground newspaper, *Arbeiter-Zeitung,* to issue a circular in both English and German:

REVENGE!
WORKING MEN, TO ARMS!!!
The masters sent out their bloodhounds—the police; they killed six of your brothers at McCormicks this afternoon. They killed the poor wretches because they, like you, had the courage to disobey the supreme will of your bosses. They killed them because they dared ask for the shortening of the hours of toil. They killed them to show you, "Free American Citizens" that you must be satisfied and contented with whatever your bosses condescend to allow you, or you will get killed!

You have for years endured the most abject humiliations; you have for years suffered unmeasurable iniquities; you have worked yourself to death; you have endured the pangs of want and hunger; your Children you have sacrificed to the factory lord—in short: you have been miserable and obedient slave(s) all these years: Why? To satisfy the insatiable greed, to fill the coffers of your lazy thieving master? When you ask them now to lessen your burdens, he sends his bloodhounds out to shoot you, kill you!

If you are men, if you are the sons of your grand sires, who have shed their blood to free you, then you will rise in your might, Hercules, and destroy the hideous monster that seeks to destroy you. To arms we call you, to arms!
YOUR BROTHERS

Tuesday morning, May 4, a crowd of some three thousand people assembled in Haymarket Square. Some of them undoubtedly had been influenced by another radical newspaper of the time, *Alarm,* which ran the statement:

Dynamite! Of all the good stuff, this is the stuff. Stuff several pounds of this sublime stuff into an inch pipe, plug up both ends, insert a cap with a fuse attached, place this in the immediate neighborhood of a lot of rich loafers who live by the sweat of other people's brows, and light the fuse. A most cheerful and gratifying result will follow.

A particularly hated cop, Inspector John Bonfield, brought 180 policemen in to break up the gathering. As the crowd was ordered to disperse, a bomb was thrown from some point on the sidewalk, exploding in the midst of the policemen, wounding 66, 7 of whom later died. The police "opened fire hysterically" killing several people and wounding 200. Within a few days radical ringleaders were arrested, and many other people, including the printers of *Arbeiter-Zeitung,* were taken into custody.

In August a jury found eight men—August Spies, Michael Schwab, Samuel Fielden, Albert R. Parsons, Adolph Fischer, George Engle, Louis Lingg, and Oscar Neebe—guilty of conspiracy to commit murder, and all but Neebe were sentenced to hang. Fielden and Schwab later had their sentences commuted to life imprisonment, joining Neebe at the State Penitentiary at Joliet. Lingg escaped the scaffold on the day before the execution by exploding a dynamite tube in his mouth.

Judge Gary asked the men if they had any reasons that their sentences should not be pronounced. Albert Parsons replied:

this verdict is the verdict of passion, born in passion, nurtured in passion, and is the sum total of the organized passion of the city of Chicago. . . . Now what is passion? Passion is the suspension of reason; in a mob upon the streets, in the broils of the saloon, in the quarrel on the sidewalk, where men throw aside their reason and resort to feelings of exasperation, we have passion. There is a suspension of the elements of judgment, of calmness, of discrimination requisite to arrive at the truth and the establishment of justice. I hold that you cannot dispute the charge which I make, that this trial has been submerged, immersed in passion from its inception to its close, and even to this hour, standing here upon the scaffold as I do, with the hangman awaiting me with his halter, there are those who claim to represent public sentiment in this city—and I now speak of the capitalistic press, that vile and infamous organ of monopoly, of hired liars, the people's oppressor—even to this day these papers, standing where I do, with my seven condemned colleagues, are clamoring for our blood in the heat and violence of passion. Who can deny this? Certainly not this court. The court is fully aware of these facts.

Said Louis Lingg:

I tell you frankly and openly, I am for force. I have already told Captain Schaack, "If they use cannon against us, we shall use dynamite against them." I repeat that I am the enemy of the "order" of today, and I repeat that, with all my powers so long as breath remains in me, I shall combat it. I declare again, frankly and openly, that I am in favor of using force. You laugh! Perhaps you think, "You'll throw no more bombs," but let me assure you that I die happy on the gallow, so confident am I that the hundreds and thousands to whom I have spoken will remember my words; and when you shall have hanged us, then, mark my words, they will do the bomb-throwing! In this hope do I say to you: "I despise you. I despise your order, your laws, your force-propped authority." Hang me for it!

But the longest expression of radical eloquence was reserved for August Spies:

If you think that by hanging us you can stamp out the labor movement—the movement from which the down-trodden millions, the millions who toil and live in want and misery—the wage slaves—expect salvation—if this is your opinion, then hang us! Here you will tread upon a spark, but there, and there, and behind you and in front of you, and everywhere, flames will blaze up. It is a subterranean fire. You cannot put it out. The ground is on fire upon which you stand. You can't understand it. You don't believe in magical arts, as your grandfathers did, who burned witches at the stake, but you do believe in conspiracies: you believe that all these occurrences of late are the work of conspirators! You resemble the child that is looking for his picture behind the mirror. What you see and what you try to grasp is nothing but the deceptive reflex of the stings of your bad conscience. You want to "stamp out the conspirators"—the agitators? Ah! stamp out every factory lord who has grown wealthy upon the unpaid labor of his employees. Stamp out every landlord who has amassed fortunes from the rent of overburdened working-men and farmers. Stamp out every machine that is revolutionizing industry and agriculture, that intensifies the production, ruins the producer, that increases the national wealth, while the creator of all these things stands amidst them, tantalized with hunger! Stamp out the railroads, the telegraph, the telephone, steam and yourselves—for everything breathes the revolutionary spirit. You, gentlemen, are the revolutionists. You rebel against the effects of social conditions which have tossed you, by the fair hand of fortune, into a magnificent paradise. Without inquiring, you imagine that no one else has a right in that place. You insist that you are the chosen ones, the sole proprietors. The forces that tossed you into the paradise, the industrial forces, are still at work. They are growing more active and intense from day to day. Their tendency is to elevate all mankind to the same level, to have all humanity share in the paradise you now monopolize. You, in your blindness, think you can stop the tidal wave of civilization and human emancipation by placing a few policemen, a few Gatling guns, and some regiments of militia on the shore —you think you can frighten the rising waves back into the unfathomable depths whence they have arisen, by erecting a few gallows in the perspective. You, who oppose the natural course of things, you are the real revolutionists. You and you alone are the conspirators and destructionists! Call your hangman! Truth crucified in Socrates, in Christ, in Giordano Bruno, in Huss, in Galileo, still lives—they and others whose number is legion have preceded us on this path. We are ready to follow.

More than twenty-five thousand working people marched to the graves of the condemned men, and they heard defense counsel William P. Black say:

I loved these men. I knew them not until I came to know them in the time of their sore travail and anguish. As months went by and I found in the lives of those with whom I talked the witness of their love for the people, of their patience, gentleness, and courage, my heart was taken captive in their cause. . . . I say that whatever of fault may have been in them, these, the people whom they loved and in whose cause they died, may well close the volume, and seal up the record, and give our lips to the praise of their heroic deeds, and their sublime self-sacrifice.

Of course Black was right. The working people did write a living epitaph in the labor union movement, giving a new dignity to the workingman. But as labor unions grew, they forgot their roots, and today the words of August Spies could be spoken at union meetings on behalf of black folks and other minorities. Like the Declaration of Independence, the rhetoric of the union movement did not apply to blacks. Today blacks continue to be systematically excluded from union membership, along with Puerto Ricans and others, the building trades unions being the most glaring example. In 1964, New York Local 28 of the Sheet Metal Workers, AFL-CIO, was ruled to have "automatically excluded" blacks over the entire seventy-eight years of its existence. A year later, NAACP studies of AFL-CIO building trades unions in Cincinnati revealed: the Electrical Workers—no blacks; the Plumbers—no blacks; the Pipe Fitters—no blacks; the Sheet Metal Workers—no blacks; the Asbestos Workers—no blacks; the Structural and Ornamental Iron Workers—no blacks; the Millwrights—no blacks. In Pittsburgh the NAACP found virtually the same situation, but some token blacks were discovered: two in Bricklayers Local 2; eighteen in Cement Masons Local 526; three in Painters Local 6; four in Tile Layers and Helpers Local 20; and thirty-five in Construction and Common Laborers Local 373.

So as northern union leaders, such as Harry Van Arsdale of New York, marched south for civil rights demonstrations during the 1960's, blacks back home still had a hard time getting into their unions. The dawn of a new decade has not changed the practice of union discrimination. The free enterprise system is still very much a myth for black folks in America as Robert S. Browne has indicated: "Powerful congressional committees, along with the military-industrial complex, the White House, the 153 families and the corporations run the country. Blacks have no fingerhold on any one of these levers of power."

> "There is no king who has not had a slave among his ancestors, and no slave who has not had a king among his."
>
> HELEN KELLER, 1902

VIII

THE MYTH OF EMANCIPATION
or Liberation Now

Even when traditional American history moves from pure myth toward a semblance of reality, admitting, for example, the injustice of slavery as a legal institution or the long denial of women's voting rights, the supposed "correction" of such injustices becomes the ingredient for constructing a new myth. So black and white schoolchildren today continue to receive the instruction that President Abraham Lincoln did away with the injustice of slavery with the signing of the Emancipation Proclamation, September 22, 1862, and that women were given their equal rights with the ratification of the Nineteenth Amendment to the United States Constitution in time for women to vote in the 1920 national elections.

Dictionary definitions make "emancipation" synony-

mous with "liberation," and that equation is the heart
of the myth. Neither "freedom" nor "liberation" resulted from the emancipatory acts of Congress regarding black folks and women, though slave testimony
indicates liberated expectations swept plantations in
the wake of the Emancipation Proclamation. "We was
free. Just like that, we was free," remembers one slave
quoted in B. A. Botkin's *Lay My Burden Down.* "We
knowed freedom was on us, but we didn't know what
was to come with it." Louisa Bowes Rose remembers,
"Daddy was down to the creek. He jumped right in
the water up to his neck. He was so happy he just
kept on scoopin' up handfulls of water and dumpin' it
on his head and yellin', 'I'se free! I'se free! I'se free!' "
And Fannie Berry recalls, "Niggers shoutin' and
clappin' hands and singin'! Chillun runnin' all over the
place beatin' time and yellin'! Everybody happy. Sho'
did some celebratin' . . ."

But when the truth of "emancipation" became clear,
former slave testimony and reaction took a different
turn. Another slave, Patsy Michener, uses an analogy
reminiscent of the Indian myth recited in Chapter II:
"Two snakes full of poison. One lying with his head
pointing north, the other with its head pointing south.
Their names was slavery and freedom. The snake
called slavery lay with his head pointed south and the
snake called freedom lay with his head pointed north.
Both bit the nigger and they was both bad."

Former slave Rhody Holsell questioned the strategy
of emancipation:

I believe it would have been better to have moved all the
colored people way out west to themselves. Abraham
Lincoln wanted to do this. It would have been better on
both races and they would not have mixed up. But the
white people did not want the "shade" taken out of the

country. Many of the bosses after the freedom couldn't stand it and went in the house and got a gun and blew out his brains. If Lincoln had lived, he would have separated us like they did the Indians. We would not have been slaughtered, burned, hanged, and killed if we had been put to ourselves and had our own laws. Many a person is now in torment because of this mixup. God give us a better principle and we could have had thousands of whites slaughtered, but we didn't after the freedom.

More bitter is the reaction of Thomas Hall, whose testimony was gathered by the Federal Writers' Project in 1938:

Lincoln got the praise for freeing us, but did he do it? He give us freedom without giving us any chance to live to ourselves and we still had to depend on the southern white man for work, food and clothing, and he held us out of necessity and want in a state of servitude but little better than slavery. Lincoln done but little for the Negro race and from a living standpoint, nothing. White folks are not going to do nothing for Negroes except keep them down. Harriet Beecher Stowe, the writer of *Uncle Tom's Cabin*, did that for her own good. She had her own interests at heart and I don't like her, Lincoln, or none of that crowd. The Yankees helped free us, so they say, but they let us be put back in slavery again.

When I think of slavery it makes me mad. I do not believe in giving you my story, 'cause with all the promises that have been made, the Negro is still in a bad way in the United States, no matter in what part he lives. It's all the same. Now you may be all right; there're a few white men who are, but the pressure is such from your white friends that you will be compelled to talk against us and give us the cold shoulder when you are around them, even if your heart is right towards us.

You are going around to get a story of slavery conditions and the persecutions of Negroes before the Civil War and the economic conditions concerning them since that war. You should have known before this late day all about that. Are you going to help us? No! You are only helping yourself. You say that my story may be put into a book, that you are from the Federal Writers' Project. Well, the Negro will not get anything out of it, no matter where you are from. Harriet Beecher Stowe wrote *Uncle Tom's Cabin.* I didn't like her book and I hate her. No matter where you are from I don't want you to write my story, 'cause the white folks have been and are now and always will be against the Negro.

THE GREAT EMANCIPATOR

In his excellent updated account of black resistance, *Look Out Whitey! Black Power's Goin' Get Your Mama,* Julius Lester explodes the myth of the Great Emancipator, Abraham Lincoln, in a single paragraph:

Blacks have no reason to feel grateful to Abraham Lincoln. Rather, they should be angry at him. After all, he came into office in 1861. How come it took him two whole years to free the slaves? His pen was sitting on his desk the whole time. All he had to do was get up one morning and say, "Doggonnit! I think I'm gon' free the slaves today. It just ain't right for folks to own other folks." It was that simple. Mr. Lincoln, however, like Mr. Kennedy (take your pick) and Mr. Eastland, moved politically, not morally. He said that if he could keep the Union together by maintaining slavery, he'd do it. If he had to free the slaves to keep the Union together, he'd do that, too. But he was in office to preserve the Union, not free the slaves. (Nowadays they say preserve law and order, not see that blacks get a little justice.)

Though Lester's observation captures the reality quite well, we should take a closer look at the opinions and actions of the Great Emancipator. First of all, the Emancipation Proclamation itself. It didn't free black folks per se, nor did it make any claim to having done so. The Emancipation Proclamation, put into effect January 1, 1863, applied only to the slaves in those states that had seceded from the Union—which left some 800,000 unaffected:

Now, therefore, I, Abraham Lincoln, President of the United States, by virtue of the power in me vested as Commander-in-Chief of the Army and Navy of the United States in time of actual armed rebellion against the authority and government of the United States, and as a fit and necessary war measure for suppressing said rebellion, do, on this 1st day of January, A.D. 1863, and in accordance with my purpose so to do, publicly proclaimed for the full period of one hundred days from the first day above mentioned, order and designate as the States and parts of States wherein the people thereof, respectively, are this day in rebellion against the United States the following, to wit:

Arkansas, Texas, Louisiana (except the parishes of St. Bernard, Plaquemines, Jefferson, St. John, St. Charles, St. James, Ascension, Assumption, Terrebonne, Lafourche, St. Mary, St. Martin, and Orleans, including the city of New Orleans), Mississippi, Alabama, Florida, Georgia, South Carolina, North Carolina and Virginia (except the forty-eight counties designated as West Virginia, and also the counties of Berkeley, Accomac, Northhamption, Elizabeth City, York, Princess Anne, and Norfolk, including the cities of Norfolk and Portsmouth), and which excepted parts are for the present left precisely as if this proclamation were not issued.

The Great Emancipator urged the newly released black folks to be nonviolent and leave the killing to white folks:

And by virtue of the power and for the purpose aforesaid, I do order and declare that all persons held as slaves within said designated States and parts of States are, and henceforward shall be, free; and that the Executive Government of the United States, including the military and naval authorities thereof, will recognize and maintain the freedom of said persons.

And I hereby enjoin upon the people so declared to be free to abstain from all violence, unless in necessary self-defense; and I recommend to them that, in all cases when allowed, they labor faithfully for reasonable wages.

To credit Abraham Lincoln with being the Great Emancipator, or the supreme abolitionist of his time, is pure myth. Many factors led to the Emancipation Proclamation, not the least of which was the factor that determines so many of America's decisions—military necessity. Abraham Lincoln never favored unconditional abolition, was always sensitive to the interests of the South, did not hate slaveholders—though he was absolutely opposed to slavery spreading into the territories—and was at best a "reluctant" emancipator reacting to the Northern abolitionist pressures because of the sensitivities of the office he held.

Regarding the difference between Northern abolitionists and Southern slaveholders, Lincoln suggested that if New England had proved to be the best place to raise cotton, slavery would have existed there. Or if Northerners had lived instead in the South, they too would have gone along with slavery.

Lincoln made his own position concerning the institution of slavery quite clear in his reply to abolitionist Horace Greeley, who had written an open letter to the President entitled "The Prayer of Twenty Millions," published in the New York *Tribune,* August 19, 1862. Greeley suggested:

Had you, sir, in your Inaugural Address, unmistakably given notice that, in case the Rebellion already commenced were persisted in, and your efforts to preserve the Union and enforce the laws should be resisted by armed force, *you would recognize no loyal person as rightfully held in Slavery by a traitor,* we believe the Rebellion would therein have received a staggering if not fatal blow.

Then Greeley reminded his President of some Civil War facts:

The Rebels are everywhere using the late anti-negro riots in the North, as they have long used your officers' treatment of negroes in the South, to convince the slaves that they have nothing to hope from a Union success—that we mean in that case to sell them into a bitterer bondage to defray the cost of the war. Let them impress this as a truth on the great mass of their ignorant and credulous bondmen, and the Union will never be restored—never. We cannot conquer Ten Millions of People united in solid phalanx against us, powerfully aided by Northern sympathizers and European allies. We must have scouts, guides, spies, cooks, teamsters, diggers and choppers from the blacks of the South, whether we allow them to fight for us or not, or we shall be baffled and repelled.

Lincoln replied in a letter to the newspaper on August 22, 1862:

I would save the Union. I would save it the shortest way under the Constitution. The sooner the national authority can be restored, the nearer the Union will be the Union as it was. If there be those who would not save the Union, unless they could at the same time save slavery, I do not agree with them. If there be those who would not save the Union, unless they could at the same time destroy slavery, I do not agree with them.

My paramount object is to save the Union, and not either to save or destroy slavery. If I could save the Union without freeing any slaves, I would do it; and if I could save it by freeing all slaves, I would do it; and if I could save it by freeing some and leaving others alone, I would also do that. What I do about slavery and the colored race, I do because I believe it helps to save this Union, and what I forbear, I forbear because I do not believe it would help to save the Union.

I shall do less whenever I shall believe I am doing hurt to the cause, and I shall do more whenever I believe more will help the cause. I shall try to correct errors when shown to be errors, and I shall adopt new views as fast as they shall appear to be true views. I have here stated my purpose according to my view of official duty, and I intend no modification of my oft-expressed personal wish that all men everywhere could be free.

Greeley was asking President Lincoln to make a blanket application of the Confiscation Bill (July 17, 1862), a bill "to suppress insurrection, to punish treason and rebellion, to seize and confiscate the property of rebels," of which slaves were a part. On July 22, Secretary of War Edwin M. Stanton issues the executive order of the President:

That military commanders within the States of Virginia, South Carolina, Georgia, Florida, Alabama, Mississippi, Louisiana, Texas and Arkansas, in an orderly manner, seize and use any property, real or personal, which may be necessary or convenient for their several commands, for supplies or for other purposes, and that while property may be destroyed for proper military objects, none shall be destroyed in wantonness or violence.

That military and naval commanders shall employ as laborers, within and from said States, so many persons of African descent as can be advantageously used for Military or naval purposes, giving them reasonable wages for their labor.

That as to both property and persons of African descent, accounts shall be kept sufficiently accurate and in detail to show quantities and amounts, and from who both such property and such persons have come, as a basis upon which compensation can be made in proper cases, and the several Departments of this Government shall attend to and perform their appropriate parts towards the execution of these orders.

Blacks began to meet the Union troops in large numbers, effecting what was a general work strike. Without black labor in the fields, it would be extremely difficult to feed Confederate troops. The Committee of the American Freedman's Union Commission described the phenomenon: "Imagine, if you will a slave population . . . coming garbed in rags or in silks, with feet shod or bleeding, individually or in families and larger groups,—an army of slaves and fugitives. . . . The arrival among us of these hordes was like the oncoming of cities."

"It was," said W. E. B. Du Bois, "a general strike that involved directly in the end perhaps a half a million people." Early Union practice during the Civil War was not to interfere with slaveholders and their property. Union officers returned runaway slaves to their masters. On the Fourth of July 1861, Colonel Pryor of Ohio delivered a speech to the people of Virginia saying,

I desire to assure you that the relation of master and servant as recognized in your state shall be respected. Your authority over that species of property shall not in the least be interfered with. To this end, I assure you that those under my command have pre-emptory orders to take up and hold any Negroes found running about the camp without passes from their masters.

But the black work stoppage changed all that and made the Union armies emancipators even before their Commander-in-Chief was ready to draft and release his Proclamation. Thus Du Bois explained:

The North started out with the idea of fighting the war without touching slavery. They faced the fact, after severe fighting, that Negroes seemed a valuable asset as laborers, and they therefore declared them "contraband of war" (property belonging to the enemy and valuable to the invader). It was but a step from that to attract and induce black labor to help the Northern armies. Slaves were urged and invited into Northern armies; they became military laborers and spies; not simply military laborers, but laborers on the plantations, where the crops went to help the Federal army or were sold North. Thus where Northern armies appeared, Negro laborers came, and the North found itself actually freeing slaves before it had the slightest intention of doing so, indeed when it had every intention not to.

The Emancipation Proclamation, then, was a wartime measure, issued in the midst of a difficult war. Antidraft riots (which featured the lynching of black folks) by white folks in the Northern cities necessitated the enlistment of black fighting men. War Department records show that there were 178,595 blacks regularly enlisted in the Union army, 36 per cent of the free black population, taking part in over four hundred military engagements during the Civil War. Add to that the large numbers of blacks in direct support of the Union army and the figure soars to a million. There is no doubt that the large number of blacks with access to arms was a determining factor in the Union's successful termination of the rebellion.

Europe was posing a problem with possible interference. Some sentiment in England favored recognizing the South as an independent nation, and warships were being prepared for Confederate use. An antislavery declaration was needed to swing British public opinion strongly in favor of the Union and to ward off British interference. And abolitionist pressure was demanding a clear antislavery issue as a rallying point against the South. Only as a wartime measure did the Emancipation Proclamation make sense anyway. No President can declare the Constitution null and void, and Abraham Lincoln knew that. However, in an existing state of war the President can declare emergency measures, even if they are unconstitutional. Such measures cannot remain in effect longer than the state of war. Permanent abolition of slavery, of course, required constitutional amendment.

All of thsee factors were being batted back and forth in Lincoln's mind as he decided whether or not to become the "Great Emancipator." A delegation representing a public meeting of "Christians of all denominations," held in Chicago, Sunday, September 7, 1862, met with President Lincoln on September 11, urging national emancipation. Lincoln asked the delegation:

What good would a proclamation of emancipation from me do, especially as we are now situated? I do not wish to issue a document that the whole world will see must be inoperative, like the Pope's bull against the comet! Would *my word* free the slaves when I can not even enforce the Constitution in the rebel states? Is there a single court, or magistrate, or individual that would be influenced by it there? And what reason is there to think it would have any greater effect upon the slaves than the late law of Congress, which I approved, and which offers protection and freedom to the slaves of rebel masters who come within our lines? . . . And suppose they could be induced by a proclamation of freedom from me to throw themselves upon us, *what should we do with them?* How could we feed and care for such a multitude? General Butler wrote me, a few days since, that he was issuing more rations to the slaves who have rushed to him, than to all the white troops under his command. They *eat,* and that is all;

though it is true General Butler is feeding the whites also, by the thousand; for it nearly amounts to a famine there. . . . Understand, I raise no objection against it, on legal or constitutional grounds; for as commander-in-chief of the army and navy, in time of war, I suppose I have a right to take any measure which may best subdue the enemy. Nor do I urge objections of a moral nature, in view of possible consequences of insurrection and massacre at the South. I view the matter as a practical war measure, to be decided upon according to the advantages or disadvantages it may offer to the suppression of the rebellion.

The delegation reminded President Lincoln "that when the proclamation should become widely known [as the law of Congress has not been] it would withdraw the slaves from the rebels, leaving them without laborers, and giving us both laborers and soldiers." They further insisted that General Butler's difficulties were the inevitable result of "half way measures."

Abraham Lincoln summed up the meeting in these words:

I admit that slavery is the root of the rebellion, or at least its *sine qua non*. The ambition of politicians may have instigated them to act, but they would have been impotent without slavery as their instrument. I will also concede that emancipation would help us in Europe and convince them that we are incited by something more than ambition. I grant further that it would help *somewhat* at the North, though not so much, I fear, as you and those you represent imagine. Still, some additional strength would be added in that way to the war. And then unquestionably it would weaken the rebels by drawing off their laborers which is of great importance; but I am not so sure we could do much with the blacks. If we were to arm them, I fear that in a few weeks the arms would be in the hands of the rebels; and indeed thus far we have not had arms enough to equip our white troops. I will mention another thing, though I meet only your scorn and contempt. There are fifty thousand bayonets in the Union armies from the Border Slave States. It would be a serious matter, if, in consequence of such a proclamation as you desire, they should go over to the rebels. I do not think they all would—not so many indeed as a year ago, or as six months ago—not so many to-day as yesterday. Every day increases their Union feeling. They are also getting their pride enlisted, and want to beat the rebels. Let me say one thing more: I think you should admit that we already have an important principle to rally and unite the people in the fact that constitutional government is at stake. This is a fundamental idea, going down about as deep as anything.

Eleven days later Abraham Lincoln wrote the Emancipation Proclamation, which was issued the first of the following year. He proved to be a man of his word. Lincoln did exactly what he told Horace Greeley he might do—free some slaves and leave others untouched. And of course in reality he didn't free any slaves at all. Those slaves who were in the Union, over whom he had immediate authority, Lincoln did not free, as his abovementioned "Border State" concerns prevailed. Those slaves he did declare to be free were the property of the rebel states over whom Lincoln did not have immediate authority. The North had to defeat the South in battle before such authority would be restored. But then the war would be over, and an emergency measure would not be in effect; thus, the whole issue became a matter of constitutional amendment.

A month before the Emancipation Proclamation became effective, Abraham Lincoln proposed constitutional amendments in his annual message to Congress, December 1, 1862. Lincoln's plan involved compensation to slaveholders from government funds, and relocation of black people "on the continent or elsewhere," also with government funds. Lincoln had long been intrigued with the idea of sending black folks back to Africa (or *to* Africa, since most of them were at least a generation removed from their native soil). Or sending them to any other convenient place, for that matter.

On April 16, 1862, an act abolishing slavery in the District of Columbia was approved by Abraham Lincoln. Said Lincoln: "I have ever desired to see the National Capital freed from the institution in some satisfactory way." Section XI of the act designated

That the sum of one hundred thousand dollars, out of any money in the treasury not otherwise appropriated, is hereby appropriated, to be expended under the direction of the President of the United States, to aid in the colonization and settlement of such free persons of African descent now residing in said District, including those to be liberated by this act, as may desire to emigrate to the Republics of Hayti or Liberia, or such other country beyond the limits of the United States as the President may determine; *Provided*, The expenditure for this purpose shall not exceed one hundred dollars for each emigrant.

Thus the law that "emancipated" slaves in Washington, D.C., immediately encouraged them to get out. Life for "free" blacks in Washington was designed to encourage them to want to leave. When Lincoln was assassinated, the Washington City Council ordered that blacks be excluded from the funeral procession. The Assistant Secretary of War interceded on their behalf, so a quota was set on the number of blacks officially allowed to mourn their departed Emancipator. Even that was better than New York City, where city officials refused to permit any black men to walk in the funeral procession for Lincoln there.

Thursday afternoon, July 14, 1862, President Lincoln gave audience at the White House to a "committee of colored men." The President informed his guests that a sum of money had been placed at his disposal by Congress for the purpose of colonizing people of African descent, "or a portion of them," in some other country, "making it his duty as it had long been his inclination to favor that cause."

Why [asked the President] should the people of your race be colonized? Why should they leave this country? . . . You and we are different races. We have between us a broader difference than exists between almost any other two races. Whether it is right or wrong, I need not discuss, but this physical difference is a great disadvantage to us both, as I think your race suffers very greatly, many of them, by living among us, while ours suffers from your presence. In a word, we suffer on each side. If this is admitted, it affords a reason at least why we should be separated.

President Lincoln urged his "colored" delegation to take the initiative in getting out for the good of white and black folks, even though they might not want to go. Lincoln's suggested colonization site was in Central America. Lincoln urged:

I suppose one of the principal difficulties in the way of colonization is that the free colored man can not see that his comfort would be advanced by it. You may believe you can live in Washington or elsewhere in the United States the remainder of your lives, perhaps more so than you can in any foreign country, and thence you may come to the conclusion that you have nothing to do with the idea of going to a foreign country. This is (I speak in no unkind sense) an extremely selfish view of the case.

There is an unwillingness on the part of our people, harsh as it may be, for you free colored people to remain with us. Now, if you could give a start to white people, you would open a wide door for many to be made free. If we deal with those who are not free at the beginning, and whose intellects are clouded by slavery, we have very poor materials to start with. If intelligent colored men, such as are before me, would move in this matter, much might be accomplished. It is exceedingly important that we have men at the beginning capable of thinking as white men, and not those who have been systematically oppressed.

Lincoln even got in a sly dig blaming black folks for all the trouble in the land:

See our present condition—the country engaged in war; our white men cutting one another's throats, none knowing how far it will extend, and then consider what we know to be the truth. But for your race among us there could not be war, although many men engaged on either side do not care for you one way or the other. Nevertheless, I repeat without the institution of slavery and the colored race as a basis the war could not have an existence.

The "colored" delegation said they would think about the President's suggestion and give him an answer "in a short time." Frederick Douglass, as always, had a nitty-gritty reply on the tip of his tongue:

A horse thief pleading that the existence of the horse is the apology for his theft or a highway man contending that the money in the traveller's pocket is the sole first cause of his robbery are about as much entitled to respect as is the President's reasoning at this point. No, Mr. President, it is not the innocent horse that makes the horse thief, nor the traveller's purse that makes the highway robber, and it is not the presence of the Negro that causes this foul and unnatural war, but the cruel and brutal cupidity of those who wish to possess horses, money and Negroes by means of theft, robbery, and rebellion.

But Abraham Lincoln was very slow to give up on the idea of voluntary black deportation. When the Central America plan failed to materialize, he thought of black colonies in Texas and Florida. Haiti remained a strong possibility in the President's mind. In fact some four hundred blacks were taken to Haiti, but most of them died in a smallpox epidemic. Some blacks did go to Africa after the war and founded the Republic of Liberia. And in the same month of his assassination, April 1865, Lincoln was again corresponding with his old Union officer friend Benjamin Franklin Butler asking him to work out the logistics of shipping black folks to Haiti or Liberia. Butler wrote in reply: "Mr. President, I have gone carefully over my calculations as to the power of the country to export the Negroes of the South and I assure you that, using all your naval vessels and all the merchant marine fleet to cross the seas with safety, it will be impossible for you to transport to the nearest place . . . half as fast as Negro children will be born here."

Abraham Lincoln did not live to see the ratification of the Thirteenth Amendment to the United States Constitution, which abolished slavery officially; though the amendment did not include either compensation to slave owners or the relocation of blacks. Today the name of Abraham Lincoln is revered in America as the Great Emancipator, while the names of black groups and individuals advocating separatism, such as the Black Muslims, are reviled. But the Honorable Elijah Muhammad and Abraham Lincoln, though a century apart in history, are very close politically. Both men reject false notions of emancipation in the interest of true black liberation, and both consider separatism a necessary prerequisite.

That emancipation is no substitute for liberation

was witnessed almost immediately after the Civil War. Southern states began enacting "black codes" and "peonage" laws which in effect returned the freed slaves to the control of their former masters. Blacks were forced to work as hired farm hands and domestic servants or to face being arrested on charges of vagrancy. Vagrants were "bound out," rented as laborers, giving their employers the right to pay their fines in place of serving jail sentences. Blacks could not testify in court against white men and could serve as court witnesses only in cases involving other blacks.

With the former masters now the employers, Frederick Douglass summed up the situation: "The employers retained the power to starve them to death, and wherever this power is held, there is the power of slavery."

YOU'VE COME A LONG WAY, BABY?

Whenever the word "emancipation" appears in the pages of traditional American history books, the reader should always be suspicious. It is usually used as a cover to discourage any further thought of liberation. No clearer example in American history can be found than the so-called emancipation of women. It simply means women obtained their long overdue right to vote as a result of suffrage agitation in the late nineteenth and early twentieth centuries. The liberation of women has yet to be accomplished.

Women waged a courageous struggle against the injustice at the polling places of America, just as they have continued to engage in the struggle for justice and human dignity ever since. Today women of all ages swell the ranks of demonstrators against the war in Vietnam, they have become the backbone of the peace movement, and they cannot be accused of being in the struggle out of selfish interests. They do not face the immediate problem of being drafted. Yet they put themselves on the line because the cause is right, and they want to stand alongside men in protesting continued injustice.

Spending as much time as I do on college campuses all over the country, I am continually reminded of the second-class status of women. Almost every campus I visit has different dormitory regulations for women and men. Women have to abide by an 11 P.M. curfew. Men can stay out all night, which means male students can sneak into the library after hours on the night before a big test, if they happen to have a friend working at the library who can let them in. Yet male and female students take the same test together. Women do not get a 30 per cent headstart on each test.

Women come to college as students, not as women, and they should obviously be treated on an equal basis with men students. And if parental pressure is responsible for college curfews, if parents do not trust their sons and daughters to be treated equally as students on campus, they should keep them home and watch them themselves.

But discrimination against women on campus is merely a reflection of the discrimination that exists in society. Women work just as hard as men to earn their degrees, it takes them just as long to obtain a doctorate, yet they know in advance they will never make the same salaries as men holding the same degree. Women pay the same food prices as men; the same hospital fees, doctor bills, and rent. Obviously salaries should also be equal.

Marlene Dixon, writing in the December 1969 issue of *Ramparts* magazine, clearly demonstrates the salary inequity of working women, especially nonwhite working women. She says:

Women, regardless of race, are more disadvantaged than are men, including non-white men. White women earn $2600 less than white men and $1500 less than non-white men. The brunt of the inequality is carried by 2.5 million non-white women, 94 percent of whom are black. They earn $3800 less than white men, $1900 less than non-white men, and $1200 less than white women.

For further documentation of the deprivation and degradation of women, Marlene Dixon cites the decline in educational achievement at the very time when higher educational levels are demanded. She says:

In 1962 . . . while women constituted 53 percent of the graduating high school classes, only 42 percent of the entering college class were women. Only one in three people who received a B.A. or M.A. in that year was a woman, and only one in ten who received a Ph.D. was a woman. These figures represent a decline in educational achievement for women since the 1930's when women received two out of five of the B.A. and M.A. degrees given, and one out of seven of the Ph.Ds. While there has been a dramatic increase in the number of people, including women, who go to college, women have not kept pace with men in terms of educational achievement. Furthermore, women have lost ground in professional employment. In 1960 only 22 percent of the faculty and other professional staff at colleges and universities were women —down from 28 percent in 1949, 27 percent in 1930, 26 percent in 1920. 1960 does beat 1919 with only 20 percent—"you've come a long way baby"—right back to where you started! In other professional categories: 10 percent of all scientists are women, 7 percent of all physicians, 3 percent of all lawyers, and 1 percent of all engineers.

That 3 per cent figure in the lawyer category strikes home to me personally, as every time I appear in court and watch my attorney Jean Williams in action, I am once again reminded of the courtroom competence of women.

A recently published government study entitled *American Science Manpower 1968: A Report of the National Register of Scientific and Technical Personnel* gives ample documentation of salary discrimination in the field of science against women of equal scholastic standing with men. The 1968 figures show that roughly 9 per cent of the nation's registered scientists are women, which seems to be a drop of 1 per cent since 1960. The median annual income for the registered women scientists is $10,000. The median annual income for all scientists in $13,200. There is no special breakdown for the median annual income for male scientists, but since women were included in the "all scientists" category, obviously the median salary for men is higher than $13,200.

Government units came the closest to giving women a fair deal in salaries: $10,600 on the average compared with $11,200 for men. Nonprofit agencies such as foundations were farthest out of line with $10,000 versus $14,700. Industry was almost identical in salary sex discrimination to nonprofit agencies. And the report indicated disparities up to 35 per cent between salaries paid men and women with Ph.D. degrees.

Society's discrimination against women, placing them in the category of sex objects rather than individual human beings, begins at a very early age. Little kids are indoctrinated with society's sickness. An adult will ask a little boy: "What do you want to be when you grow up?" The same adult will turn to a little girl and say "Who's your boy friend?" It is a sick male-oriented society that will push sex that close to the cradle.

Then from the cradle to the grave society tells women that their role is to be pretty, feminine, and domestic and to stay behind their men. Multibillion-dollar cosmetic and fashion industries encourage the role, insisting that women wear lipstick, rouge, perfume, and other types of cosmetics, and wear pretty clothes. But such superficialities have nothing to do with a woman's stature as a full human being. I could wear all those things also, and it would not make me a woman.

Sexism and racism are closely allied, and both are the enemies of true human liberation. People are born into this world as human beings first and sexual beings second. The quality of a person's life determines whether a male will grow into the full stature of manhood or a woman will grow into the full stature of womanhood. Males and females can engage in sexual activities whether or not they ever reach the level of manhood and womanhood.

Sexism and racism are best symbolized by America's current confusion regarding the American flag, and pseudo-patriotic claims upon that flag indicate an opposition to true human liberation. Many Americans are upset at seeing the American flag treated with disrespect; burning it, tearing it, soiling it, or other forms of desecration. But what is a flag, after all, but a piece of cloth. Personally I have always had more respect for human beings than I have had for a piece of cloth. When all Americans grow to the full stature of manhood and womanhood, and learn to salute each other as *human beings,* that is the day *all* flags will be safe.

For such salutary behavior would indicate the dawn of a liberated America. An America in which Muham-

mad Ali could reign as heavyweight champion of the
world regardless of his religious or political beliefs. An
America where a man's religious beliefs are respected
regardless of the color of the believer. An America
where churches would *live* the gospel of Jesus Christ
rather than merely *preach* that word, where Felipe
Luciano and the Young Lords would not have to assume the burden, facing arrest and persecution, of in-
carnating the gospel the churches ignore. An America
where Cesar Chavez would be recognized as a saint and
a statesman rather than tormented as a rabblerouser
in the grape fields. In short, an America where patriotism is expanded beyond love of country to embrace
a love and devotion to worldwide humanity.

> "Religion and race define the next stage in the evolution of the American peoples. But the American nationality is still forming: its processes are mysterious, and the final form, if there is ever to be a final form, is as yet unknown."
>
> DANIEL PATRICK MOYNIHAN, 1963

> "The time may have come when the issue of race could benefit from a period of 'benign neglect.'"
>
> DANIEL PATRICK MOYNIHAN, 1970

IX

THE MYTH OF THE BOOTSTRAP
or The Melting Pot Boils Over

In the waiting room of the airline terminal in Newark, New Jersey, a city where over half the population is black, a sign over the shoeshine stand reads "BOOT-BLACK." All boots are not black, of course, nor is the polish used to shine them. But blacks are sometimes called "boots," and all of the young men shining shoes in the Newark terminal are black. So the sign seems to have racial connotations.

It is just one more reminder of the myth of the bootstrap. How does that particular myth run? Well, America is the land of opportunity. It is the great melting pot of the world. People come to these shores from every land at the invitation of the Statue of Liberty, who speaks for America's government and citizenry,

Thus the words of Emma Lazarus are enshrined on Miss Liberty herself:

> Give me your tired, your poor, your huddled masses
> yearning to breathe free;
> The wretched refuse of your teeming shore.
> Send these,
> The homeless, tempest tossed to me.
> I lift my lamp beside the Golden Shore.

Once these homeless, tempest-tossed folks land in America, go through the necessary immigration procedures and get settled, they are given the opportunity of their lives to prove what they are worth. If they are willing, the myth says, to work hard, engaging in honest, decent labor, they will melt in with the rest of America's already established citizenry and enjoy the unique freedom and benefits that accompany living in a democracy. Those who come to America should not except to be given handouts. They should pitch in and make it on their own, as everybody else in America has done; hence the phrase "pick yourself up by your own bootstraps."

The classic articulation of America as the caldron of democracy is found in the 1908 play by Israel Zangwill entitled *The Melting Pot*. In the play David Quixano, a Russian-Jewish immigrant who has escaped to New York City, exuberantly outlines the myth:

> America is God's Crucible, the great Melting Pot where all the races of Europe are melting and reforming! Here you stand, good folk, think I, when I see them at Ellis Island, here you stand in your fifty groups with your fifty languages and histories, and your fifty blood hatreds and rivalries, but you won't be long like that brothers, for these are the fires of God you've come to—these are the fires of God. A fig for your feuds and vendettas! German

and Frenchman, Irishman and Englishman, Jews and Russians—into the Crucible with you all! God is making the American. . . .

The real American has not yet arrived. He is only in the Crucible, I tell you—he will be the fusion of all the races, the coming superman.

The careful reader will notice a significant omission from that bubbling pot of freedom. The mixture is pure vanilla, and no pretense is made of adding chocolate. As a result, the melting pot is boiling over.

POT LUCK

Color is the crucial ingredient in the recipe for America's melting pot. If your pot luck has been to be born white, you can expect better treatment even when the country is gripped by the throes of hysteria. During World War II, after the Japanese attack on Pearl Harbor, West Coast Americans were living in fear of imminent invasion. Japanese submarines were being "seen" off the west coast of the United States with more frequency than flying saucers are sighted today. As a result, America really turned up the heat in her crucible. America dipped into her melting pot, pulled out everyone of Japanese ancestry, dried them off, and herded them into concentration camps. The whole ugly process is described in Morton Grodzins' book *Americans Betrayed*:

One hundred ten thousand Americans of Japanese ancestry were evacuated. Aliens and citizens, children and adults, male and female, were moved on short notice from their lifetime homes to concentration centers. No charges were ever filed against these persons and no guilt ever attributed to them. The test was ancestry applied with the greatest rigidity. Evacuation swept into guarded camps orphans, foster-children in white homes, Japanese married to caucasians, the offspring of Japanese ancestry, and American citizens with as little as one-sixteenth Japanese blood. Evacuation was not carried out by lawless vigilantes or by excited local officials. The program was instituted and executed by military forces of the U.S. with a full mandate of power from both the executive and the legislative branches of the national government.

One military leader, General DeWitt, testifying before a subcommittee hearing of the House Naval Affairs Committee, April 13, 1943, sounded as though he felt the melting pot experiment had been a big mistake with regard to Orientals. Said the General (echoing the sentiments of General Custer before him):

I don't want any of them [Japanese] here. They are a dangerous element. . . . It makes no difference whether he is an American citizen, he is still a Japanese. American citizenship does not necessarily determine loyalty. You need not worry about the Italians at all except in certain cases. Also, the same for the Germans except in individual cases. But we must worry about the Japanese all the time until he is wiped off the map.

This type of thinking spawned the McCarran Act, which has been on the books since 1950 and at the time of this writing is still the law of the land. Title II, Section 100, of the McCarran Act provides that under certain conditions, the President may, on his own judgment, proclaim the existence of a "national internal security emergency" throughout the land. He can do so if: there is a declaration of war by Congress; there is an "insurrection" within the United States; there is an "imminent invasion" of the United States or any of its possessions. Upon doing so, the President's political appointee, the Attorney General, is required immediately to "apprehend and detain *any person* as to whom there is reasonable ground to believe that such person *probably* will engage in, or *probably* will conspire with others to engage in acts of espionage or of sabotage." The emphases are in the original wording of the Act itself. About a million dollars has been spent to establish internment camps (in Allenwood, Pennsylvania; Avon Park, Florida; Wittenburg and Florence, Arizona; El Reno, Oklahoma; and Tule Lake, California) just in case a President comes along who decides to implement the McCarran Act.

Concentration camps in America are the symbols of the fallacy of the melting-pot myth. The American recipe is still very conscious of the color of the ingredients. Obviously Japanese-Americans were pulled out of the melting pot for a cruel form of preferential treatment because they were *nonwhite*. After all, America was also at war with white Europeans during World War II, specifically Germans and Italians. And it is not as though the Germans in America were behaving themselves. Dating from the 1930's, some German-Americans and German aliens living in the United States had organized chapters of the German-American Bund, an organization which openly proclaimed loyalty to Germany and Adolf Hitler, sang the Nazi rallying "Horst Wessel Song" and the national anthem "Deutschland Über Alles," and gave the Nazi salute. In spite of such grounds for suspicion, German-Americans were not herded off to concentration camps. And all the while America was rounding up Japanese-Americans, she was telling the world how inhumane Hitler was for placing Jews in concentration camps!

America continues to display reactions today which indicate a belief in Hitler's doctrine of Nazi superiority. Not long ago in Chicago, Illinois, police raided the headquarters of the racist-oriented American Nazi party.

Police said they had been keeping the Nazis under surveillance for more than three weeks. The raid netted rifles, shotguns, twelve thousand rounds of ammunition, swords, bayonets, photos of Adolf Hitler, and hate-filled literature.

It was an orderly raid, conducted in broad daylight. Five white men were arrested and were not harmed in the process. A few months earlier the Chicago police had conducted another raid. That raid took place in the early morning hours, under the cover of darkness. Police broke into an apartment and did not hesitate for a moment to fire their guns repeatedly. After the raid was over, Illinois Black Panther Chairman Fred Hampton and Defense Captain Mark Clark lay dead. So it is safer to be a white Nazi in this country that defeated Hitler than it is to be a black American.

It is a sad day for the melting-pot image when black Americans must realize that America will show more respect and consideration for her enemies than she does for her own black children. A white German who fought in World War II as a Nazi storm trooper could come to America today and move into a neighborhood that would not accept a black American who fought in the same war *against* the Nazi storm trooper. And America's enemies treat black Americans with more equality than they receive at home. If a white American soldier and a black American soldier are fighting side by side, and they are both killed, the enemy will kick both dead bodies into a ditch without making a color distinction. They will be viewed merely as two dead American enemies. Yet if those two dead bodies were shipped home to America, there are cemeteries in this country where they could not be buried side by side. And if the white American soldier and the black American soldier survive the war, they cannot live together at home even though they can fight together abroad. It is a sad realization that a black American is granted more equality as a dead casualty in a foreign war than as a live citizen at home.

Zangwill's play is correct in one respect. The "fires of God" are indeed smoldering in America. But those fires are as apt to be flames of judgment as heat applied in the refining process of creating the real American. Two alternatives face America. She can either become the *true* melting pot, where *all* Americans are melted together and refined according to the principles of justice, equality, freedom, human dignity, and liberation. Or she can acquiesce in the other alternative. Someone from the outside will throw America into a pot. And the country will be cooked. Americans must come up with a new recipe or cook together in destruction. Or, to paraphrase a famous sentiment voiced by Benjamin Franklin: "We must, indeed, all melt together, or most assuredly we shall all cook separately."

THE DOUBLE STANDARD

During the summer of 1967 the American melting pot reached a rapid boil. Some 150 American cities experienced disorders in black, and in some cases Puerto Rican, ghettos. President Lyndon Johnson appointed a blue ribbon panel, headed by Governor Otto Kerner of Illinois and Mayor John V. Lindsay of New York City, to find out what was happening. Why had black folks become rioters and looters?

It was not as though the melting pot had not boiled rapidly before. America had experienced riots and civil disorders since prerevolutionary days. A particularly hot riot period occurred during the 1840's, the 1850's, and the 1860's. Hardest hit were the cities on the east coast. Baltimore had twelve riots, Philadelphia (the City of Brotherly Love) had eleven, New York City had eight, and Boston had four. Rioting occurred for all sorts of reasons: labor riots, election riots, antiabolitionist riots, anti-"Negro" riots, anti-Catholic riots, and riots involving inflamed volunteer firemen.

During the 1860's anti-Civil War draft riots took place which make today's demonstrations against the war in Vietnam look like games at a Sunday School picnic by comparison. For five days in July 1863, New York City was the scene of the bloodiest rioting in American history. "East side, west side, all around the town," white folks poured out into the streets killing police and soldiers, burning buildings and looting stores, hanging, burning, beating, and killing any black folks unlucky enough to be found outside. The enraged mob even broke into a black orphans' home looking for little kids to kill. Most of the children had escaped. But the mob found one frightened little black girl hiding under her bed and promptly killed her.

In James McCague's book *The Second Rebellion* an eyewitness to the rioting reports: "Boys went through the streets, flourishing and firing off pistols, men brandished guns, and mad and hoarse with passion and bad spirits, cursed and swore and threatened everyone disagreeing with them in their excesses. Some threatened to kill every 'Black-Republican-nigger-worshiping s—— of a b——,' and burn their houses."

McCague describes the crazed white mob in action:

Several Negroes were chased to the roof of a building. Their pursuers put the torch to it and waited, howling in insane glee while flames drove the poor fugitives to the eaves, then over the eaves, and at last burned their hands so they could hang on no longer. One by one they fell to the ground and the crowd flung itself on them, stamping and clubbing, and so they died.

. . . The area was a slum with a large population of Negroes. Many had fled. . . . But William Jones had not fled. He stole out, early in the morning that still was warm and muggy after the storm, to buy a loaf of bread for breakfast. And a mob of prowling troublemakers caught him. Someone threw a rope around his neck. Someone else tossed its end over a handy tree limb. Eager hands took hold and heaved away. The women were the worst: over and over again that would be the story told by shocked witnesses of the rioting. A fire was lighted beneath the dying man and they capered around it, shrieking as they pelted the body with stones and sticks and clods. Tiring of that, the mob went on. . . . It was said that they [the police] found his charred loaf of bread still clutched under one arm.

In 1877 a nationwide railroad strike, which began along the Baltimore and Ohio Railroad and spread to the Far West, spurred a series of riots, and great sections of Pittsburgh were left in smoking ruins. The modern urban police system was created in response to the riots of the 1830's, the 1840's, and the 1850's, and the present National Guard system was developed in response to the uprisings of 1877. It is little wonder the police-community relations are so frayed today, since modern urban police systems were developed after communities had already broken down, and are designed to keep those communities under control rather than to help them grow and mature.

So the melting pot had been boiling for quite some time, and, with the exception of riots in Harlem (New York City) in 1935 and 1943, white folks had always been the aggressors and black folks had provided the list of casualties. When white folks were doing the rioting, considerable death and killing resulted. During the uprisings of 1967, where black initiative was displayed, concentration was upon destruction of property rather than of white lives. So a blue ribbon panel was obviously necessary to try to understand why *anyone* would place more value on human life than on property.

The Report of the National Advisory Commission on Civil Disorders, commonly called the "Kerner Report," came up with some answers and some suggested solutions. The Kerner Report recognized that the image of the melting pot has always been a myth with regard to black folks. Once that myth is exploded, all of white America's favorite clichés with regard to black folks are destroyed with it. A few excerpts from the Kerner Report will indicate the double standard applied to white and black America:

When the European immigrants were arriving in large numbers, America was becoming an urban-industrial society. To build its major cities and industries, America needed great pools of unskilled labor. The immigrants provided the labor, gained an economic foothold, and thereby enabled their children and grandchildren to move up to skilled, white collar, and professional employment.

Since World War II, especially, America's urban-industrial society has matured; unskilled labor is far less essential than before, and blue-collar jobs of all kinds are decreasing in number and importance as a source of new employment. The Negroes who migrated to the great urban centers lacked the skills essential to the new economy; and the schools of the ghetto have been unable to provide the education that can qualify them for decent jobs. The Negro migrant, unlike the immigrant, found little opportunity in the city; he had arrived too late, and the unskilled labor he had to offer was no longer needed.

... Well before the high tide of immigration from overseas, Negroes were already relegated to poorly paid, low status occupations. Had it not been for racial discrimination, the North might well have recruited Southern Negroes after the Civil War to provide the labor for building the burgeoning urban-industrial economy. Instead, Northern employers looked to Europe for their sources of unskilled labor. Upon the arrival of the immigrants, the Negroes were dislodged from the few urban occupations they had dominated. Not until World War II were Negroes generally hired for industrial jobs, and by that time the decline in the need for unskilled labor had already begun. European immigrants, too, suffered from discrimination, but never was it so pervasive as the prejudice against color in America, which has formed a bar to advancement unlike any other.

Today, whites tend to exaggerate how well and how quickly they escaped from poverty, and contrast their experience with poverty-stricken Negroes. The fact is, among many of the Southern and Eastern Europeans who came to America in the last great wave of immigration, those who came already urbanized were the first to escape from poverty. The others who came to America from rural backgrounds, as Negroes did, are only now, after three generations, in the final stages of escaping from poverty. . . .

. . . their [Negroes'] escape from poverty has been blocked in part by the resistance of the European ethnic groups; they have been unable to enter some unions and to move into some neighborhoods outside the ghetto because descendants of the European immigrants who control these unions and neighborhoods have not yet abandoned them for middle-class occupations and areas. . . .

. . . The immigrant who labored long hours at hard and often menial work had the hope of a better future, if not for himself then for his children. This was the promise of the "American dream"—the society offered to all a future that was open-ended; with hard work and perseverance, a man and his family could in time achieve not only material well-being but "position" and status.

So the Kerner Report indicated that, instead of a melting pot, America is really a crucible of white racism. A double standard, whch is clearly based upon a white and nonwhite distinction, pervades America. And the clichés which flow so easily from the lips of whites to the ears of blacks are formulated by a white racist mentality.

"Why don't you stop all this rioting, looting and burning and pick yourselves up by your own bootstraps?" white America asks black folks. Black folks should quickly answer, "Why don't you give us some boots with some zippers on them?" White America is forever telling black folks to grab their own boots, but white America always wants to control the shoe allotment.

Not long ago in Washington, D.C., Mrs. Richard Nixon sipped tea with several hundred members of the Congressional Wives Club. Outside, guests' cars were double-parked. The social event happened to be taking place across the street from Pride, Inc., a black youth organization led by Marion Barry which is really trying to do something concrete about the business of picking folks up by their own bootstraps. Yet every day police discourage the bootstrap efforts of the Pride workers who, in a hurry, happen to double-park outside their offices and are immediately ticketed. No tickets were written across the street for the Congressional Wives.

Marion Barry went to the party and told Mrs. Winston Prouty, wife of the Republican Senator from Vermont, "If you can do it, we want to do it too!"—meaning, of course, double-park. Mrs. Prouty asked Barry why he wanted to cause the good ladies all this grief. Then she stated a grievance of her own. She warned Barry that if he and his cohorts didn't behave a little bit better, some of the husbands of the disturbed wives might "think twice about [Pride] appropriations."

Pick yourself up by your own bootstraps, you see, but behave yourself while you are doing it. Otherwise white folks in control might snatch away the boots.

Then the clichés of white America proceed to explain to black folks why they are not quite ready to be trusted with boot-lacing responsibility. "Education is your problem," says white America to black folks. "Equal opportunity means equal responsibility, and you have to be educated to assume the responsibilities of freedom." But white America does not believe that cliché. If there were really a relationship between education and freedom, America would have her schoolteachers in Vietnam instead of her soldiers. And if education were really the key, the Jews would own this country!

"Not only are you black folks uneducated, but you are also culturally deprived," continues white America. That phrase "culturally deprived" is the current pet socialogical phrase in America and one more example of a white mentality which is forever analyzing black folks and applying a white rhetoric to that analysis.

I grew up in a black ghetto, and when I was five years old, I not only knew what a prostitute looked like, I had watched one turn a trick. At five years old I knew what the junkie, the dope pusher, the pimp, and the hustler looked like. That was my ghetto culture. After seeing all those things at five years old, my problem was I had *too much* culture. There are a lot of things wrong with the black ghetto, but cultural deprivation, as white folks understand it, is not one of them.

My overexposure to ghetto culture affected my ability to learn in school. In school the white mentality dictated the content of my textbooks. As a result I almost didn't learn how to read. After watching a prostitute at age five, the "Dick and Jane" first-grade reader just didn't interest me at six. I came to school without breakfast, hungry and hostile, and was told to read a story about little Jane feeding her dog. Later on in school I was given the story of *Black Beauty* to read. It was a story about a white girl kissing a horse, and I knew that same white girl wouldn't kiss me. What was supposed to be educational material was really hate literature for me.

One day I was given a problem in arithmetic class. The teacher said, "If Betty Jane had five apples and little Billy had seven, how many objects did they have?" I couldn't answer, and the teacher thought I must be stupid. But if the problem had been reworded to fit my ghetto culture, I could have easily answered. "If five junkies are standing on one corner and seven cops are standing across the street, how many folks are out there?"

Daniel Patrick Moynihan, counselor to the President with cabinet rank, has provided some new clichés for white America to apply to black America. His memo to President Nixon urging a policy of "benign neglect" concerning racial matters is one cliché. His earlier Moynihan Report spoke of the "matriarchal society" which pervaded the black ghettos in America, and it was widely accepted by white folks and some black folks. The new cliché suggested that one of the problems in the black community was that the black woman was stronger than the black man.

Such an observation only sounds plausible to white-indoctrinated ears. The black woman has never been *stronger* than the black man. When is the last time you heard of a black woman playing college football, let alone making All-American? Who was the last black female heavyweight champion of the world? The black woman in America has never been stronger than the black man. The black woman in the black ghetto has been more *responsible* than the black man. But the rhetoric of the white system has an aversion to applying the word "responsibility" to black womanhood, so the concept is changed to "strength."

The black woman has been the most responsible woman in this country over the years. And her responsibility has been necessary for black survival in a racist system. When the black man found an eight-hour job and each day he was subjected to the insult of being called "nigger," "coon," and "boy" and rubbed on the head for luck, his concept of manhood was destroyed. So when the black man left the job on Friday to return to the black ghetto with his week's pay in his pocket, on the way home he sought to recapture his lost manhood. He thought all the women he could have on the way home made him a man. He thought all the whisky he could drink, all the craps he could shoot, all the fights he could get into on his way home to his black woman made him a man.

So at two o'clock in the morning on payday night he ended up at his door drunk, broke, and hurt, all because of a false search for manhood brought on by a racist system. And when his black woman opened the door, the black man jumped on her and knocked her to the floor. Through her tears of hurt and understanding, the black woman said to her man, "Baby, the kids just went to bed." And the black man shouted with the assumed authority of wounded dignity, "What were they doing up so late!?" And his woman gently replied, "Honey, you know it's Friday night. They were waiting for you to bring something special home for dinner."

The black man confessed, painfully but confident that his woman would understand, "Baby, I'm sorry, but I'm broke." And the black woman got up off the floor, went into the kitchen, and took oatmeal out of the pantry. She cooked that breakfast food, not with *strength*, but with so much love and responsibility that when she woke the kids up and sat them down at the table to eat, they didn't know they were eating ordinary oatmeal, but thought that daddy had brought something special home for them. That is responsibility and not strength, and it has allowed black folks to survive a racist system; a system that has refused to allow black folks to share the American Dream and has erected every conceivable barrier to survival.

But black folks have survived. And black folks in America today are not asking white folks to do us any favors. We are asking them to do America some favors. As beautiful as the Kerner Report is on the whole, it still bears close scrutiny. The report suggests that to solve the problems of the black ghettos in America an expenditure of some fifty billion dollars is necessary. I hope white America has enough sense to recognize that fifty billion dollars will not solve the problems of the black ghettos.

To solve the problems of the black ghettos, America must first do something that will not require her to spend a nickel on black folks. For the first time in history America must create an atmosphere where black folks will trust white folks. The only way America can create such an atmosphere is to go up on the Indian reservation and free my red brother; to give my Puerto Rican brother his constitutional rights; to liberate my Mexican and Oriental brothers; and to free all women. And last, but not least, America must restore human dignity to my Jewish brother. The Jew in America deludes himself about his status in society. But he should paint his face as black as mine one day and come with me to hear what that gentile says about him every day. Then the Jew will recognize that he is in the same trick bag with the rest of us.

When America has liberated all our brothers and sisters of other ethnic origins, black folks will be able to say, "Yes, my white brother, come into my ghetto and *together* we will solve our problems." But if America is not willing to follow that pattern, black folks are telling America to keep her fifty billion dollars and spend it on the biggest guns money can buy. Beyond a shadow of a doubt America will need them.

> "All the ills of democracy can be cured by
> more democracy."
>
> ALFRED E. SMITH, 1937

> "We must be the great arsenal of democracy."
>
> FRANKLIN DELANO ROOSEVELT, 1940

X

THE MYTH OF THE GOOD NEIGHBOR

or Black Jack and Depreciation

In 1933, when the Cuban government was overthrown,
Sumner Welles contacted President Franklin D. Roosevelt from the Unied States embassy in Havana, asking
him to send a naval armada and suggesting the landing
of troops. FDR sent some thirty ships, but he would not
sanction even limited military intervention. Troubled by
his decision, the President sought the counsel of his Vice
President, John N. Garner. Garner told him not to
intervene. "But suppose they kill Americans?" FDR
worried. "Wait and see who the Americans are," Garner
replied.

Whether the exchange between FDR and his Vice
President was real or apocryphal, the statement attributed to Garner is the key to understanding the myth

of America as the "good neighbor." America is a good neighbor when such a stance keeps property values up in her worldwide neighborhood. But America's "good neighbor" myth is exploded in the eyes of the world as her treatment of neighbors at home is exposed.

Suppose I was a convicted child molester, and I moved next door to you after being released from jail. We might get along quite well as neighbors. We might be friendly, go out together socially, and have a good relationship. But if I came to you one day looking for a job as a baby-sitter for your children, you would naturally be reluctant to hire me. I might have been rehabilitated and completely cured of molestation tendencies, but you would still be reluctant to trust me with your children because you knew my past record. And nothing I could say would convince you otherwise.

America has a record of molesting her children which has long been exposed to public view. It begins with the inhumane institution of slavery and continues through countless lynchings and murders of black people. It includes gunning civil rights workers down in the streets and shooting peace demonstrators on college campuses. It is a violent record which contradicts all the sweet-sounding rhetoric of freedom and democracy. It is only natural that countries all over the world, even though they recognize America as a neighbor, know her record of past molestation of her own children and do not want America "baby-sitting" for their freedom.

On December 2, 1823, President James Monroe made certain statements in his annual message which have since been elevated to form the Monroe Doctrine. That Doctrine established the United States more as the Big Brother than the Good Neighbor of the American continents:

... the American continents, by the free and independent condition which they have assumed and maintain, are henceforth not to be considered as subjects for future colonization by any European powers.

The political system of the allied powers is essentially different ... from that of America ... we should consider any attempt on their part to extend their system to any portion of this hemisphere as dangerous to our peace and safety. With the existing colonies or dependencies of any European power we have not interfered and shall not interfere.

In the wars of the European powers in matters relating to themselves we have never taken any part, nor does it comport with our policy so to do.

Thus the Monroe Doctrine issued a clear warning to Europe not to colonize in the Americas, but it left the door open for Big Brother to colonize in his own neighborhood. As so often happens among siblings, Big Brother assumed protection and control even when Little Brother did not ask for it. Isidro Fabela in *Las Doctrinas Monroe y Drago,* calls the Monroe Doctrine "a political opinion, the public expression of a desire which does not imply a doctrine; for the North American people it is a counsel, for the Latin Americans a protection not asked for and not even based on consultation with them."

The Monroe Doctrine, influenced by Secretary of State John Quincy Adams, was really a way of establishing the United States as an independent power in the eyes of the world unencumbered by an alliance with Great Britain. In the wake of the Napoleonic era the United States was apprehensive on a number of fronts. Czar Alexander I of Russia might want to claim the northwestern coast of North America. Spain, bolstered by the strength of France, might want to reconquer Latin America. British Prime Minister George Canning played upon United States apprehensions and suggested that Great Britain and the United States team up to tell France to keep its hands off Latin America.

John Quincy Adams seemed to feel that America was a grown child now, did not need momma Britain any longer, and could act alone. To Prime Minister Canning he said, "We proposed to your government to join us some time ago, but they would not, and now we shall see whether you will be content to follow us!" Canning's proposal had stipulated that England "aimed at the possession of no portion of the colonies for herself." Adams did not want the United States to be limited by such a self-denying statement—just in case the opportunity for annexing Cuba or some other Latin American territories might present itself at some future date.

Thus the United States emerged as the independent power of the Americas, bold and strong enough to issue hands-off warnings to the rest of the world—a stance she steadfastly maintains today. Yet even though the United States was saying "hands off" to others, she has always had itchy fingers herself.

By the time the Franklin Roosevelt administration rolled around, with its Good Neighbor policy toward Latin America, wealthy United States families had established a strong enough commercial foothold south of the border to make plausible Vice President Garner's words, "Wait and see who the Americans are." The arrogance of the northern "good neighbor" was highlighted during President Nixon's administration when New York Governor Nelson Rockefeller was appointed to represent the United States on a fact-finding tour through Latin America. Everywhere the Governor went, his motorcade was hounded by Latin American students and young folks. They knew that if it were not for the Rockefellers and their Standard Oil interests, the entire Third World could breathe easier and taste the fruits of freedom and self-determination.

America must realize that her credibility as "good neighbor" of the world will *never* be established until she cleans up neighborhood activities at home. The phrase "making the world safe for democracy" echoes abroad with a particularly hollow ring as long as America's brand of democracy continues to breed so much dissatisfaction and civil turmoil within her own shores. Any objective, neutral outside observer would never be able to reconcile the American rhetoric of making the world safe with daily American newspaper accounts reporting that the streets of American cities are unsafe; the air Americans breathe is unsafe; the water in America is unsafe for drinking and bathing; and holding unpopular political beliefs is increasingly unsafe. It is like having a safety patrolman who helps little kids to cross the street but does not have the sense of coordination to avoid being hit by a car when he tries to cross the street himself.

Consider an America that claims to be a "good neighbor" of Latin America yet has permitted the neighborhood activity in the grape fields of California which has oppressed, degraded, and dehumanized Mexican-American grape workers. And when those grape workers banded together in their struggle for human dignity—a struggle now close to triumph—organizing a strike in those vineyards of oppression, the Nixon administration responded by purchasing grapes of wrath: eighty-nine million dollars' worth of grapes to be shipped to Vietnam—four pounds of grapes per soldier—thus piling oppression on top of oppression. If such arrogant governmental disregard for human dignity forces the grape workers to blow up the vineyards to be heard, perhaps President Nixon can sell the dirt to underdevolped nations.

Consider an America that spends billions of dollars and invests millions of young American lives to make Indochina safe for democracy, while supporting and fighting alongside a military dictatorship in South Vietnam. A government that holds "free" elections and after the votes have been counted imprisons a losing candidate. A government that allows one of its "peace officers" to place a gun to the side of the head of a suspected Vietcong in the streets of downtown Saigon, pull the trigger, and blow the suspect's brains out.

Consider an America whose supposed love for democracy allowed her to stand by and watch democracy fall in Greece and eventually to support the new dictatorial regime.

So the nations of the world are taking a second look at the desirability of including "good neighbor" America in the worldwide neighborhood. She might depreciate moral properties.

THE NEW DEAL

The Franklin Roosevelt administration, which spawned the name Good Neighbor policy, attempted to change some neighborhood activities at home. Roosevelt's New Deal was not so much a new game of cards as it was a reshuffling of the old American deck which had always been stacked against certain players—especially the workingman, the farmer, and the small shopkeeper. It was still a white folks' game, and no attempt was made to shift from "strip poker" to "black jack." No specific New Deal legislation appeared on behalf of black folks. But in the process of helping white folks, the New Deal did help *some* black folks.

Though Roosevelt was called everything from a fascist to a communist during his lifetime, Carl N. Degler reminds us that the President "was certainly not prepared to overturn the status quo; he had come to save the system, no to destroy it."

The system was about as close to collapse as one could imagine. The hard times of the Depression had left folks shivering and hungry. William E. Leuchtenburg describes those hard times:

By 1932, the unemployed numbered upward of thirteen million. Many lived in the primitive conditions of a pre-industrial society stricken by famine. In the coal fields of West Virginia and Kentucky, evicted families shivered in tents in midwinter; children went barefoot. In Los Angeles, people whose gas and electricity had been turned off were reduced to cooking over wood fires in back lots. Visiting nurses in New York found children famished; one episode, reported by Lillian Wald, "might have come out of the tales of old Russia." A Philadelphia storekeeper told a reporter of one family he was keeping going on credit: "Eleven children in that house. They've got no shoes, no pants. In the house, no chairs. My God, you go in there, you cry, that all.". . .

On the outskirts of town or in empty lots in the big cities, hopeless men threw together makeshift shacks of boxes and scrap metal. St. Louis had the largest "Hooverville," a settlement of more than a thousand souls, but there was scarcely a city that did not harbor at least one. Portland, Oregon, quartered one colony under the Ross Island bridge and a second of more than three hundred men in Sullivan's Gulch. Below Riverside Drive in New York City, an encampment of squatters lined the shore of the Hudson from 72nd Street to 110th Street. In Brook-

lyn's Red Hook section, jobless men bivouacked in the
city dump in sheds made of junked Fords and old barrels.
Along the banks of the Tennessee in Knoxville, in the
mudflats under the Pulaski Skyway in New Jersey, in
abandoned coke ovens in Pennsylvania's coal counties, in
the huge dumps off Blue Island Avenue in Chicago, the
dispossessed took their last stand. . . .

. . . In Chicago, a crowd of some fifty hungry men
fought over a barrel of garbage set outside the back door
of a restaurant; in Stockton, California, men scoured the
city dump near the San Joaquin River to retrieve half-
rotted vegetables. The Commissioner of Charity in Salt
Lake City disclosed that scores of people were slowly
starving, because neither county nor private relief funds
were adequate, and hundreds of children were kept out of
school because they had nothing to wear. "We have been
eating wild greens," wrote a coal miner from Kentucky's
Harlan County. "Such as Polk salad. Violet tops, wild
onions, forget-me-not wild lettuce and such weeds as cows
eat as a cow won't eat a poison weed."

Those fortunate enough to be employed were not
much better off. Department stores were paying clerks
five or ten dollars a week. A study of the wages of working girls in Chicago revealed that most of them were
working for less than twenty-five cents an hour, a fourth
of them for less than ten cents an hour. Domestic servants received room and board and ten dollars a month.
First-class stenographers in New York saw their salaries
drop from thirty-five or forty-five dollars a week to sixteen dollars. After unskilled workers had been clob-
bered, white collar workers, technicians, and profes-
sionals felt the squeeze. Physicians and lawyers saw
their incomes drop 18 to 30 per cent below their 1929
level.

To stem the rising tide of poverty and unemployment
the New Deal enacted programs for work relief and to

benefit organized labor, such as the Civilian Conservation Corps, the Works Progress Administration, the National Recovery Act, and the National Labor Relations Act. Since white folks seem to have a hangup about working for their relief money, shovels were put into their hands, and into the hands of some black folks, and they all began to dig in. Jacob Baker explained, "Construction work exactly suits the American temperament."

Relief workers built waterworks, sewage systems and garbage-disposal plants, irrigation ditches, hospital buildings, swimming pools, stadiums, and athletic fields. They laid streetcar lines and electric power lines and built airports. They rehabilitated and redecorated state capitols and built community centers.

Black folks were disproportionately high on the lists of unemployed and disproportionately low on the rolls of work relief. The Civilian Conservation Corps enlisted only about 8 per cent of its total work force of two and one-half million from the ranks of young black men. Blacks were at least 10 per cent of the total population. The Works Progress Administration did a little better. Since it, unlike the CCC, did not have a quota on blacks, in January 1935 blacks constituted some 30 per cent of the WPA work force. Some New Deal agencies built housing, hospitals, and schools in black communities and extended some loans to black colleges and universities.

Though there was no official mandate from the White House to improve the lot of black folks, the New Deal did have its effect in black communities. Black folks shifted their allegiance from the Republican to the Democratic party, for one thing. Even in the election of 1932, in the midst of the Depression, most black folks voted Republican. By 1936 black voting allegiance, to the extent that blacks were allowed to vote at all, had switched to the Democrats.

The New Deal also marked the beginning of a steady decline in the number of lynchings of black people in this country. There has always been a black reaction pattern to lynchings. Whenever a brutal lynching occurred, large numbers of black people would move out of the community immediately thereafter. New Deal programs improved the economic lot of enough black folks for them to establish credit for the first time. And also for the first time it was to the advantage of white folks *not* to have large numbers of black folks leaving town with unpaid bills. The unprecedented phenomenon occurred of white folks gathering at the city limits to block the exit of black folks! And lynching began to lose its popularity, because for the first time it was economically potentially dangerous.

An editorial from the Memphis (Tenn.) *Commercial-Appeal,* August 5, 1913, illustrates that even before the New Deal some white folks were beginning to realize lynching was bad for business:

The killing of Negroes by white people in order to fatten the average ought to be stopped, and killing Negroes just because one is in a bad humor ought also to be stopped.

Two apparently inoffensive Negroes, good farm hands, real wealth producers, were assassinated near Germantown a few days ago. The Negroes had furnished no possible motive for the deed. So far as any one knows they were quiet and orderly, as country people of their class usually are. They worked and played and loafed, just like other country Negroes.

Now, the Negro is about the only dependable tiller of the soil in these parts. Competition for existence is not keen enough to force many white people into the harder work.

The Negro also is very useful as a distributor of money. About all he gets goes through his fingers.

Commercially, then, he is a very valuable asset. It is not good business to kill them.

When the Negro enters into the contest with the white man he is already at a disadvantage, and therefore the truly brave white man never seeks a quarrel with Negroes. He knows the Negro is at a disadvantage, and he does not desire to take advantage of him.

Furthermore, the white man of courage can most always control the Negro without being compelled to resort to violence.

The May 10, 1940, issue of the *New York Times* reported the startling data that the South had gone a whole year without a lynching, though New Deal reforms were not credited with having produced the strange new phenomenon:

The modern South ended its first year without a lynching last midnight, and today a foe of mob rule credited this new record to effective education, plus swift work of police radio patrols.

Mrs. Jessie Daniel Ames, executive secretary of the Association of Southern Women for the Prevention of Lynching, said midnight marked the close of the first twelve-month lynchless period since tabulations were started in 1882.

In contrast to this is the peak mark of 231 mob killings recorded in 1892.

. . . She declared the twelve months just past, and the previous year's record of only three lynchings, represented the fruits of long years of campaigning to bring about "lynch-consciousness." Formerly, she said, lynchings were "hushed up" and therefore soon forgotten.

"Now, however, we get the facts and see that they are publicized," she added. "When we hear a lynch-mob has assembled, we make a direct appeal to law enforcement officials, so that a lynching cannot take place without the authorities knowing of it."

The association, representing about 41,000 Southern women and now in its tenth year, Mrs. Ames said, campaigned especially against public opinion that has "accepted too easily the claim of lynchers that they acted solely in the defense of women."

Of the previous year's lynchings, she asserted, none involved a crime against women.

Perhaps most significant, the New Deal marked the beginning of rising black expectations. The First Lady, Eleanor Roosevelt, made her stand against racial discrimination publicly known. New Deal agencies had black officials or black advisers. Black potential federal appointees began to be brought to the attention of the President, such as William H. Hastie, the first black man appointed to the federal judiciary.

Later legislation of the Kennedy and Johnson administration specifically designed to improve the condition of black folks has its historic roots in the New Deal. But black expectations were higher than anything the government was willing to implement by law. Though the New Deal reshuffled the deck, the rules of the game remained too much the same as far as black folks were concerned. Now black folks are realizing they must deal their own hand. When that happens, the game can never be the same.

> "I have nothing more to offer than what George Washington would have had to offer had he been taken by the British officers and put to trial by them. I have ventured my life in endeavoring to obtain the freedom of my countrymen. I know that you have predetermined to shed my blood. Why then all this mockery of a trial?"
>
> A SLAVE DURING GABRIEL'S REVOLT, 1800

XI

THE MYTH OF AMERICAN RHETORIC

or White Man Speaks with Forked Tongue

THE DECLARATION OF INDEPENDENCE AND THE UNITED STATES CONSTITUTION

The traditional mythology of American history tends to lump together treasured American documents as though they were all the same. As a result such documents are *revered* rather than *read*. Two of America's most treasured documents are the Declaration of Independence and the United States Constitution. Unfortunately the two documents have become so enshrined in American patriotic mythology that most Americans fail to recognize the basic difference in their rhetoric.

The United States Constitution is a right-wing document. The Declaration of Independence is a left-wing document. The Constitution is a *physical* document, whereas the Declaration of Independence is a *spiritual* document. The Constitution describes and outlines a physical entity, a definite and specific form of government. The Declaration of Independence tells what must be done when any form of government fails to deliver its promises. The Constitution displays a respect for a certain form of government and clearly shows the proper way of functioning *within* it. The Declaration of Independence issues a radical appeal to conscience, stating what government *should* be and calling for the abolition and destruction of any form of government that becomes tyrannical and oppressive.

Thus the Constitution was the document of the civil rights movement of the 1960's. The Declaration of Independence is the document of ghetto revolts, campus demonstrations, and radical youth. The civil rights movement articulated the demand of black folks for their rights under the Constitution. The civil rights movement was born in the South, and it called for an end to *physical* abuse. Blacks and their white supporters marched and sang "We Shall Overcome," demonstrating for full expression of constitutional guarantees to all Americans. In the South the enemy was clear, because the South had always imposed physical abuse upon black folks. The enemy was the bigoted, red-necked cracker who would seek to physically destroy civil rights demonstrators who demanded constitutional rights. In the South the enemy was a man, who could be identified, confronted, and resisted. The battle lines were clearly drawn, since the South represented a system of physical abuse where black folks were concerned.

In the North the battle lines were never so clear. Whereas in the South the black man was abused physically, in the North he was abused mentally. The enemy in the South was a man; in the North the enemy was a system. The North had always given lip service to constitutional guarantees, but the system of institutionalized racism was deeply entrenched. The North, for example, produced a pattern of neighborhood racial segregation which did not exist in the South. In many areas of the South, black folks and white folks have always lived side by side. Thus in the South white folks have always approved buses being used to transport white kids and black kids to separate schools. Northern white folks are opposed to busing and insist upon neighborhood schools, because a neighborhood school will be a racially segregated school, since neighborhoods themselves are segregated.

Thus in the North it is very difficult to demonstrate under the United States Constitution, to use the strategies and tactics applicable to the civil rights movement in the South, to sing "We Shall Overcome" to a racist system. Consequently the spirit of the Declaration of Independence was adopted in the northern ghettos as a reaction to northern mental abuse, and the cry "Burn, baby, burn" echoed the sentiments of the founding fathers who urged the destruction of an oppressive system.

Demonstrating under the Constitution asks the system to change. Demonstrating under the Declaration of Independence seeks to change the system. The Declaration of Independence finds support among those revolutionary spirits who recognize that the system has broken down; that the national body is in a state of illness and decay; and that health cannot be restored short of immediate and radical action. Thus the Declaration of Independence best expresses the attitude of American youth, who have taken a good look at their mother country and have come to the conclusion that momma is sick.

America looks at today's youth and says they are *revolutionaries;* they are trying to bring about a *revolution.* But America does not realize that young folks today are merely the products of nature. Revolution is nothing more than the natural extension of evolution. Evolution is the slow process of natural change which leads into quick change, or *revolution.* Evolution and revolution represent the natural order.

When a woman becomes pregnant, the nine-month gestation period is evolution. But when that period of evolution is up, quick change occurs, the baby arrives, and that is revolution. Anyone who thinks he can stop a natural revolution by means of repression should muster all the National Guardsmen he can find, tell them to cross a pregnant woman's legs, and see if they can stop that baby from being born. Nature dictates that the baby will arrive, even if it means death to the mother and the child.

Nature also has a way of telling the mother when the revolution is at hand. At the end of the period of evolution the mother develops labor pains. Labor pains are nature's way of saying, "Hey, lady, don't go to the party tonight. You are about to become a mother." Of course, someone might invent a pill to kill the labor pains, to deaden the pain for the expectant mother. But it would not stop nature's revolution. It would just mean that a pregnant woman would be shopping at Saks Fifth Avenue one day and all of a sudden a baby would drop out.

America's evolutionary period is drawing to a close, and now she is feeling the labor pains. She hears her children saying, "Momma, you're not well." Of course America had been told she was sick before by prominent sociologists, psychologists, political scientists, psychiatrists, and the like, who analyzed the national body and warned concerning the state of its health. But America did not listen, because the marks of her illness were not yet clearly visible. Nor does America want to listen to the warning of her own children. Instead momma says to her kids, "How do you know I'm sick? You're no doctors."

But momma's kids have a convincing answer. They say, "We've read your health chart, momma. That health chart left for us by the founding fathers called the United States Constitution. It tells us what you would be like if you were well."

So because the kids love their momma, they begin to plead with her to take care of herself. "Stop drinking, momma," the kids are saying, "and get some rest. Relax and lie down on the couch. Take your right foot out of Vietnam and your left foot out of Cambodia. Take your head out of Europe and your fingers out of the pockets of the poor. Try some breathing exercises and get all that pollution out of your lungs. We love you, momma, and we want to see your health chart get back to normal."

But still momma refuses to listen and will not let up. Her ankles swell into Laos. Her breathing becomes more and more difficult as she refuses to clear out the pollution. Her fingers become twisted and gnarled in the pockets of poverty, and the arthritic inflammation spreads deep into the Third World.

So America's children, seeing that momma will not listen, are saying, "Momma, you're not only sick. You're crazy. You've lost your mind." But the kids love momma so much they refuse to leave her bedside and insist she receive treatment for her own good. "Those same founding fathers who left us the health chart," momma's children are telling her, "also left us a prescription. It's called the Declaration of Independence. It tells us what to do when you become sick and insane. It says it is our duty to abolish and destory an unhealthy government and to reconstitute a more healthy human environment. And we're going to make you take your medicine, momma, even if you resist us every step of the way."

". . . WITH LIBERTY AND JUSTICE FOR ALL"

The original pledge of allegiance first appeared in the September 8, 1892, issue of the weekly magazine *Youth's Companion*. Subsequent changes have been made in the original pledge—the phrase "my flag" was changed some thirty years later to "the flag of the United States of America," and a 1954 Act of Congress inserted the words "under God"—so that the current official version reads:

I pledge allegiance to the flag of the United States of America and to the republic for which it stands, one nation under God, indivisible, with liberty and justice for all.

Authorship of the original pledge remained in dispute for many years, but a 1957 report issued by the Library of Congress attributes authorship to Francis Bellamy, a former member of the *Youth's Companion* editorial staff. So today schoolchildren and their elders continue to insist that the American flag symbolizes a godly, undivided nation which represents "liberty and justice for all." As a result many churches display the flag prominently near the cross of Jesus Christ, and the red, white, and blue adorns all American courtrooms as America's brand of justice is meted out.

The working rule of America's system of justice is that a defendant in court is innocent until proved guilty. The dictionary definition of a defendant is "a person required to make answer in an action or suit." Article VI of the United States Constitution further insists that the defendant has a right "to have the assistance of counsel for his defense." Every man has a right to have a lawyer on his side, though it is not required that he have legal counsel. He may handle his own defense if he chooses. In America's legal system it is the right and duty of the defendant to defend himself against his accusers.

The myth of American legal rhetoric was most dramatically called into question during the courtroom procedures of the Chicago conspiracy trial, which began September 26, 1969. Eight men, one black and seven white, were charged with conspiring to cross state lines to incite to riot as a result of their activities in protest demonstrations during the 1968 Democratic Convention in Chicago. The black defendant was Bobby G. Seale, national chairman of the Black Panther party. The seven white defendants were represented by William Kunstler, renowed civil rights lawyer. Bobby Seale asked to be represented by his own lawyer, Charles Garry. Mr. Garry was ill at the time, and Bobby Seale requested that the trial be delayed until Mr. Garry was physically able to represent him.

Instead the court assigned Bobby Seale's case to be represented by Mr. Kunstler and his colleague Leonard Weinglass. Repeatedly Bobby Seale protested, saying that if Mr. Garry could not represent him, he would handle his own defense. Bobby Seale was trying to uphold and represent the right and duty of every defendant in America—namely the right to *defend* himself. Bobby Seale's own words, from the official court transcript, tell the story. At one point, Mr. Weinglass was addressing the court and Bobby Seale stated emphatically:

BOBBY SEALE: Hey, you don't speak for me. I would like to speak on behalf of my own self and have my counsel handle my case in behalf of myself. How come I can't speak in behalf of myself? I am my own legal counsel. I don't want these lawyers to represent me.

THE COURT: You have a lawyer of record and he has been of record here since the 24th.

BOBBY SEALE: I have been arguing that before the jury heard one shred of evidence. I don't want these lawyers because I can take up my own legal defense and my lawyer is Charles Garry.

The responsibility and duty of upholding the words of the pledge of allegiance and the spirit of the United States Constitution, "with liberty and justice for all," fell upon the shoulders of one black man. And the Chicago federal court resisted the spirit of justice. Every time Bobby Seale rose to exercise his right to defend himself, he was ordered to be silent, to sit down, and not to *disrupt* the courtroom proceedings. It seemed to matter little that the entire system of legal justice in America was being disrupted.

Finally, when it became clear that Bobby Seale would not stand by and allow his rights to be violated or the system of American justice to be mocked, he was tied to his chair and his mouth was gagged so that he could not speak. The one black man out of two hundred million people in this country who stood up for the legal rights of *all* Americans was silenced in the most brutal way imaginable by a federal court. Yet most Americans stood silently by and allowed such a mockery of justice to happen.

Suppose instead that courtroom scene had happened in Moscow, Russia. Suppose a man had stood up in a Russian courtroom and asked that his rights not be violated. And suppose further that man was bound, gagged, and chained to a chair, and the pictures of him shackled in the courtroom appeared in American newspapers. The same Americans who allowed Bobby Seale to be silenced would look at those pictures from a Russian courtroom, shake their heads in horror and disbelief, and say, "Well, that's communism for you."

But the scene didn't happen in a Russian courtroom. It happened in an American federal court. Honest Americans must shake their heads and say, "That's democracy for you." And they must further recognize that when one man's rights are so denied, America is slipping dangerously close to the time when *every* American's rights will be in jeopardy.

Bobby Seale's case was severed from the rest of the defendants. And the Chicago conspiracy trial became known as the "trial of the Chicago Seven." At the conclusion of the trial, before the jury had rendered its decision, presiding judge Julius Hoffman levied contempt-of-court sentences upon the seven defendants and their lawyers. Numerous charges of contempt were read along with the date upon which each contempt charge occurred. All the charges were tallied, and sentences were meted out accordingly. Again, such a procedure mocks the concept of liberty and justice for all.

The court has a right to insist that an atmosphere of sanity prevail in the courtroom so that the ends of justice can *really* be served. But if the establishing of such an atmosphere were the purpose of the court, each time a contempt incident occurred, the trial would be stopped, the sentence passed, and the trial delayed until the sentence was served. Instead the Chicago court chose to keep a record of contempt incidents and add them up at the conclusion of the trial. Such an act makes one believe the court had something else in mind other than establishing a sane atmosphere in the courtroom and serving the ends of justice.

Suppose I am lecturing in a classroom and shoot someone sitting on the front row. Each successive day I come into the classroom and shoot somebody else in the room. Then at the end of the term law enforcement officers come into the classroom and arrest me for murder, reading the list of people I have killed and the dates when I did the shooting. Obviously such law enforcement officers would not be interested in preserving life, and making the classroom safe, or they would have arrested me the first time I pulled a gun.

Finally the concept of liberty and justice for all is most decisively mocked by the expense involved in taking a conviction up to the Supreme Court on appeal. Most of the cases handled by the Supreme Court are "big money" cases. Though the Supreme Court's civil and human rights decisions are highly publicized, such cases are actually a small minority of the Supreme Court calendar. Carrying an appeal all the way up to the Supreme Court costs something in the neighborhood of $25,000. Only those Americans with access to considerable wealth can afford such an appeal. Rich corporations, for example, can afford a payroll that includes legal researchers and consultants or even entire law firms.

If liberty and justice for all were really taken seriously in America, legislation would be passed to make it possible for *every* citizen, rich and poor alike, to have his case heard by the Supreme Court. Legislation should be immediately enacted to provide the opportunity for lawyers and legal researchers to take any case on file and bring it up to the Supreme Court, and if a reversal of an original decision results, government funds would be used to pay such lawyers and legal researchers. But until such legislation is enacted, an honest pledge of allegiance would speak of "justice for all who can afford it."

Liberty and justice are in real danger in America. It is both curious and frightening to notice that what used to be minority problems have now become majority problems. Every time you turn around you notice someone else is losing his civil liberty.

I have had personal experience with this obsession. I have been arrested many times, and I have been convicted of so-called "crimes." So I am a convict. But I am not a criminal. Many of the real criminals, those who daily commit actual crimes, have never been convicted—Mafia leaders, big-business capitalists, politicians, and the like. The very people who place the moral, decent folks in jail are the real criminals. But America does not realize that when a man has been convicted for his convictions, he develops a moral strength that will eventually overcome the criminals who have thus far escaped conviction. When people are placed in jail for doing right, the jail itself becomes the prisoner. If America continues along her present course of repression, one day there will be enough moral convicts to rise up and make convicts out of the *real* criminals in this country.

THE 1964 CIVIL RIGHTS ACT

The Civil Rights Act of 1964 is heralded as the great document of freedom and equality, completing the intent of the Emancipation Proclamation. Yet a closer look at the Civil Rights Act reveals a rhetoric that can only be called racial madness.

The Public Accommodation Section of the 1964 Civil Rights Act, Title II, covers:

(1) any inn, hotel, motel, or other establishment which provides lodging to transient guests, other than an establishment located within a building which contains not more than five rooms for rent or hire and which is actually occupied by the proprietor of such establishment as his residence;

(2) any restaurant, cafeteria, lunchroom, lunch counter, soda fountain, or other facility principally engaged in selling food for consumption on the premises, including, but not limited to, any such facility located on the premises of any retail establishment; or any gasoline station;

(3) any motion picture house, theater, concert hall, sports arena, stadium or other place of exhibition or entertainment; and

(4) any establishment (A) (i) which is physically located within the premises of any establishment otherwise covered by this subsection, or (ii) within the premises of which is physically located any such covered establishment, and (B) which holds itself out as serving patrons of such covered establishment.

Thus the act covers hotels, motels, restaurants, lunch counters, theaters, stadiums, etc., but it doesn't cover bars and taverns. Consider the potential insanity of that omission.

Not long ago a Russian spy was apprehended in Seattle, Washington. Let's assume that Russian spy had been operating not in Seattle, but rather in Mississippi. Let's further assume that the spy was being pursued by a black FBI agent. And during the final moments of the chase, the white Russian spy ducked into a Mississippi tavern. Do you begin to understand the potential insanity? The black FBI agent would not be permitted to enter the tavern to capture the white Russian who had stolen America's security secrets. It is certainly total madness that would permit more freedom for a white Russian spy, committed to the overthrow of America, than for a black FBI agent, dedicated to the protection of our government.

THE 1968 CIVIL RIGHTS ACT

The Civil Rights Act of 1964 began the congressional practice of granting freedom to black folks on the installment plan. The 1965 version covered voting rights, and the 1968 version was intended to cover housing. The tragic assassination of Dr. Martin Luther King figured prominently in the passing of the 1968 civil rights installment. Housing legislation was a memorial to Dr. King; the "antiriot" rider attached to the act was a response to the ghetto revolts that swept some cities in the wake of Dr. King's death.

The 1968 Housing Act exposes the myth of American rhetoric when one realizes it covers only some 80 per cent of the housing in America. Such a division of civil rights is ludicrous. I sent a letter to the State Department asking if I am only covered in 80 per cent of the nation's housing, does that mean 20 per cent of me can be Communist? Or if I am drafted and asked to serve in Vietnam, can I leave 20 per cent of me at home with my wife and family?

When Communists come to this country, they do not need civil rights bills or fair housing bills to be free. When Stalin's daughter, Svetlana Alliluyeva, came to this country from Russia, she didn't need any special legislation to live anywhere she chose. The foreign exchange students who come to this country from Russia do not need fair housing legislation to find lodging in racist college towns. Yet when they go back home, they will use their newly acquired knowledge to help their government kill American soldiers. Given such "fair housing" contradictions, is it any wonder black people want to destroy *all* houses, block by block and brick by brick?

So Congress attached an "antiriot" rider to the 1968 Housing Act making it a federal offense (five years, $10,000) to cross state lines with the *intention* of inciting, promoting, encouraging, or participating in a riot, which is defined as any assemblage of three or more persons in which one or more persons injure another person (or more) or damage property, or threaten to do so. Clearly the rider was anti-Rap Brown and anti-Stokely Carmichael. White America accepted and approved the "antiriot" rider because they were sure it was intended to curb the activities of black militants.

Yet the first court test of the new "antiriot" legislation put on trial seven whites and one black. That should give all white folks some pause for reflection. For years white college students from all over the country have been traveling to Fort Lauderdale, Florida, during their spring vacation. And each year those students tear up the town. Since most of them cross state lines, and considerable property damage results, students on a spring lark had better re-evaluate their favorite pastime. Local Florida law enforcement officials might have a different attitude since the passing of the new "antiriot" legislation.

The "antiriot" legislation is applied quite discriminately. It makes a big difference *who* is assembling or creating a disturbance and *why* they are doing it. When youthful demonstrators assembled at the Democratic Convention in Chicago in 1968, protesting the war in Vietnam and other injustices, the assemblage was judged disruptive and gave rise to the first court test of the "antiriot" legislation. Yet the Shriners convene in Chicago quite often. Every time they meet, high-spirited Shriners are seen drunk on the streets of Chicago, create havoc in downtown hotels, throw water and other objects out of hotel windows, and otherwise harass passersby. Yet the Shriners are never clubbed by police or greeted with tear gas and Mace. Why? Because the Shriners do not come to Chicago to *change* anything, only to *buy* something. If a person is supporting the capitalistic system in America by spending money, anything he does is seemingly all right. But if a person is trying to change the system, it is an entirely different matter.

Thinking of the moral issues involved, who do you suppose spent more money on whores and prostitutes while they were in Chicago—the youthful demonstrators or the Shriners? Who do you suppose committed more adultery while they were in Chicago—the hippies and the yippies or the Shriners? Certainly not the youthful demonstrators, because their main concern was with an American system that has prostituted itself to the almighty dollar.

About a month after the Democratic Convention in Chicago, another assembly took place in the financial district of New York City. For days word had been circulating through the lunch hour crowd in the Wall Street area that at precisely 1:28 P.M., a shapely girl in a tight sweater would ascend the steps of the BMT subway station near the New York Stock Exchange and walk to work at the Chemical Bank New York Trust Company on Broadway.

Every day the crowd of onlookers grew larger. They gathered to gawk at 5-foot 4-inch, twenty-one-year-old Francine Gottfried, an IBM machine operator. Miss Gottfried's measurements of 43–25–37 became much more important to the Wall Street business community than the Dow Jones average. And her daily appearance posed an increasing threat to domestic tranquillity.

On September 20, 1968, more than five thousand brokers, bankers, and beige-jacketed Stock Exchange clerks mobbed the four corners of Broad and Wall Streets in advance of Miss Gottfried's appearance. She was a few minutes late. At 1:34 P.M. when she emerged from the Broad Street subway station, crowds were so thick that hundreds of passersby were shoved against buildings. Traffic was stopped. People stood on cars to get a better view of her intoxicating measurements, and some of the cars were damaged.

Brokers peered out of the windows of the Stock Exchange. The steps of the Subtreasury were mobbed. The windows of the majestic Morgan Guaranty Trust Company building were filled with expectant faces. Spectators roamed rooftops and clung to light poles.

Plainclothes police were waiting to protect Miss Gottfried from the unlawful assembly. They escorted her safely to work as the eager mob followed.

The incident received thorough newspaper and television coverage. As a result crowds the next day tripled. More than fifteen thousand people jammed the same area, covering ten blocks standing elbow to elbow. More blocking of traffic. More damage to parked cars. But no Miss Gottfried. Her civil rights were so obviously threatened the day before that it was no longer safe for her to go to work.

No arrests were made. Police did not wade into the crowd with nightsticks nor did they make an effort to disperse the assembly. FBI chief J. Edgar Hoover did not get on television and say, "Tittie-watching is definitely Communist-inspired." Yet the Wall Street crowd far outnumbered the demonstrators at the Democratic Convention in Chicago and any campus demonstration to date. And it was a lawless assembly which displayed open contempt for traffic regulations and damaged personal property. Only a sick, degenerate America would show more respect for a crowd gathered to look upon a woman with lust than for citizens gathered to insist that *love* and *justice* be incorporated into national policy.

Of course, if Sister Francine wanted to disperse the crowd of degenerates and make sure she was never bothered again, she could have easily done it. All she would have had to do is hang two signs from her bosom. One would read, "Free all political prisoners," and the other would read, "Bring the boys home from Vietnam."

The December 7, 1968, issue of the *New Republic* contained the following report:

A city relatively free of civil disorders finally erupted into a major riot on the weekend before last. Over 6,000 citizens of Columbus, Ohio, took to the streets in a demonstration that lasted more than nine hours. . . . Traffic on the city's main street was stopped; motorists had their cars walked on, painted, overturned. Store windows were broken. Police officers were manhandled by young rioters; bystanders were hit by flying bottles and bricks.

And the mayor . . . joined the festivities. Columbus newspapers, whose editorials quivered with outrage after hippies marched in Chicago, reported property damage without concern and pronounced the whole affair delightful. The police joyfully escorted the demonstrators. Governor Rhodes, who calls out the national guard at the slightest provocation, felt it had been a great day for Ohio. In short, this was a good riot. Well-scrubbed young Americans were celebrating the football victory of Ohio State over Michigan.

So "antiriot" legislation does not seem to apply to Wall Street brokers and sports enthusiasts. It is reserved for those people who refuse to accept the myth of American rhetoric and who demand that America practice what she preaches.

THE UNITED NATIONS GENOCIDE CONVENTION

On December 9, 1948, the General Assembly of the United Nations adopted the United Nations Convention for the Prevention and Punishment of Genocide. It became part of international law when it was later ratified by twenty nations. The United States of America signed the Convention but has not yet ratified, although the Nixon administration requested the Senate to do so.

The Genocide Convention includes:

Article I: The contracting parties confirm that genocide, whether committed in time of peace or in time of war, is a crime under international law which they undertake to prevent and punish.

Article II: In the present Convention, genocide means any of the following acts committed with intent to destroy, in whole or in part, a national, ethnical, racial or religious group as such:
  a) Killing members of the group;
  b) Causing serious bodily or mental harm to members of the group;
  c) Deliberately inflicting on the group conditions of life calculated to bring about its physical destruction in whole or in part;
  d) Imposing measures intended to prevent births within the group;
  e) Forcibly transferring children of the group to another group.

Article III: The following acts shall be punishable:
  a) Genocide;
  b) Conspiracy to commit genocide;
  c) Direct and public incitement to commit genocide;

d) Attempt to commit genocide;
e) Complicity in genocide.

The myth of American rhetoric sees membership in the United Nations as an illustration of America's commitment to a peaceful and humane world order, although today's pseudo patriots see it as a sign of weakness and a concession to communism. Perhaps the Genocide Convention is the real reason for opposition to the United Nations. America's oppressive and genocidal policies stand clearly exposed in violation of international law.

Who can deny the past and continuing violations of the Genocide Convention perpetrated against the Indian American? Indian reservations are a deliberate inflicting of conditions of life calculated to bring about physical destruction, and those conditions most certainly cause serious bodily and mental harm. The deliberate transfer of Indian children from reservations to other homes remains accepted official policy. And who can fail to see violations of the Genocide Convention reflected in life in the black ghettos of America, where programs of birth control are encouraged by government, schools are overcrowded and deteriorated, and the unemployment statistics among young blacks continues to rise? No matter what rationalizations might be offered by the United States government, "complicity in genocide" seems irrefutable.

THE SPIRIT OF AMERICAN RHETORIC

Let us close this chapter by taking one example of American rhetoric at face value. Meeting in Atlanta, Georgia, June 9, 1970, the National Committee of Black

Churchmen adopted a statement to be issued on the Fourth of July. Using the Declaration of Independence as their guide, the Black Churchmen spoke to white and black America:

In the Black Community, July 4, 1970

A Declaration

By concerned Black Citizens of the United States of America in Black Churches, Schools, Homes, Community Organizations and Institutions assembled:

When in the course of human Events, it becomes necessary for a People who were stolen from the lands of their Fathers, transported under the most ruthless and brutal circumstances 5,000 miles to a strange land, sold into dehumanizing slavery, emasculated, subjugated, exploited and discriminated against for 351 years, to call, with finality, a halt to such indignities and genocidal practices —by virtue of the Laws of Nature and of Nature's God, decent respect to the Opinions of Mankind requires that they should declare their just grievances and the urgent and necessary redress thereof.

We hold these truths to be self-evident, that all Men are not *only* created equal and endowed by their Creator with certain unalienable rights among which are Life, Liberty, and the Pursuit of Happiness, but that when this equality and these rights are deliberately and consistently refused, withheld or abnegated, men are bound by self-respect and honor to rise up in righteous indignation to secure them. Whenever any form of Government, or any variety of established traditions and systems of the Majority become destructive of Freedom and of legitimate Human Rights, it is the Right of Minorities to use every necessary and accessible means to protest and to disrupt the machinery of Oppression, and so to bring such general distress and discomfort upon the oppressor as to the Offended Minorities shall seem most appropriate and most likely to effect a proper adjustment of the society.

Prudence, indeed, will dictate that such bold tactics should not be initiated for light and transient Causes; and, accordingly, the Experience of White America has been that the descendants of the African citizens brought forcibly to these shores, and to the shores of the Caribbean Islands, as slaves, have been patient long past what can be expected of any human beings so affronted. But when a long train of Abuses and Violence, pursuing invariably the same Object, manifests a Design to reduce them under Absolute Racist Domination and Injustice, it is their Duty radically to confront such Government or system of traditions, and to provide, under the aegis of Legitimate Minority Power and Self-Determination, for their present Relief and future Security. Such has been the patient Sufferance of Black People in the United States of America; and such is now the Necessity which constrains them to address this Declaration of Despotic White Power, and to give due notice of their determined refusal to be any longer silenced by fear or flattery, or to be denied justice. The history of the treatment of Black People in the United States, is a history having in direct Object the Establishment and Maintenance of Racist Tyranny over this People. To prove this, let Facts be submitted to a candid World:

The United States has evaded Compliance to Laws the most wholesome and necessary for our children's education.

The United States has caused us to be isolated in the most dilapidated and unhealthful sections of all cities.

The United States has allowed election districts to be so gerrymandered through these black districts that the Right to Representation in the Legislature is almost impossible of our attainment.

The United States has allowed the dissolution of school districts controlled by blacks when blacks opposed with manly Firmness the white man's Invasions of the Rights of our People.

The United States has erected a Multitude of Public Agencies and Offices, and sent into our ghettos Swarms of Social Workers, Officers and investigators to harass our People, and eat out their Substance to feed Bureaucracies.

The United States has kept in our ghettos, In Times of Peace, Standing Armies of Police, State Troopers and National Guardsmen, without the consent of our People.

The United States has imposed Taxes upon us without protecting our Constitutional Rights.

The United States has constrained our black sons, taken Captive in its Armies, to bear arms against their black, brown and yellow Brothers, to be the Executioners of these Friends and Brethren, or to fall themselves by their Hands.

The Exploitation and Injustice of the United States has excited domestic Insurrections amongst us, and the United States has endeavored to bring on the Inhabitants of our ghettos, the merciless Military Establishment, whose known Rule of control, is an indistinguished shooting of all Ages, Sexes and Conditions of Black People.

For being lynched, burned, tortured, harried, harassed and imprisoned without Just Cause.

For being gunned down in the streets, in our churches, in our homes, in our apartments and on our campuses, by Policemen and Troops who are protected by a mock Trial, from Punishment for any Murders which they commit on the Inhabitants of our Communities.

For creating, through Racism and Bigotry, an unrelenting Economic Depression in the Black Community which wreaks havoc upon our men and disheartens our youth.

For denying to most of us equal access to the better Housing and Education of the land.

For having desecrated and torn down our humblest dwelling places, under the Pretense of Urban Renewal, without replacing them at costs which we can afford.

The United States has denied our personhood by refusing to teach our heritage, and the magnificent contributions to the life, wealth and growth of this Nation which have been made by Black People.

In every stage of these Oppressions we have Petitioned for Redress in the most humble terms; Our repeated Petitions have been answered mainly by repeated Injury. A Nation, whose Character is thus marked by every act which may define a Racially Oppressive Regime, is unfit to receive the respect of a Free People.

Nor have we been wanting in attentions to our White Brethren. We have warned them from time to time of Attempts by their Structures of Power to extend an unwarranted, Repressive Control over us. We have reminded them of the Circumstances of our Captivity and Settlement here. We have appealed to their vaunted Justice and Magnanimity, and we have Conjured them by the Ties of our Common Humanity to disavow these Injustices, which would inevitably interrupt our Connections and Correspondence. They have been deaf to the voice of Justice and Humanity. We must, therefore, acquiesce in the Necessity, which hereby announces our Most Firm Commitment to the Liberation of Black People, and hold the Institutions, Traditions and Systems of the United States as we hold the rest of the societies of Mankind, Enemies when Unjust and Tyrannical, when Just and Free, Friends.

We, therefore, the Black People of the United States of America, in all parts of this nation, appealing to the Supreme Judge of the World for the Rectitude of our Intentions, do, in the Name of our good People and our own Black Heroes such as Nat Turner, Richard Allen, Frederick Douglass, Marcus Garvey, Malcolm X, Martin Luther King, Jr., Absalom Jones, James Varick, and all Black People, past and present, great and small, Solemnly Publish and Declare, that we shall be, and of Right ought to be, FREE AND INDEPENDENT FROM THE INJUSTICE, EXPLOITATIVE CONTROL, INSTITUTIONALIZED VIOLENCE AND

RACISM OF WHITE AMERICA, that unless we receive full Redress and Relief from these Inhumanities we will move to
renounce all Allegiance to this Nation, and will refuse, in
every way, to cooperate with the Evil which is Perpetrated
upon ourselves and our Communities. And for the support
of this Declaration, with a firm Reliance on the Protection
of divine Providence, we mutually pledge to each other
our Lives, our Fortunes, and our sacred Honor.

Signed by Order and in Behalf of
Black People

"Even voting for *the right* is *doing nothing* for it. It is only expressing to men feebly your *desire* that it should prevail."

HENRY DAVID THOREAU, 1849

"No reform is possible within the existing parties. History has proven that no reform was ever yet worked inside the party or sect in which originated the corruption complained of."

STEPHEN SMITH, SECRETARY
FARMER STATE ASSOCIATION OF ILLINOIS, 1873

"The political philosophy of black nationalism means: we must control the politics and the politicians of our community. They must no longer take orders from outside forces. We will organize and sweep out of office all Negro politicians who are puppets for the outside forces."

MALCOLM X
NEW YORK CITY PRESS CONFERENCE, MARCH 1964

XII

THE MYTH OF FREE ELECTIONS

or The Course of Human Events

The late President John F. Kennedy once observed that every mother wants her son to grow up to become President, but no mother wants her boy to become a politician in the process. The myth and the reality of politics in America, the operations of government and the elective process are captured in JFK's wry observation.

Mythical thinking in America extols the virtues of representative government. Americans have not only the right, but the solemn duty to cast their secret ballot for the candidate of their choice. Those elected officials then become directly responsible to the voters who put them in office. Such representation produces a governmen "of the people, by the people and for the people." Any man from the ranks of the people, the myth says, has the chance to be elected to the nation's highest office.

The American myth further extols the virtues of the two-party system. The two-party system is supposed to be a built-in guarantee of healthy debate among the American electorate. Voters have the choice between two divergent points of view, two different political philosophies. Voting becomes not only a sacred *right* but an opportunity to exercise a real *choice*. Thus the myth of free elections continues to cloud the minds of those who might otherwise recognize democracy in decay.

SELECTING THE ELECT

Perhaps I am more sensitive to the reality of free elections since I happen to live in Chicago, Illinois. In many places voting is a right. In Chicago it's a sport. I always invite my out-of-town friends to visit me during election time. I tell them I'll take them around to see the various polling places, and they can vote if they like! They say "old soldiers never die," but in Chicago the same thing applies to "old voters."

The myth of "free" elections is a twofold lie. Far from being free, elections today are outrageously expensive. And though American voters have the right to cast their ballot, to *elect* the candidate of their choice, they are not free to *select* the candidates from which to choose.

Back in 1931 satirist Will Rogers observed, "Politics has got so expensive that it takes a lot of money even to get beat with." Senator Thruston B. Morton of Kentucky remembers those days when he used to go campaigning with his grandfather and what a politician mainly needed was "a big cigar, a shadbelly vest and a constitution that permitted you to stand out in the hot July sun and talk for two and a half or three hours . . . before a couple of hundred or a couple of thousand people."

Those days of relatively "free" elections and campaigning seem to be gone forever. Today's candidate must have strong financial backing, either personal wealth or the support of considerable wealth; pursestrings that will undoubtedly be pulled to remind the candidate of his personal obligations once he has been elected to office. A candidate for any major elected office must buy radio and television time, advertising agencies and experts, speech writers, public opinion pollers to uncover the most popular issues and to determine the candidates' strengths and weaknesses, research specialists to study those issues, and a veritable army of clerks, secretaries, and helpers to man multiple campaign headquarters and arrange campaign logistics.

Spending huge sums of money to get elected has become an accepted practice in America today. Back in 1918, Senator Truman H. Newberry of Michigan was forced to resign from the Senate because he openly spent $195,000 to defeat an opponent who (unlike Spiro Agnew) was an established household word—Henry Ford. But nobody batted an eye when Governor Nelson Rockefeller of New York announced that he had spent $5.2 million to get re-elected in 1966. Personally, I think a man has to be slightly stupid to spend $5 million to get a $50,000-a-year job! If I had $5 million to spend on the campaign, I could run for God—and win!

So any man from the ranks of the people cannot be elected to the nation's highest office, or even to the lesser offices, within the current political system. Any man who can get his hands on a lot of money has a chance of being considered. Which means, of course, that wealth determines political decisions and defines governmental operations in America.

Both major political parties have become increasingly open about publicizing the fact that large financial contributions will ensure privileged status for the contributor. The Democrats formed the President's Club, an organization whose members have contributed $1,000 or more to the national Democratic party. During President Kennedy's administration the promises made to President's Club members were rather limited; just a little social prestige—a chance to meet JFK personally (under whom the club was started), invitations to White House cocktail parties and possible formal dinners.

But when the President's Club became such a financial success—in 1964 four thousand members were pumping $4 million into the Democratic party national coffers—bigger and better promises were made. Clifton F. Carter, former executive director of the Democratic National Committee, wrote to potential President's Club members that those who joined were "assured a direct relationship with President Johnson. Members who want to talk to the President, the Vice President or one of their assistants have only to contact my office. Members will immediately be put in contact with whomever they want to reach."

So contributing large sums of money to the ongoing process of "free" elections assures a hearing from elected officials. How *much* money a person controls determines how carefully those elected officials will listen. Since elections are not free financially, elected officials are not free to make their own decisions without regard to financial commitments and obligations. Economic considerations dominate and control both elections and governmental decisions. Moral considerations take a back seat to what is good for business.

One example is sufficient. The government has heard for a long time that the birth control pill is "the most dangerous drug ever introduced for use by the healthy," as one medical journal put it. Yet the pill is still on the market. The moral consideration of what it does to the mother is secondary. Yet the pill is a violation of the supreme act of nature—intercourse between a man and a woman to produce new life.

Now suppose the capitalists in America found a way to reproduce instantly a multimillion-dollar 747 jet airplane. Two 747's would fly close to one another, and the new process would allow the planes to hook up, and from the product of that union another 747 would be reproduced. Then suppose someone came along with an invention to stop the new 747 reproduction process— perhaps a pill slipped into the gas tank. Not only would the man who invented that pill be run out of the country by the airline industry, but immediate legislation would be passed to make sure the jet control pill was never used. America has more respect for a commercial fuselage which will make some money than it does for a woman's body.

THE PARTY'S OVER

America places so much emphasis on the right to vote, the right to *elect* a candidate, that the important right to select a candidate is bypassed completely. Obtaining the right to vote has always been a hard struggle for black folks in the South. Black folks have traditionally been openly denied voting rights, barred from the polls, kept from registering through literacy tests and poll taxes, and threatened or attacked if they tried to exercise their voting right.

An example of planned voter intimidation is found in the campaign strategy of the South Carolina Democratic Party before the elections of 1876. Article XII of the campaign strategy stated: "Every Democrat must feel honor-bound to control the vote of at least one Negro, by intimidation, purchase, keeping him away or as each individual may determine, how he may best accomplish it." And Article XVI of the same document said: "Never threaten a man individually. If he deserves to be threatened, the necessities of the times require that he should die. A dead Radical is harmless—a threatened Radical or one driven off by threats from the scene of his operations is often troublesome, sometimes dangerous."

In the North black folks by and large have always had the right to vote (though many blacks have been kept off the voter registration rolls through various kinds of intimidation), but they have never enjoyed the equally important right to select the candidate who appears on the ballot. The right to vote is a shallow civil liberty if you have no say in determining the candidates. Northern candidates are selected by political machines, party bosses and organizations, all under the control of white folks. The right to vote for Northern black folks means the right to choose between some candidates white folks have selected.

Free elections will never be possible in America as long as the decadent dominance of the two-party system prevails. Americans do not choose their candidates for President. The candidates are chosen at national party conventions. The back room discussions at party convention halls are much more important in the making of a President than the family discussions in American living rooms. The two-party system in America produces politicians rather than statesmen. Politics is the art of compromise, and politicians in America today are well schooled in that art. They compromise to get nominated, they compromise to get elected, and they compromise after they are elected, to stay in office.

There is a big difference between a statesman and a politician. In times of crisis the politician responds by flexing his muscle. The statesman, on the other hand, in times of crisis responds by flexing his mind. The sad war in Indochina is a good example of politicians flexing their muscle. And that war illustrates another truth about the American political system: the higher up one travels in the two-party system, the closer together party distinctions blend. In 1968, America changed from a Democratic to a Republican President. Yet America remained involved in the same old war she was fighting under the old administration. Perhaps President Nixon gave a clue to the nonpartisan force really in control of the American political system when he slipped and told the nation he was shown rooms in the White House after he became President-elect that he had never seen while he was Vice President. One cannot help wondering what those rooms are being used for, if no one but the President-elect and those conducting his tour are allowed to peek in.

The 1968 Democratic Convention was a good example of party politics at work. The mood of the country was about as anti-Johnson administration as it could possibly be. Primaries across the country had registered a great popularity for Senator Eugene McCarthy of Minnesota. Yet the power mechanisms of convention politics produced a nomination victory for Vice President Hubert Humphrey, closely identified with the very administration which was in such disrepute.

The two-party system does not offer real choice for the American voters. It merely raises alternatives, frequently forcing the voter to choose the lesser of two evils. But to be forced to vote for the lesser of two evils is really to have no choice at all. Adolf Hitler was elected as a lesser evil, as was Lyndon Johnson. Under such circumstances the only real choice a person has is to exercise his right *not* to vote; to boycott the polls and refuse to participate in a process that mocks the concept of free elections.

Look at it this way. Suppose you were given a choice of marrying one of two women. One of the women is a prostitute seven days a week, and the other woman practices her trade only on weekends. If you were interested in choosing the lesser of two evils, you would choose to marry the weekend prostitute. But you really have no choice at all, because whatever choice you make you still end up being married to a whore. The only real choice you have is to decide to remain single.

So most Americans end up voting for the party a candidate represents rather than for the man himself. Free elections in America under the two-party system are at best an expression of party allegiance. Since the American voter really has very little to say in determining the candidates representing his party, the voter has little interest in what those candidates themselves say during the campaign. But when a candidate comes along who is willing to buck the two-party system, "free elections" begin to move from myth to reality.

The candidacy of George Wallace during the 1968 presidential election was a real blow to the two-party system. Voters accustomed to following party allegiance turned on their television sets to find out what George Wallace was saying. And in the process of finding out what George Wallace was up to, those voters also heard the candidates of their own party. An interest developed in the candidates themselves rather than the parties they represented. And voters quickly realized what a shallow choice was being offered on election day. Such voter awareness is the beginning of a death blow to the two-party system.

One cannot help wondering if the Nixon administration has finally realized how deeply the two-party system is in trouble; and is beginning to sense the spirit of independence takin root among the American electorate. A "confidential memorandum" from the Washington, D.C., office of the Urban Coalition dated June 9, 1970, refers to the possibility of "free elections" being canceled in 1972:

A variety of extremely disturbing rumors from several highly reliable sources have become so recurrent that they deserve immediate attention. The substance of the referenced communications is outlined as follows:

1. An article in the April 27, 1970, issue of *The Nation* magazine states that the Rand Corporation has been commissioned by the Nixon administration to study the feasibility of not holding a presidential election in 1972. . . .

2. A former employee of the State Department (now president of a consultant firm) maintains that at a recent meeting at the State Department, it was revealed that the current administration has commissioned MIT to do a survey of the country's registered voters to determine voter reaction to the possibility of not holding an election in 1972.

3. A well known lobbyist on Capitol Hill is in receipt of information from a colleague whose father, a retired (and very right-wing) general from Pennsylvania advised her to take an extended vacation out of the country because he claimed to have learned: a) that in 18 months Nixon plans to declare martial law, suspend the constitution, dismiss the Congress, and institute a legal military

government. b) That this state of emergency would be created by a series of planned incidents in ten major metropolitan areas, in which 40,000 people would be killed. The general claimed, additionally, to have the names of the people who would be targets in the Philadelphia area.

4. This same lobbyist was contacted by a close friend who is a law student in a class taught by the Vice-president of the New York Bar Association. She said that in a recent class discussion, her teacher mentioned that the New York Bar Association had been asked by the Nixon administration to study the constitutionality of declaring martial law under certain circumstances. . . .

Those "disturbing rumors" have captured national attention and seem to sound more and more plausible as bombings increase in major metropolitan areas and the Black Panther party announces a Labor Day Constitutional Convention *in Philadelphia*. National concern has been strong enough to produce a denial of the validity of a similar memo allegedly from the office of Vice President Spiro Agnew. The Vice President's denial was supported by Attorney General John Mitchell. Even the Rand Corporation felt compelled to deny any involvement in election cancellation studies.

So perhaps the party's over. The myth of free elections is exploded once and for all when large numbers of Americans can harbor the private belief that the administration which invests billions of dollars and thousands of lives to guarantee free elections in Indochina would display the supreme irony of canceling them at home.

In such an atmosphere it is well to remember the beginning words of the Declaration of Independence: "When in the Course of human events, it becomes necessary for one people to dissolve the political bands which have connected them with another . . ."

> "Loyalty to petrified opinions never yet broke a chain or freed a human soul in *this* world— and never will."
>
> MARK TWAIN, 1885

Epilogue

FROM MYTH TO REALITY

Living by myth, or "petrified opinions," to use Mark Twain's words, is dangerous and self-destructive. It is one thing to lie. But when a nation lies about itself so long that its people believe the lie, that nation is in deep trouble.

America seems to be the only nation around today that openly lies about herself to the rest of the world. Premier Kosygin and his cohorts in Russia make no other claim than to be committed to worldwide communism. His predecessor, Premier Khrushchev, openly announced that he intended to "bury" America. Mao Tse-tung does not claim to be anything other than a communist and a revolutionary. Fidel Castro openly declares his revolutionary intentions. Even Hitler in all his madness did not lie about his Nazi regime. He let the whole world know that he felt the Germans were a superior race and that he hated Jews to the extent of wiping them out. Only America announces to the world that she represents a true democracy, committed to freedom and equality for all people. Then she denies it all by the way she treats oppressed minorities at home.

America's mythical understanding of herself is summed up in *The American's Creed,* by William Tyler Page:

I believe in the United States of America as a government of the people, by the people, for the people; whose just powers are derived from the consent of the governed; a democracy in a republic; a sovereign nation of many sovereign states; a perfect union, one and inseparable; established upon those principles of freedom, equality, justice and humanity for which American patriots sacrificed their lives and fortunes. I therefore believe it is my duty to my country to love it, to support its constitution, to obey its laws, to respect its flag and to defend it against all enemies.

This mythical creed is firmly believed by many Americans as illustrated by their support of America's tragic involvement in the war in Indochina. When demonstrations were held in the Lower Manhattan section of New York City by construction workers and others supporting President Nixon's war policy, the *New York Times* interviewed one demonstrator, a printer by trade and a World War II veteran. Asked why he was demonstrating, the patriotic American said: "We've got to beat the Communists somewhere. So we're fighting them. Victory. No substitute for victory."

The demonstrators' attitudes are based upon a dangerous myth. America has been in Vietnam for sixteen years. Red China and Russia have remained untouched, so America cannot be said to be turning back the tide of communism. All the while some $30 billion a year is being spent on the war; the body count of American soldiers rapidly approaches 50,000 killed and 300,000 wounded.

The idea of "victory" is itself a myth. After all, the government has told us over and over again that "we are fighting a limited war for limited objectives." We are not in an all-out war against communism nor are we likely to engage in such a war. A nuclear war with Russia would be suicidal for both countries. By 1980 the Red Chinese will number a billion. They would consider nuclear war a form of birth control. Even now the Red Chinese have more census-takers than we have people!

The American mythical creed speaks of "honoring commitments," yet the United States has not signed any binding treaty to provide military assistance to South Vietnam. There is no official commitment. Behind the myth lies the reality of an America approaching bankruptcy because of the war in Indochina, and a nation divided against itself.

Pseudo-patriotic rhetoric in America is always talking about Communist infiltration and Communists trying to destroy this nation from within. The same people who are most worried about a Communist takeover in America also support America's actions in Vietnam. Yet that war is destroying America beyond the wildest schemes or dreams of the Communists. The war has caused demonstrations in the streets and on the campuses, leading to the beating and killing of young people, and setting Americans at each other's throats as never before in history. And that interior destruction of America hasn't cost the Red Chinese or the Russians a single life nor have they had to fire any shots. They can let the police and the National Guard do their shooting for them. Such is the price a nation pays for believing its own myths.

Myth and reality in America were called into question quite dramatically when British troops invaded the tiny island of Anguilla in the Caribbean in March 1969. Not many in America protested the invasion. I imagine former President Lyndon Johnson sat sullenly at the ranch trying to figure out what English Prime Minister Harold Wilson knew that he didn't. If LBJ had invaded St. Thomas or St. Croix with American troops—as he did Santo Domingo—the voices of protest would have echoed from American shores all the way around the world.

Anyone who really believed his own rhetoric about human rights would see the Anguilla invasion as an ideal focal point of protest. True opponents of colonialism, those who detest seeing imperialistic interests dominate the human spirit yearning for freedom, should have felt considerable revulsion at seeing a tiny population of six thousand being forcibly occupied by a major world power.

And anyone who sees a relationship between racism, imperialism, and military solutions should have found a ready-made protest issue considering that the occupied population was black and the occupying troops were white; to say nothing of a display of military muscle by a nation whose racial tensions at home get hotter every day.

The right-wing press in America was more critical of the British occupation of Anguilla than were the left-wing students. When America sends troops into Vietnam or continues to hold the Third World under the thumb of oppression, left-wing students call it "imperialism." Are they really against "imperialism," or are they merely against *American* imperialism? If students were really opposed to *imperialist* actions, and not just concerned with a *particular* national expression of imperialism, they would not have let the invasion of Anguilla slip by.

When Russian tanks rolled into Prague, Czechoslovakia, in 1968, United States senators and congressmen called the action a denial of freedom and a violation of human rights. Yet the senators and congressmen were silent when British troops moved into Anguilla. Were those earlier congressional voices being raised to advance the cause of human rights, or were they merely expressing anti-Communist sentiments?

There is a profound difference between name-calling, or labeling, and a real moral crusade for human rights. Protests based on certain "anti" sentiments will never contain a moral revolution for a new world order. Such protests only serve to make clear the distinction between *dissent* and *revolution*. If right-wing Americans are preoccupied with the myth of anti-Communism and left-wing Americans are preoccupied with the myth of anti-Americanism, they will both fail to comprehend fully the reality of a worldwide revolution to end *all* oppression and denial of human dignity.

THE COST OF MYTHICAL THOUGHT

America's most current mythical preoccupation is her supposed concern for "law and order." Considerable confusion surrounds the increasingly popular "law and order" cry. Most people seem to think that law and order is a white folks' issue. Nothing could be further from reality.

Black folks have been screaming for law and order for years, and they taught white folks to take up the same plea. For decades, as thousands of black people were being lynched in America, black folks voiced the urgent cry "law and order!" When Medgar Evers was shot in the back, black folks again screamed "law and order!" But the cry fell upon deaf ears. Medgar Evers' murderer still walks free and is probably complaining about "crime in the streets" of America today.

When Malcolm X was gunned down, black folks took up the "law and order!" cry once again. When Martin Luther King was felled, an agonizing plea for "law and order!" arose from the black community. For decades, black folks have urged the law-and-order issue upon America in the interests of justice.

But white America demonstrated no real enthusiasm for law and order while the killing of black people was going on. White resistance to law and order produced the inevitable result of violent eruption in the black ghettos of this nation. Violent rebellion was the avenue of last resort. White folks had demonstrated such an immunity to law and order that black folks had given up on their ever hearing that plea.

All of a sudden, in response to ghetto violence, white America began to demand law and order. Though the words were the same, white America's posing of the issue was considerably different. White folks did not raise the cry of law and order in the interest of justice as black folks had been doing for so long. Rather, white America insisted upon law and order even in the *absence* of justice. When black America was threatened by the prevalence of lawlessness, white America did not hear our law-and-order cry. Now that white America feels itself threatened by black lawlessness, white folks will not listen to any other issue.

Law and order seems to be the symptomatic utterance of a sick society. When black folks raised the cry, it was a warning. Violence is a social disease, and killing is a testimony to the failure of human reason and compassion. Black folks begged America to recognize that lynchings and assassinations represent a terrible social sickness, even a sickness unto death. Black folks were telling America that even as she remembers and honors her war dead, she should also recognize and admit the lynchings of thousands and thousands of innocent black people. If all the unknown black folks in America who have been martyred and lynched were given official recognition, our TOMB OF THE UNKNOWN BROTHER would make Arlington Cemetery look like a thimble.

Now that white folks have finally taken up the law-and-order cry, it again points to America's sickness. To demand law and order, while refusing to attack the cancerous conditions in the national body, is an open admission that America cannot solve her social problems.

The law-and-order campaign rhetoric of national and local elections (witness the 1968 presidential election and subsequent elections in Minneapolis, Los Angeles, and New York City) is a frightening symptom of the condition of the national body. Law-and-order advocates are now justifying their own use of violence and killing rather than trying to find a way to put an end to both. The Democratic candidate for mayor of New York City in the 1969 election wanted to *restore* the death penalty. But retribution and retaliation are no substitutes for justice.

Law-and-order campaign rhetoric bears the mark of national death because it is used to hide the real social conditions; just as treating a symptom rather than the disease can result in the death of a patient. I imagine many good-thinking and decent Germans who listened to Adolf Hitler knew his campaign rhetoric was pure myth, but they stood silently by and watched the Nazis have a field day because they were afraid to open their mouths. But one day they looked up in the sky and saw the bombers open up on Berlin. It must have been a terrible realization that not one of those falling bombs was labeled, "For bad Germans only."

History seems to have a way of turning the tables in its repetition, and those who choose to ignore the horrors of one historical era can almost expect to be the victims of the same horror the second time around. White folks in America are just beginning to realize fully the terrible price one must pay for choosing to ignore certain problems or remaining silent about them.

Twenty years ago, when the crime syndicate in America was restricting its dope-pushing activity to black ghettos, black parents cried out to white America, "Please stop those syndicate hoodlums from pushing reefers and heroin to young black kids." But white America looked the other way. Little did white America realize that if it permitted the syndicate hoodlums to push dope to young black kids without fear of reprisal, it would only be a matter of time before the same hoodlums would be pushing dope to young white kids.

Now it is white America's turn to live with the tragic results of that earlier silence. Newspaper editorials and magazine feature stories are finally recognizing the terrible problem of narcotics—now that young white kids are becoming addicted. Some of white America's most prominent families—in government, in the entertainment industry, in high society—have been touched by narcotics addiction. Yet it is odd to notice that narcotics addiction in the black community has decreased during the last decade, or so statistics of the Federal Bureau of Investigation say. A decrease in the black use of narcotics has resulted in spite of the silence and apathy of the white community.

It is also ironic that dope addiction has traditionally been a problem only in the most impoverished black communities. Middle-income and upper-middle-income black families, those who benefited from higher education and good jobs, seldom had to worry about their kids being hooked on dope. Black kids who suffered most from addiction were the children of poverty-stricken, uneducated black folks.

Now that it is white folks' turn to be plagued by the horrors of dope addiction, it is the children of upper-income families who are getting hooked. Young white kids in Appalachia are not turning on and getting high. Odd, isn't it, that when it comes to dope addiction at least, white folks' *best* seems to equal black folks' *worst*.

For years, white folks stood by in silent approval as buses were used to transport white kids *and* black kids in the interest of maintaining segregated schools. Now that busing is being used as a strategy to promote school *integration*, white folks act like black folks invented buses.

Black folks, too, are beginning to realize fully the high price one must pay for being silent. The sad truth of the matter is that black folks, too, sat by for years and watched this American system oppress and destroy the Indians without raising a voice of outraged protest. If black folks did not protest the system's genocide against the Indian, they can hardly be surprised when the same system becomes openly genocidal against them.

Presidential adviser Daniel Patrick Moynihan and others are fond of pointing to the progress blacks have made during the past decade. It is true that black folks have made *physical* progress during the 1960's. But a more important consideration is what the past decade did to blacks *mentally*.

The great event of the 1950's which began to formulate a black attitude of expectation was the Supreme Court decision (1954) on public school desegregation. A year later "all deliberate speed" indicated a positive change in the posture of government, a momentum that might be reflected in the mentality of society at large.

So the 1960's began with the election of President John F. Kennedy. That election itself was a further indication of change in process, the acceptance of young leadership, a young leader who happened also to be a Roman Catholic. Such a national election at the very dawn of the decade, even though the electoral margin was slim, gave black folks a further indication that something really positive might happen.

But the bubble of expectation was burst a third of the way through the sixties, when the new young leader was assassinated. Pending civil rights legislation had not yet been validated. Full and real implementation of the 1954 Supreme Court decision had not been accomplished. The murder of promise was a shocking reminder that resistance is not easily eliminated.

The late fifties and early sixties represented the infancy stage of black expectation. It was as though I were a child walking down the street with my brand-new balloon. I am happy with my new balloon and thrill to see it floating above me, blowing freely in the breeze. And then a man comes by smoking a big cigar and takes that cigar and breaks my new balloon—for no apparent reason. I am terribly disappointed, but sadly and tragically I reach a new level of maturity. I have faced cruelty directly, and I develop an attitude that governs my reaction in future confrontations.

As the 1960's progressed, black folks continued to struggle and grow. Further promises appeared in the form of installments of civil rights legislation. Blacks pushed for implementation of promise, as they matured into the adolescent stage of the struggle for freedom and were greeted with greater acts of cruelty. Open struggle took the form of street demonstrations, usually peacefully conducted, and violent resistance intensified. Dogs, fire hoses, and tear gas were used to discourage demonstrators. Blacks and white sympathizers were killed during open struggle or during dark and silent moments of night raids. George Wallace emerged as a national symbol of intensified resistance. Churches were blown up, and little black children became innocents slaughtered while learning their Sunday School lessons.

So the middle and late sixties represented the adolescent stage of black expectation. No longer was the image of bursting a balloon appropriate to describe the intensified resistance. It was as though a man took a brick and threw it, breaking my stained-glass window. The middle and late sixties saw the destruction of those promises and persons black folks had treasured and admired most.

But the dominant black attitude of the 1970's carries the level of maturity of black expectation a step further. The bursting of the balloon represented the deflation of the promise of my individual rights. The breaking of the stained-glass window represented the destruction of those I admired and treasured, though I was not personally and individually involved.

The black attitude for the 1970's is formulated by more personal and individual feelings. For the first time in history the word "genocide" is receiving wide utterance in the black community. It began as a whisper in the black community with the murder of Dr. Martin Luther King, Jr., undeniably the most widely revered black man in America. And it became more and more audible as a large number of Black Panthers across the nation were killed by police, one of them while lying asleep in his own bed. With the recognition that blacks are the intended victims of a planned program of genocide in this nation, a new image is required to represent this final extreme of intensified resistance to the struggle for black liberation.

The latest stage of black expectation is best represented by a man taking a knife and ripping up my masterpiece. This man who has been attacking me all my life, from the cradle to the grave, has now done about all that he can do. He has burst my balloon, broken my stained-glass window, and now scarred my masterpiece. His last act shows me clearly that he intends to destroy me personally, because each individual person is a masterpiece. Before, the man was only breaking what I treasured. Now he is after me.

There is a sense of urgency now in the black community as never before in history. Every person born into the world is a masterpiece. And every person in every ethnic group should recognize both himself and his people as a masterpiece. Black folks now realize that there is a cruel, evil, and repressive force in this country, and the word "genocide" echoes louder and louder. If you place a teakettle on a stove, you will notice that when the water starts to boil the teakettle will make a noise. The escaping steam will cause the teakettle to whistle. If you try to repress that whistle by plugging up the hole in the teakettle, an explosion will result. There is no way to avoid that explosion unless you turn off the heat underneath the teakettle.

America today has become a one-room kitchenette

and the boiling kettle of protest is on the stove. Governmental acts of repression are merely efforts to plug up the last safety valve left in America. But the explosion will occur just the same unless the system changes and the heat causing the kettle to boil is turned off.

Although repression is a futile *solution*, it is a legitimate *reaction*. All men have the basic right to be afraid, regardless of how wrong, how degenerate, or how insane they are. And all men have the right to react to their fears. If I am speaking in a crowded auditorium and I think I see a ghost, I have the right to react to my fear and run for the door. If I knock down twelve people as I run for the door, I will not be arrested for assault, because I am merely reacting to a legitimate fear.

The government resorts to repressive measures because its representatives are afraid. The social and political sickness in America is not measured by legitimate reactions to fear. It is measured rather by the reason for that fear. When a nation becomes so depraved that its government fears voices calling for justice, dignity, and morality, that nation is on the verge of destruction.

IT'S LATER THAN YOU THINK

America's sickness has reached a very advanced stage. If a man has cancer and finds out about it in the early stages, it is possible for the man to rid himself of the cancer and save his life. Not long ago I attended a conference in California of hundreds of people who had been cured of cancer. One of the marks of America's sickness is the fact that certain known cures for cancer—nature's own medicine, such as apricot seeds —are suppressed from general knowledge.

But sometimes a man has had cancer in his body for a long time and doesn't know it. One day he wakes up in the morning, and he is unable to talk, move his legs, has sharp pains, and can't get out of bed. When the doctor examines the man, he gets a grave look on his face, shakes his head, and tells his patient, "It's probably too late." And that is the only way to describe America today. The sickness of the national body has reached the kind of advanced stage which afflicted the Egyptians, the Greeks, and the Romans in ancient history. Those societies also became afraid of morality and righteousness, and though they had the mightiest armies on the face of the earth, they crumbled to ashes because of deterioration and destruction from the inside.

The best way to diagnose America's sickness is to read *The Decline and Fall of the Roman Empire* (1776–1788) by Edward Gibbon. The Roman Empire did not crumble overnight. It was a long time declining. During that period of decline many events occurred that have their parallels in America today.

For one thing, Rome had a "bad money" problem. Silver got so scarce that coins were made with copper and given a silver coating. If you looked closely at a coin, around the edges you would see the telltale marks of brown showing through. A clear parallel is America's current condition of inflation, with white collar workers being laid off by the thousands and a stock market as unpredictable as the next ghetto revolt. And have you looked at your own coins lately?

Gibbon analyzes the decline of Rome as follows:

But the decline of Rome was the natural and inevitable effect of immoderate greatness. Prosperity ripened the principle of decay; the causes of destruction multiplied with the extent of conquest; and as soon as time or accident had removed the artificial supports, the stupendous fabric yielded to the pressure of its own weight. The story of its ruin is simple and obvious; and instead of inquiring *why* the Roman empire was destroyed, we should rather be surprised that it had subsisted so long. The victorious legions, who, in distant wars, acquired the vices of strangers and mercenaries, first oppressed the freedom of the republic, and afterwards violated the majesty of the purple. The emperors, anxious for their personal safety and the public peace, were reduced to the base expedient of corrupting the discipline which rendered them alike formidable to their sovereign and to the enemy; the vigour of the military government was relaxed and finally dissolved by the partial institutions of Constantine; and the Roman world was overwhelmed by a deluge of barbarians.

So Rome's involvement in "distant wars" finally did her in, causing a corruption of the form of government that made her great and a repression of freedom at home and abroad. Doesn't that sound quite familiar? Gibbon sounds as if he could be resident scholar for the Youth International Party.

The corruptions of government in America today are too numerous to list. Our government "of the people, by the people and for the people" has deteriorated to a group of men occupying the corridors of the Capitol building in Washington who act as though it were *their* government, while young folks stand out in the streets calling for "Power to the people."

One example of Capitol Hill corruption will suffice. Tourists in Washington, D.C., are guided through the halls of the Capitol and told the myth of American history. The great sandstone and marble building is described as the shrine preserving America's hard-won freedom and demonstrating true democracy to the rest of the world. But the lower levels of the Capitol building are not shown to tourists. Joseph Trento, writing in the May 1970 issue of *Signature*, the Diners Club magazine, gives a printed tour of those lower levels.

The bowels of the Capitol building contain a vast network of discount stores, free services, and transportation systems provided at taxpayers' expense for members of Congress and their staffers. Free haircuts for senators and congressmen and the minimal charge of $1.25 for staff members. No wonder there are so few longhairs in Congress. Free long-distance telephone calls for homesick secretaries and congressional aides. Stationery is available at huge discounts, and free booze is provided by friendly Capitol Hill police to senior members of Congress. It's all free, that is, to those who enjoy congressional privilege (including a few favorites from the press). The American taxpayer really pays the bill.

The stores and services in the underground Congress are not government-owned. Many operate at a substantial loss. But then Congress appropriates tax money to cover the deficit. The taxpayer pays the tab, but no private citizen can avail himself of the services. The chief of the 616-man Capitol Hill police force (which, by the way, outnumbers the total number of senators and congressmen as well as the state police force of New Hampshire) said it all: "Things are not always done exactly by the rules here, but this is an important place and you have to bend. After all, the people we protect are *special* Americans. Most people know how to give and take." So the Capitol Hill police spend their time escorting tourists across the street, delivering portables to members of Congress, and changing automobile license plates for important congressional staffers.

Maintaining the underground and aboveground ac-

tivities in the Capitol building costs the American taxpayer about $700,000 per year per member of Con-
gress. That's $374,500,000 annually. There is another
underground taking firm root in America that would
like to get its hands on such a budget.

Gibbon cites the emergence of police state tactics as
further evidence of the decline of the Roman Empire:

> Two or three hundred *agents* or messengers [to the
> provinces] were employed, under the jurisdiction of the
> master of the offices, to announce the names of the an-
> nual consuls, and the edicts or victories of the emperors.
> They insensibly assumed the licence of reporting whatever
> they could observe of the conduct either of magistrates
> or of private citizens; and were soon considered as the
> eyes of the monarch and the scourge of the people. Under
> the warm influence of a feeble reign they multiplied to
> the incredible number of ten thousand, disdained the mild
> though frequent admonitions of the laws, and exercised in
> the profitable management of the posts a rapacious and
> insolent oppression. These official spies, who regularly
> corresponded with the palace, were encouraged, by favour
> and reward, anxiously to watch the progress of every
> treasonable design, from the faint and latent symptoms of
> disaffection, to the actual preparation of an open revolt.
> Their careless or criminal violation of truth and justice
> was covered by their consecrated mask of zeal; and they
> might securely aim their poisoned arrows at the breast
> either of the guilty or the innocent, who had provoked
> their resentment, or refused to purchase their silence. . . .
> The ordinary administration was conducted by those
> methods which extreme necessity can alone palliate; and
> the defects of evidence were diligently supplied by the
> use of torture.

Many people have been talking and writing about
the police state atmosphere in America. Those who
look for signs of increasing police state maneuvers in

this country are fond of citing such things as the "no-knock" section of the Controlled Dangerous Substances Act of 1969, the presence of concentration camps authorized under the McCarran Act with its vague reference to "possible" saboteurs, and the Federal Bureau of Investigation computer banks on groups and individual Americans. Until very recently, few Americans were aware of the extent to which the United States Army has engaged in, and perfected, the highly technical art of citizen-watching and reporting.

Christopher H. Pyle, who served two years as a captain in Army intelligence, gave America an eye-opening glimpse of the role and the results of soldier-agent activities. Since Mr. Pyle's exposure the Army has admitted its activities. "Military undercover agents," wrote Mr. Pyle, "have posed as press photographers covering antiwar demonstrations, as students on college campuses, and as 'residents' of Resurrection City. They have even recruited civilians into their service—sometimes for pay but more often through appeals to patriotism." So Uncle Sam might not only be watching you; he might also have your best friend gathering the information.

America's army agents have many advantages over the agents in the Roman Empire. A highly developed technological advantage for one. Army information gathering about the doings of the private citizenry now employs an extensive teletype reporting system which will soon be linked to a computer data bank. The computer, to be installed at the Investigative Records Repository at Fort Holabird in Baltimore, Maryland, will be able to produce instant print-outs of information in ninety-six separate categories.

Much like the activity in the Roman Empire which Gibbon described, the army intelligence file, which contains material devoted exclusively to describing the lawful political activity of civilians, is not subject to congressional or presidential supervision and thereby enjoys uninhibited freedom for growth. Yet the army file is located in one of the government's main libraries for security-clearance information, and access to it is not limited to Army personnel. Personnel files can be readily available to any federal agency issuing security clearances, conducting investigations, or enforcing laws.

In commenting upon the Army's civilian-watching activity, Pyle quoted the words of John Stuart Mill spoken over a century ago: "A state which dwarfs its men, in order that they may be more docile instruments in its hands, even for beneficial purposes, will find that with small men no great things can really be accomplished."

It would be well to carry John Stuart Mill's observation a step further. The small men of history, those of insane vision and limited morality, who eventually succeeded in destroying their own nations, always began their insane exploits by setting up police state measures which specialized in keeping close watch on the private citizenry. Then individual rights and any semblance of human freedom disappeared. John Stuart Mill is quite correct. No really great things can be accomplished in such an atmosphere. Only loud, noisy, clamorous, and sure destruction.

There are other striking similarities between the fall of Rome and the decline of America. During the period of the decline and fall of Rome, garbage piled up in the streets, and people refused to remove it. Political assassinations became more and more common. Fire swept through sections of Rome, as well as famine and disease—"conflagration and pestilence" to use Gibbon's words.

In America today, assassinations are commonplace. And America's reaction to those assassinations reveals her sickness. Most Americans were outraged and upset when John F. Kennedy, Robert F. Kennedy, and Martin Luther King, Jr., were murdered. But hardly anyone was equally outraged and upset when Malcolm X and George Lincoln Rockwell were assassinated. The same people who were so upset about the killing of Martin Luther King would not be dismayed if George Wallace were assassinated. Americans are not against assassination. They only become upset when somebody they *like* is killed. A healthy nation would be upset by the act of assassination—period. Otherwise it has no right to be upset about the assassination of anyone.

But there is an even closer parallel. Dr. King was killed in Memphis, Tennessee, where he was demonstrating in support of the garbage workers who had gone on strike. The lessons of ancient and modern history seem to tell us that garbage, death, and destruction are related. Garbage piling up breeds rats which in turn spread disease.

The settling of a garbage strike always creates a famine crisis for rats. A rat has a governor in his head which determines the size of its litter of young according to the amount of food the rat eats. Rats infest poor communities, slums, and ghettos, because there is more food to be found. Poor folks have lived with rats for so long they have learned how to strike a bargain. Poor parents leave food out for the rats so they won't bite little babies in their cribs. Whenever you read that a little baby was bitten by a rat, you will know that the child was hungry also, because there was no food to leave out for the bargain.

When a rat's belly is full, it is afraid of noise; it frightens easily. But when the rat is hungry, nothing will scare it. Rats are like humans in that respect. Suppose a man decides to hold up a bank, but he doesn't really need the money desperately. If the slightest little thing goes wrong, a strange noise or a suspicious move, the bank robber and his accomplices will run out of the bank. They are not desperate enough to take unnecessary risks. But if a man who desperately needs the money to survive holds up a bank, the moment he hears a strange noise or sees something suspicious, he will fire his gun and kill anything moving. And he will order his accomplices to do the same thing.

So when garbage collectors go on strike and uncollected garbage piles up, rats find more to eat and the governors in their heads are turned on, causing their litters of young to be much larger. By the time the litters are due, the garbage workers have settled the strike, with the result that there are far more rats than there is food. The rats cannot stay in their old slum neighborhood. They have to move out, in their search for food, to the white neighborhood. But a rat lying in the gutter waiting for the garbage to pile up in a white neighborhood would starve to death. The rat doesn't know that garbage collection is better in the white neighborhoods than in the slums and ghettos. And certainly the rat has never heard of garbage disposal units.

But the rat finds something in the white community it didn't find back in the old slum neighborhood. The rat finds many pets—poodles, cats, monkeys, and chihuahuas. So the rat bites the pets just as it did the babies in their cribs back in the old neighborhood. When the owners find their precious little pets bitten, they don't know what really happened, so they will be petting, hugging, and kissing their pets, trying to comfort them. And that's how the rat's famine problem spreads disease—bubonic plague!

A few months after a garbage workers strike was settled not long ago in New York City, a story appeared on the wires of national news services telling of rats coming up to Park Avenue. Everyone thought it was a cute and quaint expression of the rats' striving for upward mobility. Little did they realize the deeper meaning of the phenomenon.

Then came America's mild form of the plage. The nation was gripped by an epidemic of "Asian" flu. America has a habit of naming diseases after people she doesn't like. If it was really *Asian* flu, why do you suppose Red China didn't come down with it? If Mayor Daley of Chicago, for example, would name a disease "Gregoryitis," and the disease infected Evanston, Illinois, but none of my own kids contracted it, obviously the mayor would be trying to create a situation where folks wouldn't like me. He would be naming a plague after what's been plaguing him. The Asian flu struck New York City and the east coast first. Then it spread across the country. Since winds blow from west to east, if the flu really came from Asia, it would have started in California.

America also has a habit of giving sweet-sounding names to the marks of her own destruction. The Nixon administration is a good example. Every racist, bigoted decision is called "conservative" or a "Southern strategy."

And the fires or "conflagrations" that marked the latter days of the Roman Empire are recurring today under a new name. During the reign of the Emperor Nero a great fire swept through Rome. Everyone remembers it today as a time when "Nero fiddled while Rome burned." Gibbon describes the slum conditions at the time of the fire with these words: "Innumerable buildings, crowded in close and crooked streets, supplied perpetual fuel for the flames." Gibbon also describes the policy of Nero's government in the wake of the fire and the end result of the conflagration itself:

The Imperial gardens were thrown open to the distressed multitude, temporary buildings were erected for their accommodation, and a plentiful supply of corn and provisions was distributed at a very moderate price. The most generous policy seemed to have dictated the edicts which regulated the disposition of the streets and the construction of private houses; and, as it usually happens in an age of prosperity, the conflagration of Rome, in the course of a few years, produced a new city, more regular and more beautiful than the former.

Today in America we call the destruction of slums and ghettos "urban renewal" or "slum clearance." Nero didn't have bulldozers and other types of modern machinery, so the only way he could conduct an urban renewal program was to burn the slums to the ground. But contemporary urban renewal programs follow the pattern Gibbon describes: relocation of slum families and the erection of public housing. The only difference is that American cities seldom emerge "more regular and more beautiful" than they were before. Perhaps it is because Nero seemed to be wise enough to realize that an urban renewal program cannot take place in a piecemeal manner. You have to burn the whole thing down and start over. When residents of the black ghetto, with their instinctive wisdom, do the same thing, they are called "rioters," "hoodlums," and "arsonists."

The Roman emperor who had the most peculiar affinity to present-day America was a man named Commodus. One of Commodus' favorite pastimes, Gibbon relates, was killing *panthers* for the entertainment of the multitudes:

Elated with . . . praises, which gradually extinguished the innate sense of shame, Commodus resolved to exhibit before the eyes of the Roman people those exercises which till then he had decently confined within the walls of his palace and to the presence of a few favourites. On the appointed day the various motives of flattery, fear, and curiosity attracted to the amphitheatre and innumerable multitude of spectators; and some degree of applause was deservedly bestowed on the uncommon skill of the imperial performer. . . . A panther was let loose; and the archer [Commodus] waited till he had leaped upon a trembling malefactor. In the same instant the shaft flew, the beast dropped dead, and the man remained unhurt.

Political leaders in America today continue the tradition of shafting Panthers—this time members of the Black Panther party. And national leaders in the Justice Department and elsewhere are guiding that shaft just as surely as did the hand of Commodus. History's most gruesome example of panther-killing occurred in Chicago on December 4, 1969, when Illinois Black Panther Chairman Fred Hampton and Panther Defense Captain Mark Clark were killed during a predawn raid on their apartment. The raid occurred under the cover of darkness. Fred Hampton was shot while sleeping in his own bed. At least Commodus had the decency to engage in his insane pastime during broad daylight.

The brutal killings of Fred Hampton and Mark Clark solidified the feeling many Americans had been sharing that the government is determined to exterminate the Black Panther party. Anyone in their right mind would know that if you are going to assassinate a man, you must catch him in a limousine during a parade, or standing on the balcony of a motel, or hide yourself in the crowd in a hotel kitchen, or best of all, get one of his own to kill him while he addresses a crowd gathered in a Harlem ballroom. If you sneak up on a man and shoot him while he lies asleep in his own bed, it is very difficult to hide or explain your intentions. But that is exactly what the Chicago police did, as a Grand Jury investigation has now verified. And such an act declares publicly that if the system wants a man bad enough, it will kill him in a playground while he is playing with his own kids.

The killing of Mark Clark and Fred Hampton was just one more example of a social and political system in America at war with black people. Not merely the firing of guns; it runs much deeper than that. The police in the black ghettos of America stand silently by and watch the activities of the prostitute, the dope pusher, the policy peddler, the pimp, and the hustler. Such entrepreneurs receive official approval because their business activities can only bring harm to the black community. But when the black beautiful people come to the ghetto street corner—the Rap Browns, the Stokely Carmichaels, the Malcolm Xs, the Martin Luther Kings, the Jesse Jacksons, the Ralph Abernathys, the LeRoi Joneses, or the Bobby Seales—they are either shot or jailed because they only intend good for the black community. They are talking about unifying black people for the common good; developing black pride; and attaining human dignity.

Some people try to explain that the Black Panther party has become the target of police hostility because its members talk bad about the cops, calling them "pigs," or even shooting at them on occasion. But official aggression against the Panthers obviously runs much deeper than that. After all, the Black Panther party displayed a more militant and mean stance when the organization first began than it has been displaying lately. In the early days of the party Panthers entered a California courthouse carrying rifles, displaying a "don't mess with us" attitude, and using rhetoric to match that stance. Police were not under orders to fire upon the Panthers then. The system in America is not frightened by guns, nor does it care about speaking disrespectful of cops. The same system in America which now seeks to destroy the Panthers is the system which treats the cops themselves unjustly.

It takes more than guns to frighten the system. Official hostility against the Black Panther party began to be displayed when the Panthers started their breakfast program and began *feeding* hungry black children and *teaching* them. Feeding and teaching black folks, all poor folks for that matter, is white folks' business according to the system. If the system can control the feeding and teaching programs, it can determine how much feeding will be done and what lessons will be taught.

There are two kinds of hunger: the hungry stomach and the hungry mind. The hungry stomach reacts to smell, and the hungry mind reacts to sound. A hungry man, dependent upon the system for his meager food allowance, can be expected to behave just as the system wants him to behave. He reacts to the smell of food and his reactions are geared toward getting some of that food for his hungry stomach. But when a child is fed a proper diet, he grows strong in body, and when his stomach is full, he develops a hungry mind. His mind reacts to sound, and the lessons the system teaches him just don't sound right to him any more. The child develops a strong mental determination to be free.

That is what the system in America is really afraid of, not guns. If a group of white militants went into Appalachia and began to feed and organize poor white folks to change the system in America, they would find themselves subjected to the same kind of harassment the Panthers are now experiencing. Those white militants would end up just like Chairman Fred Hampton and all the rest of the dead Panthers, because the system knows that feeding hungry poor children, and teaching them the truth about America, is the most powerful weapon of all. Governmental opposition to such activity knows no color barrier.

Consider the murder of coal mine workers organizer Jack Yablonski, along with his wife and daughter. Yablonski knew what life was like for the men who daily risked their lives to bring out the coal. He had gone to work in the mines at the age of fifteen, and his father was killed in a mine accident. He defied the regular union organization and everyone else who stood in the way of a better way of life for mine workers. He organized the workers and taught them the truth about union corruption and their own right to human dignity. Now he is dead.

Just as the system in America knows no color distinction in its opposition to truth, morality, and human dignity, neither is there a color barrier between those united and determined to change that system in America. If the tide of America's decline and decay can be stemmed and redirected, it will be because of the pure moral dedication of America's youth—black, white, brown, and yellow. The youth of America today are the most morally dedicated group of young people in America's history. That is why the system in America continually puts young people down. The system calls young folks "hippie, yippie, bearded, smelly kids." I've always wondered why the system feels wearing a beard means you must stink. Nobody ever says anything like that about Abraham Lincoln. He not only had a beard, but he was ugly, too.

The youth of America can change the system if they band together, organize, and realize the truth about the system they are dealing with. Demonstrations and carrying picket signs demanding constitutional rights will not change the system, because the system has displayed over and over again that it doesn't care about the Constitution. The youth must recognize that ours is a capitalistic system, and that to effect change they must address their grievances to the capitalists.

Young folks have long realized the essential hypocrisy in a system which says that a young man is old enough to go to war and die at the age of eighteen, but he is not old enough to vote at the same age. To make matters worse, nonvoting-age young men have been sent off to die in an unconstitutional, undeclared war. So young folks have been saying, "If I have to go to war at age eighteen, I want the right to vote at age eighteen." That's absolutely foolish! If a young man has to go to war at age eighteen, he had better get the right to vote at age seventeen. As groovy as young folks in America are today, if they got the right to vote at age seventeen, there probably wouldn't be any wars when they got to be age eighteen.

But if young folks really want the right to vote at age seventeen, they can get it. They merely have to address their grievance to the capitalists. First, young people must organize. After they have a strong youth organization, they should go to the phonograph record industry with the announcement, "If you don't go to Washington, D.C., and lobby and in two months get a seventeen-year-old voting rights bill pushed through, we're going to call a nationwide boycott on buying phonograph records for the next two years." Before the system would permit young folks to wipe out a multibillion-dollar-a-year industry, it would allow sixteen-year-olds to vote! The old right-wing conservatives don't buy phonograph records. If they do, it is one of the late Senator Dirksen's albums.

If young folks really want changes on campuses and in college administrations, again they should address their grievances to the capitalists. They should organize and announce, "If we don't get the educational changes we want by next September, we are going to boycott eating meat for five days each week." What do you suppose the multimillionaire cattle growers from Texas and the leaders of the packing-house industry would do? They may be right-wingers and despise today's youth, but they would fly into any college town and kick the door off the local college president's office and say, "Come here, boy, we want to talk to you."

Young folks in America today are stronger than anyone, including themselves, seems to realize. If President Nixon has any doubts about the strength of young folks, I suggest he make one long-distance telephone call to the LBJ ranch and ask former President Johnson about what they can do to a man's political ambitions. Youth protest against the war in Vietnam was so strong that President Johnson knew he dare not run for office again. And if young folks can run Lyndon Johnson back to his ranch, they should have no trouble sending Richard Nixon back to his New York City law office.

A beautiful alliance is beginning to emerge among young folks of all colors and ethnic backgrounds in America. There is a common recognition that poor blacks, poor whites, poor Puerto Ricans, poor Indians, poor Chicanos, and poor Orientals share a common problem. The common problem is the system in America itself. Such "rainbow coalitions" cannot help but have a profound effect upon the system, the Man in control. The old tricks the Man used in the past do not work with young folks. The system always kept poor white folks in their place by giving them black folks to look down upon and feel superior to. But as former "Negroes" are now standing tall, black, and proud, poor whites are realizing they have a right to human dignity also.

It is like a man who had two mean and vicious dogs in his backyard to protect his property. The dogs were always fighting each other, and that was the man's protection. In fact the only way the man could come out in his own backyard and get close enough to feed his dogs was to get the dogs fighting with each other so he could sneak up and put down the dish of food. As long as the dogs were fighting and hating each other, the man was safe in his own backyard, and his property was safe also.

Then one day the situation changed. The man looked out his window and saw the dogs fighting. So he went and got the plate of food and walked out in the yard. The dogs saw the man coming. One dog said to the other dog, "Look, brover, all this fighting isn't getting us anywhere. We're still trapped in this man's backyard, and we protect his property. We're dependent upon him for everything, even our food. I'll tell you what let's do. Let's just *pretend* we're fighting, and when he gets close enough with that plate of food, we'll jump on him and get our freedom. After we've got our freedom, we may decide to go back fighting each other again for real. But this time, let's get together and pretend. Let's trick this man just once."

When radical white youth demonstrated in Chicago in the fall of 1969, breaking store windows in the Loop but not stealing merchandise, the system must have realized what was happening, as it called them "mad dogs." Radical students, poor white Appalachian youths, Black Panthers, Puerto Rican Young Lords, Chicanos, Indians, and Orientals are getting together in America's backyard. No longer will they respect the Man's property at the expense of anyone's right to full humanity.

HORROR MOVIES

America is the only country in the history of the world to make a movie about her own destruction. The old *Frankenstein* movies are parables of America's destruction. The plot of the *Frankenstein* story is simple. The mad doctor, Dr. Frankenstein, pays people to go into the graveyard, dig up bodies, steal them, and bring the bodies back to him. Then Dr. Frankenstein pieces the bodies together to create a monster. He has a large laboratory, equipped with an elaborate technology, and he shoots electricity into the body of the monster to give him a new form of life.

From the very first shot of electric current, the monster is the servant of the mad doctor. The mad doctor sends his monster out to do his dirty work for him. The monster goes out and kills innocent victims, but he always brings them back to his master. The mad doctor orders the deaths and is the real freak, not the monster. Little kids instinctively realize that fact. They always want to play "monster," but a little kid never wants to be Dr. Frankenstein. Kids never want to be anything bad. That's why you never see little kids playing Santa Claus.

Then one day the mad doctor makes a mistake. He shoots too much electricity into the body of his monster, and the monster turns on his creator. When the mad doctor overshot his monster, he made his fatal mistake. A struggle takes place between the monster and his creator, resulting in the burning down of the castle and the killing of the monster *and* the mad doctor. But the mad doctor was the only one who had anything to lose in the final destruction. The monster was dead to begin with.

America is the world's mad doctor. The mad doctor paid people to sail to Africa, dig up the bodies of black folks from their native soil, steal them, and bring them back to him. The mad doctor put them in chains and made them do his bidding. He made black folks his monster, trained and controlled to do his dirty work for him.

One day during the 1960's the mad doctor began to shoot too much juice into his monster in Orangeburg, South Carolina. As the decade was in its final month, he overshot toward destruction. In that predawn raid in Chicago the destructive current began to flow. It flowed on into the seventies, and its electrocuting shock was felt in Kent, Ohio, in Jackson, Mississippi, and in Augusta, Georgia. Black folks now realize that they have nothing to lose; the doctor is indeed mad; America has become a mad scientist's laboratory. The monster must act on his own. The monster has turned and cannot be expected to be the same again.

And the mad doctor has made a monster of his own children.

DR. MARTIN LUTHER KING'S LAST MESSAGE TO AMERICA

It is altogether fitting that the final word concerning the reality of America today should come from the late Dr. Martin Luther King, Jr. Dr. King's final words to America were spoken at Mason Temple, Memphis, Tennessee, April 3, 1968. The next day he was murdered, but his vision for a humane world order will never die. The following excerpted version of Dr. King's last address is reprinted from the April 1969 issue of Renewal *magazine.*

A View from the Mountaintop

If I was standing at the beginning of time with the pulse of energy ticking, a kind of general with panoramic view of the whole of human history up to now, and the Almighty said to me, "Martin Luther King, which age would you like to live in?" I would take my mental flight by Egypt. And I would watch God's children in their magnificent trek from the dark dungeons of Egypt; across the Red Sea; through the wilderness; on toward the Promised Land, and in spite of its magnificence, I wouldn't stop there.

I would move on by Greece and take my mind to Mount Olympus. I would see Plato, Aristotle, Socrates, Euripides and Aristophanes, assembled around the Parthenon. And I would watch them around the Parthenon as they discuss the great and eternal issues of reality, but I wouldn't stop there.

I would go on even to the great heyday of the Roman Empire. And I would see developments through various emperors and leaders. But I wouldn't stop there.

I would even come up to the day of the Renaissance, and get a good picture of all that the Renaissance did for the cultural and aesthetic life of man, but I wouldn't stop there. I would even go by the way that the man for whom I am named had his habitat. And I would watch Martin Luther as he tacks his 95 theses on the door of the church of Wittenberg. But I wouldn't stop there.

I would come on up even to 1863 and watch the vacillating President by the name of Abraham Lincoln finally come to the conclusion that he had to sign the Emancipation Proclamation. But I wouldn't stop there.

I would even come up to the early thirties, and see a man grappling with the problems of the bankruptcy of this nation. And come with an eloquent cry that we have "nothing to fear but fear itself." But I wouldn't stop there.

Strangely enough, I would turn to the Almighty and say, "If you allow me to live just a few years in the second half of the twentieth century, I will be happy."

Now that's a strange statement to make because the world is all messed up, the nation is sick, trouble is in the land, confusion all around . . . that's a strange statement. But I know somehow that only when it is dark enough can you see the stars. And I see God working in this period of the twentieth century in a way that men in some strange way are responding. Something is happening in our world. The masses of people are rising up, whether they are in Johannesburg, South Africa, Nairobi, Kenya, Ghana, New York City, Atlanta, Georgia, Jackson, Mississippi, or Memphis, Tennessee, the cry is always the same: "We want to be free."

I'm happy to live in this period in which we're going to have to grapple with the problems that men have been trying to grapple with through history but the demand didn't force them to do it. Survival demands that we grapple with them. Men for years now have been talking about war and peace. But now, no longer can they just talk about it. It is no longer a choice between violence and nonviolence in this world. It's nonviolence or nonexistence. That is where we are today.

Now, I'm just happy that God has allowed me to live in this period, to see what is unfolding. And I'm happy that he's allowed me to be in Memphis. I can remember when Negroes were just going around, as Ralph [Abernathy] has said so often, "scratchin' heavy to the ditch and laughin' when they were not tearful." But that day is all over. We mean business now and we are determined to gain our rightful place in God's world.

And that's all this whole thing is about; we aren't engaged in any negative protest and in any negative arguments with anybody. We are saying that we are determined to be men, we are determined to be people.

We are saying that we are God's children, and if we are God's children, we are going to have to live like we are supposed to live. Now what does all this mean in this great period of history? It means that we've got to stay together and maintain unity.

You know, whenever Pharaoh wanted to prolong the period of slavery in Egypt, he had a favorite formula for doing it. What was that? He kept the slaves fighting among themselves. But whenever the slaves get together, something happens in Pharaoh's court, and he cannot hold the slaves in slavery; when the slaves get together, that's the beginning of getting out of slavery. Now let us maintain unity.

We've got to go on in Memphis just like that. I call upon you to be with us when we go out Monday. We'll have an injunction and we'll go on into court tomorrow morning to fight this illegal, unconstitutional injunction. All we say to "massa" is "be true to what you said on paper." If I lived in China, or even Russia, or in any totalitarian country, maybe I could understand some of these illegal injunctions. Maybe I could understand the denial of certain basic First Amendment privileges, because they have committed themselves to that over there. But somewhere I read of the freedom of assembly; somewhere I read of the freedom of speech, somewhere I read of the freedom of press, somewhere I read that the greatness of America is the right to protest for right.

What is beautiful to me is to see all these ministers of the Gospel here tonight. And I want you to thank them. Because so often preachers aren't concerned about anything but themselves. And I'm always happy to see a relevant minister. It's all right to talk about long white robes over yonder in all of its symbolism. But all too many people need some suits and dresses and shoes to wear down here. It's all right to talk about streets flowing with milk and honey. But God has commanded us to be concerned about the slums down here and the children who can't eat three square meals a day. It's all right to talk about the New Jerusalem, but one day God's creatures must talk about the new New York, the new Atlanta, the new Philadelphia, the new Los Angeles, the new Memphis, Tennessee.

This is what we have to do. Always anchor our external direction with the power of economic control. Now we're poor people. Individually we're poor, when you compare us with white society in America. We're poor. But collectively, that means all of us together, collectively we are richer than most of the nations in the world. Did you ever think about that?

After you leave the United States, Soviet Russia, Great Britain, West Germany, France, I could name others, the American Negro collectively is richer than most nations in the world. We have an annual income of more than 30 billion dollars a year, which is more than all of the exports of the United States and more than the national budget of Canada. Did you know that?

That's power right there if we know how to pool it. We don't have to argue with anybody. We don't need any bricks and bottles; we don't need any molotov cocktails. We just need to go around to these stores and massive industries in our country and say, "God sent us by here, to say to you that you're not treating his children right. And we come by here to ask you to make the first item on your agenda fair treatment where God's children are concerned. Now if you are not prepared to do that, we do have an agenda that we must follow. And our agenda calls for withdrawing economic support from you." Up to now, only the garbage men have been feeling pain. Now we must kind of redistribute the pain.

Now let me say as I move to my conclusion, that we've got to give ourselves to this struggle until the end. Nothing will be more tragic than to stop at this point in Memphis. We've got to see it through. When we go on our march, you need to be there. If it means leaving work, if it means leaving school, be there! Be concerned about your brother. You may not be on strike, but either we go up together or we go down together.

I remember when Mrs. King and I were first in Jerusalem. We rented a car to go from Jerusalem down to Jericho. And as soon as we got on that road, I said to my wife, "I can see why Jesus used this as the setting for the parable of the Good Samaritan." It's a winding, meandering road. It's really conducive for ambushing. You start out in Jerusalem which is about 1200 feet above sea level. And by the time you get down to Jericho, 15 or 20 minutes later, you're about 2200 feet below sea level. That's a dangerous road. In the days of Jesus it came to be known as the Bloody Pass.

And you know it's possible that the priest and the Levite looked over that man on the ground and wondered if the robbers were still around. It's possible that they felt the man on the ground was merely faking— acting like he had been robbed and beaten in order to lure them there for quick and easy seizure. And so the first question that the priest asked, the first question that the Levite asked was, "If I stop to help this man, what will happen to me?" But then the Good Samaritan came by. And he reversed the question. "If I do not stop to help this man, what will happen to him?" That's the question before you tonight. Not if I stop to help the sanitation workers what will happen to my job;

not if I stop to help the sanitation workers what will happen to all of the hours that I usually spend in my office every day of every week as a pastor. The question is not if I stop to help this man in need, what will happen to me. The question is, if I do *not* stop to help the sanitation workers, what will happen to them. That's the question.

Let us rise up tonight with a greater readiness. Let us stand with a greater determination. And let us move on, in these powerful days, these days of challenge, to make America what it ought to be. We have an opportunity to make America a better nation. And I want to praise God once more for allowing me to be here with you.

You know, several years ago I was in New York City, autographing the first book that I had written. While sitting autographing books, a demented woman came up. The only question I heard from her was, "Are you Martin Luther King?" And I was looking down writing. I said "yes." The next minute I felt something beating on my chest. Before I knew it, I had been stabbed by this demented woman. I was rushed to Harlem Hospital. It was a dark Saturday afternoon. X-rays revealed that the tip of the blade was on the edge of my aorta, the main artery. And once that's punctured, you drown in your own blood. That's the end of you. It came out in the *New York Times* the next morning that if I would have merely sneezed, I would have died.

Well, about four days later, they allowed me to read some of the mail that came in from all over the United States and the world. Kind letters came in. I read a few, but one of them I will never forget. I had received one from the President and the Vice President: I've forgotten what those telegrams said. I had received a visit and a letter from the Governor of New York, but I've forgotten what that letter said. But there was another letter. It came from a young girl. I looked at that letter, and I'll never forget it. It said simply: "Dear Dr. King, I am a 9th grade student at the White Plains High School."

She said, "While it should not matter I'd like to mention that I'm a white girl. I read in the paper of your misfortune and of your suffering. And I read that if you had sneezed, you would have died. I'm simply writing you to say that I'm happy that you didn't sneeze."

And I want to say tonight that I, too, am happy that I didn't sneeze. Because if I had sneezed, I wouldn't have been around here till 1960 when students all over the South started sitting in at lunch counters. And I knew that if they were sitting in, they were really standing up for the best in the American dream, and taking the whole nation back to those great wells of democracy which were dug deep by the founding fathers in the Declaration of Independence and the Constitution. If I had sneezed, I wouldn't have been down here in 1961 when we decided to take a ride for freedom and ended segregation in interstate travel. If I had sneezed, I wouldn't have been around here in 1962 when Negroes in Albany, Georgia, decided to straighten their backs up. And whenever men and women straighten their backs up, they are going somewhere; because a man can't ride your back unless it is bent. If I had sneezed I wouldn't have been here in 1963; black people down in Birmingham, Alabama, aroused the conscience of this nation and brought into being the Civil Rights bill. If I had sneezed, I wouldn't have had a chance later that year to try to tell America about a tune that I had heard. If I had sneezed, I wouldn't have been down in Selma, Alabama, to start a movement there. If I had sneezed, I wouldn't have been in Memphis to see a community rally around those brothers and sisters who were suffering. I'm so happy that I didn't sneeze.

It really doesn't matter what happens now. I left Atlanta this morning, and as we got started on the plane, there was trouble. The pilot said, over the public address system, "We're sorry for the delay. But we have Dr. Martin Luther King on the plane and to be sure that all of the bags were checked and to be sure that nothing would be wrong on the plane, we had to check out everything carefully and we've had the plane protected and guarded all night." Then I got into Memphis and some began to say the threats or talk about the threats that were out, and what would happen to me from some of our sick white brothers.

Well, I don't know what will happen now. We've got some difficult days ahead, but it really doesn't matter with me now because I've been to the mountaintop. And I don't mind. Like anybody, I would like to live a long life. Longevity has its place. But I'm not concerned about that now. I just want to do God's will. And He has allowed me to go up to the mountain. And I've looked over, and I've seen the Promised Land. I may not get there with you, but I want you to know tonight that we as a people will get to the Promised Land. So I'm happy tonight. I'm not worried about anything. I'm not fearing any man. Mine eyes have seen the glory of the coming of the Lord.

NOTES

Introduction: For White Only

The description of the bombings of Hiroshima and Nagasaki is found in Truman Nelson's *The Right of Revolution* (Boston: Beacon Press, 1968), pages 110–111.

1: The Myth of the Puritan Pilgrim

For quotations and historical narrative contained in this chapter I am especially indebted to two books: *The Growth of the American Republic,* Volume I, Samuel Eliot Morison and Henry Steele Commager (New York: Oxford University Press, 1962) and *The Historian's History of the United States,* Volume I, edited by Andrew S. Berky and James F. Shenton (New York: G. P. Putnam's Sons, 1966), especially the following essays: "The Beginnings of New England," by John Fiske; "European Background of American History, 1300–1600," by Edward P.

Cheyney; and "The Colonial Period of American History," by Charles M. Andrews.

The figure for Senator Eastland's farm subsidy is found in a government booklet, *The Department of Agriculture and Related Agencies for the Fiscal Year 1970.* The section on hearings before the subcommittee on Appropriations, United States Senate, 91st Congress, H.R. 11612, page 738, reports from the State of Mississippi, County of Sunflower, that the Eastland Plantation, Inc., received $116,978. By my calculations that is $9,748 per month. The poor baby, by the way, would receive less than $100 per year.

John Robinson's letter to Governor Bradford is found in *The Indian and the White Man,* edited by Wilcomb E. Washburn (New York: Anchor Books, Doubleday and Company, 1964), on pages 176–178. Samuel Sewall's letter is found in the same source on pages 315–316.

The Germantown Mennonite Resolution Against Slavery (1688) is found in *The Negro Almanac,* compiled and edited by Harry A. Ploski and Roscoe C. Brown, Jr. (New York: Bellwether Publishing Company, Inc., 1967), on pages 59–61.

Judge Sewall's tract "The Selling of Joseph" is found in *Civil Rights and the American Negro: A Documentary History,* edited by Albert P. Blaustein and Robert L. Zangrando (New York: Washington Square Press, Inc., 1968), on pages 13–17.

Roger Williams by Henry Chupack (New York: Twayne Publishers, Inc., 1969) proved to be a helpful resource for the section "Marks of Colonization."

2: The Myths of the Savage

Three books were of great value in providing historical and statistical information about the Indian American: *The Indian Heritage of America,* by Alvin M. Josephy, Jr.

(New York: Bantam Books, 1969), *Our Brother's Keeper: The Indian in White America,* edited by Edgar S. Cahn (Washington, D.C.: New Community Press, 1969), and *Indians of the Americas,* by John Collier (New York and Toronto: The New American Library, 1947).

The quotation by Jean Jacques Rousseau is found in Washburn, *op. cit.,* pages 415–418. The quotation by John Gorham Palfrey is found in the same source on page 444.

The myth of the "pretty colored snake" is found on page 119 of Stan Steiner's *The New Indians* (New York: Harper & Row, 1968). Also the quotations by Paul Bernal (pages 153 and 243), General Custer (pages 79–80), and Lt. James D. Conner (page 79).

The quotations from the Narrative of Black Elk and the Indian Proverb are found in Cahn, *op. cit.,* page 107.

The "wasichus" testimony of the Indians is found in Cahn, *op. cit.,* page 177. Also the excerpt from Janet McCloud's Law Day Ceremonies address, page 182.

The quotation from Peter Oliver is found on pages 448–449 of Washburn, *op. cit.* Thomas Jefferson's praise of Indian oratory is found in the same source on pages 426–428.

All quotations and ideas credited to Vine Deloria, Jr., are found in his excellent book *Custer Died for Your Sins: An Indian Manifesto* (New York: The Macmillan Company, 1969).

The testimony of Bartolomeo Vanzetti is found in *The Writing on the Wall,* Walter Lowenfels (New York: Doubleday and Company, 1969).

3: The Myth of the Founding Fathers

The quotations by Thomas Hutchinson and Benjamin Franklin are contained in Carl L. Becker's essay in Berky and Shenton, *op. cit.* The emphasis upon tea and the Revolution is derived from John C. Miller's essay "Origins of the American Revolution" in the same volume.

George Washington's Last Will and Testament is found in Ploski and Brown, *op. cit.*, page 73. His letter to Captain Thompson is contained in *100 Amazing Facts About the Negro with Complete Proof* by J. A. Rogers, independently published by Mr. Rogers (New York, 1957).

Elections and other pastimes of the Virginia aristocracy are described in *The Landmark History of the American People, by Daniel J. Boorstin* (New York: Random House, 1968), Chapter Six, "How a Few Gentlemen Ruled Virginia."

Sources for the material concerning Crispus Attucks were: *The Negro Revolution,* by Robert Goldston (New York: Signet Books, 1969), *Black History: Lost, Stolen, or Strayed* by Otto Lindenmeyer (New York: Avon Books, 1970), and *Eyewitness: The Negro in American History* by William L. Katz (New York-Toronto-London: Pitman Publishing Corporation, 1967).

Quotations from Samuel Adams are found in Moses Coit Tyler's essay "The Literary History of the American Revolution: 1763–1783," in Berky and Shenton, *op. cit.*

Background material for the lives of Peter Salem, Salem Poor, and blacks in the Continental Army is from *Pioneers and Patriots,* by Lavinia Dobler and Edgar A. Toppin (New York: Doubleday and Company, 1965), Katz, *op. cit.*, Goldston, *op. cit.*, and Lindenmeyer, *op. cit.*

Background material for the life of Benjamin Banneker comes from Dobler and Toppin, *op. cit.;* and *Black Heroes in World History* (New York: Bantam Books, 1969). The correspondence between Banneker and Thomas Jefferson is found on pages 56–59 of *The Winding Road to Freedom,* edited by Alfred E. Cain (New York: Educational Heritage Inc., 1965). Jefferson's thoughts concerning the inferiority of blacks and the immorality of slavery are found on pages 36–40 of the same volume.

Material concerning the "deleted clause" in the Declaration of Independence and Jefferson's reaction is found in *Chronicles of Black Protest*, edited by Bradford Chambers (New York: New American Library, 1968), pages 46–48.

Congressman Joseph Jonas' statement is taken from the *Congressional Record*.

Anthony Benezet's comment on the slavery clause omission is found in *Freedom's Ferment*, by Alice Felt Tyler (New York: Harper & Row, Torchbooks edition, 1962), page 466.

John Adams' evaluation of the Boston Tea Party is found in Nelson, *op. cit.*, page 22. The debate of John Quincy Adams on the floor of Congress is found in the same book on pages 128–130.

Quotations from Thomas Paine are found in Moses Tyler's essay cited above. Two other sources were used in the section concerning Thomas Paine: *The Life of Thomas Paine*, by Peter Eckler (New York: Peter Eckler, Publisher, 1892) and *Citizen Tom Paine*, by Howard Fast (New York: Duell, Sloan and Pierce, 1943).

4: The Myth of Black Content

The tale of Old John is found in *Puttin' On Ole Massa*, edited by Gilbert Osofsky (New York: Harper & Row, Torchbooks edition, 1969), page 46.

The material concerning Aesop is taken from Philip St. Laurent's article "The Negro in World History: Aesop," which appeared in the January issue of *Tuesday* magazine.

Edna McGuire's version of slavery is referred to in Lindenmeyer, *op. cit.*, pages 15–16.

The myth of the contented slave as portrayed in Goldston is found on pages 59 and 60 of his *The Negro Revolution*.

Frederick Douglass' description of slave songs is taken from *Narrative of the Life of Frederick Douglass Written by Himself* (New York: The New American Library,

1968), pages 31–32. His description of the beating of Aunt Hester is taken from the same book, pages 25–26; and the description of how slaves were tricked by their masters into equating hangovers with freedom is found on pages 84–85.

Sources for the black explorers were: Lindenmeyer, *op. cit.*; *Black Heroes in World History*, *op. cit.*; and Dobler and Toppin, *op. cit.*

Lerone Bennett's description of the slave trade is found in *Before the Mayflower: A History of the Negro in America, 1619–1964* (Chicago: Johnson Publishing Company, 1962) on page 31 (Penguin Book edition).

Kenneth Stampp's description of integration in the cotton fields is found on pages 21–22 of *The Peculiar Institution: Slavery in the Ante-Bellum South* (New York: Vintage Books, 1956). His demolishing of the myth of a black labor force as a necessity is found on page 7 of the same book.

The merchandising of servants, black and white, is described on page 41 of Lerone Bennett's *Before the Mayflower*. Goldston's *The Negro Revolution* was a most helpful source in the whole discussion of white and black servitude. Those who doubt the dumping of dead white indentured servants into the New York harbor are referred to page 45 of that book.

Melvin Drimmer's essay "Was Slavery Dying Before the Cotton Gin?" is contained in *Black History*, edited with commentary by Melvin Drimmer (New York: Doubleday and Company, 1969). The particular quotation is found on page 115.

The narratives of slave recollections of coming to America are found in Julius Lester's *To Be a Slave* (New York: The Dial Press, Inc., 1968), pages 18–22.

Material describing conditions on board slave ships draws heavily from Goldston, *op. cit.*, pages 37–42.

The quotation from Henry David Thoreau is found in Nelson, *op. cit.*, page 103.

Solomon Northrup's description of the daily ordeal of

a slave in Louisiana is found in Goldston, *op. cit.*, pages 62 and 63.

Frederick Douglass' description of slave provisions is found in his *Narrative* on page 28.

West Turner's whipping recollections are found in Lester, *op. cit.*, page 35.

The note of warning left by a loyal slave is found in Goldston, *op. cit.*, page 64.

Background sources for the slave revolts were: Lindenmeyer, *op. cit.*, Goldston, *op. cit.*, and *Black Struggle* by Bryan Fulks (New York: Dell Publishing Company, Inc., 1969).

John Brown's testimony is found in Blaustein and Zangrando, *op. cit.*, page 175.

John Copeland's last words are found in Goldston, *op. cit.*, page 99.

Frederick Douglass' Fourth of July address is printed in full on pages 88–90 of Ploski and Brown, *op. cit.*

Frederick Douglass' plan for race relations in America is found in *Black Heroes, op. cit.*, page 97.

5: *The Myth of the Courageous White Settler and the Free Frontier*

The story of the robbery at the Kansas City Fair is found in Joe B. Frantz's essay "The Frontier Tradition: An Invitation to Violence" contained in *Violence in America,* the complete official report to the National Commission on the Causes and Prevention of Violence, prepared under the direction and authorship of Hugh Davis Graham and Ted Robert Gurr (New York: The New American Library, 1969), page 119.

Resource material for the recitation of the adventures of the black cowboys is found in *The Adventures of the Negro Cowboys* (New York: Bantam Books, 1969).

Professor Frantz's essay cited above is the resource for vigilantism and the white "heroes" of the Wild West.

6: *The Myth of the Mason-Dixon Line*

Mason-Dixon line statistics are found in Morison and Commager, *op. cit.*, page 91.

I am indebted to James Baker's private collection of letters and reproductions of newspaper articles and proceedings from the Congressional Record for much of the material in this chapter.

The Montgomery *Advertiser* article is found in *100 Years of Lynchings*, by Ralph Ginzburg (New York: Lancer Books, 1962), page 73. Professor Hart's recommendation is reported on page 36 of the same book.

7: *The Myth of Free Enterprise*

Berky and Shenton's description of the wealth amassed by the few is found in the second volume of their *The Historian's History of the United States* on pages 845 and 846.

Quotations from Ferdinand Lundberg are found in *The Rich and the Super-Rich* (New York: Lyle Stuart, Inc., 1968) on pages 33, 34, 37, and 140.

Figures for oil-depletion allowances are taken from my earlier book *Write Me In!* (New York: Bantam Books, 1968).

Statistics concerning American interests in the Dominican Republic are from the research of Jack Minnis, formerly of the Student Nonviolent Coordinating Committee (SNCC) reported in *Look Out Whitey! Black Power's Gon' Get Your Mama*, by Julius Lester (New York: The Dial Press, Inc., 1968), page 130.

Resource material for the Haymarket Riot comes from Volume 4 Number 7 of *The* (Chicago) *Seed* and an essay by Samuel Yellen, "American Labor Struggles" contained in Berky and Shenton, *op. cit.*, Volume II, pages 955 through 967.

Statistics concerning black membership in unions are found in *The Negro and the American Labor Movement*, edited by Julius Jacobson (New York: Doubleday and Company, Anchor Books, 1968).

8: The Myth of Emancipation

Slave recollections of freedom are found in Julius Lester's *To Be a Slave* and *Lay My Burden Down: A Folk History of Slavery*, edited by B. A. Botkin (Chicago: The University of Chicago Press, 1945).

Julius Lester's paragraph summation of Abraham Lincoln is found in *Look Out Whitey!*, page 58.

Once again I am grateful to James Baker for making available his private collection of reproductions for much of the material in this chapter. I am also deeply indebted to Herbert Schaltegger, Sr., for allowing me to draw insight from his unpublished essay "The Decay of the American Democracy" (New Milford, Connecticut, 1968).

The quotation from W. E. B. Du Bois is found in Julius Lester's *Look Out Whitey!*, pages 61–62. Frederick Douglass' nitty-gritty reply to Abraham Lincoln is found in the same source on page 63.

9: The Myth of the Bootstrap

The quotation from Israel Zangwill is found in *Beyond the Melting Pot* by Nathan Glazer and Daniel Patrick Moynihan (Cambridge, Mass.: Massachusetts Institute of Technology Press, 1963), page 289.

The quotations from Morton Grodzin and General De-Witt is taken from the testimony of the Hon. Shirley Chisholm before the House Internal Security Committee, 1970.

The quotation from James McCague is found in his book *The Second Rebellion* (New York: The Dial Press, Inc., 1968) on pages 93, 103–104.

Excerpts from the Report of the National Advisory Commission on Civil Disorders are found in Chapter Nine, "Comparing the Immigrant and Negro Experience."

10: The Myth of the Good Neighbor

The exchange between FDR and Vice President Garner is found in *Franklin D. Roosevelt and the New Deal*, by William E. Leuchtenburg (New York: Harper & Row, Harper Torchbooks, 1963), page 208. Leuchtenburg's description of the Depression is found on pages 1–3 of the same book.

The newspaper reports from the Memphis *Commercial-Appeal* and the *New York Times* are found on pages 82–83 and 234–35 of Ginzberg, *op. cit.*

In addition to Mr. Leuchtenburg's book, *The New Deal*, edited with an introduction by Carl N. Degler (Chicago: Quadrangle Books, 1970), was a further resource aid on the New Deal period.

11: The Myth of American Rhetoric

The excerpt from the official court record of the Chicago Conspiracy Trial is found on page 38 of *The Tales of Hoffman*, edited by Mark L. Levine, George C. McNamee, and Daniel Greenberg (New York: Bantam Books, 1970).

The statement of the National Committee of Black Churchmen was given to me through the courtesy of Rev. Leon W. Watts and Rev. J. Metz Rollins.

12: The Myth of Free Elections

A helpful resource in the preparation of this chapter was *The New York Times Election Handbook*, edited by Harold Faber (New York: The New American Library, 1968).

The South Carolina Democratic Party strategy excerpts are found in Chambers, *op. cit.*, page 127.

Epilogue: From Myth to Reality

All quotations from Edward Gibbon are found in *The Decline and Fall of the Roman Empire*, a one-volume abridgement by D. M. Low (New York: Harcourt, Brace and Company, 1960), pages 524–25, 263, 201 and 53.

INDEX